WESTMAR COLLEG[E LIBRARY]
W9-BMI-443

Robert Johnson

Proprietary & Royal Governor of South Carolina

Robert Johnson
Proprietary & Royal Governor of South Carolina

by Richard P. Sherman

UNIVERSITY OF SOUTH CAROLINA PRESS
COLUMBIA 1966

F
272
.J57
S5

Library of Congress Catalog Card Number 66-25274

Copyright © 1966
BY THE UNIVERSITY OF SOUTH CAROLINA PRESS

Printed in the United States of America
BY THE STATE PRINTING COMPANY
Columbia, South Carolina

67568

To My Parents:

Louis Sherman

and

Anne Rossheim Sherman

The Author

Richard Philip Sherman is professor of history at El Camino College, Los Angeles, California, and has also taught at the University of Southern California, and at the University of California.

He is a graduate of The Citadel, the Military College of South Carolina, in Charleston, where he received his B.A. degree. Dr. Sherman holds the M.A. degree from the University of California at Los Angeles, and the Ph.D. degree from the University of Southern California.

A native of North Carolina, Dr. Sherman was born at Mt. Olive and graduated from Goldsboro High School. He saw service in World War II in the Army.

Table of Contents

Illustrations

Preface

The role of governor in colonial America was a delicate one: at best, a difficult task; at worst, untenable. Robert Johnson served twice as governor in the early history of South Carolina, during the proprietary regime and under royal rule.

In his first administration, Johnson had to deal with a variety of problems involving pirates, Indians, and a populace growing increasingly dissatisfied with proprietary overlordship. When the imminent danger of Spanish invasion helped kindle a revolution against the Lords Proprietors, Johnson was confronted with a new dilemma: should he remain loyal to the interests of the Proprietors, even though they had mistreated and ignored him; or should he join the revolution? It was a difficult choice to make, but Johnson's unequivocal decision revealed the character of the Governor and the Man.

Following a decade of hesitations and negotiations which witnessed the final transfer of South Carolina to royal hands, Robert Johnson returned to the Province from England as the King's governor.

The new status of the Province created some difficulties; and remaining were some of the same old problems, particularly those of defense against Indians and European enemies. Defense problems were aggravated by Carolina's unique position as the southern frontier of English settlement, and Governor Johnson devised and put into action further measures for improvement. He gave strong support to the Georgia settlement project to provide a buffer state for the Province; and formulated the township settlement plan as a primary defense measure.

Johnson's failure or success as governor can be assessed best by observing his competence in coping with two troublesome issues: the conflict between merchant and planter; and the governor and Council relationship with the Assembly, involving the question of royal prerogative versus assembly privilege.

Among other problems confronting the Johnson administrations was the vital land struggle. To round out the investigation and examination of land matters during his terms of office, the charges and countercharges in this area have been explored in depth.

At least the problem illustrates the futility of simply marshalling the "facts" and letting history speak for itself. The historian, to be true to his craft, must be more than a reporter of past happenings, for in a case such as this, history without interpretation fails to stop short of confusion. An interpretation, even if it ultimately turns out to be erroneous, serves as a stepping stone on the path leading out of, and away from disorder.

Interpretations of the South Carolina land struggles seem to categorize themselves into three possibilities. First, were the Governor, Council and Assembly using their official positions to engross the lands of the Province, either for their own use or for the purpose of speculation, and did St. John, Whitaker, and their associates, as defenders of His Majesty's interest, not only discover the plot but also try to put a stop to it? Or, second, was it simply a case of one group of land speculators vying with another; that is, had the government representation gotten to the lands first, thereby embittering the St. John group who determined to break the monopoly and procure the lands themselves? Or, third, was the Governor, with the cooperation of the Assembly, trying to settle equitably the land question in a manner designed to protect inhabitants in their landholdings, while the St. John associates opposed this policy because it wanted the land for speculative purposes?

Although there are a number of other possibilities, they seem to be variants on these three, main themes, which—in addition—interact among themselves.

It seems fairly evident from the extant correspondence that St. John, Whitaker and Hume represented that their interests were not self-seeking, and that they were indeed His Majesty's true servants. The Board of Trade also seems to have concurred, its attitude influenced either by the persuasiveness of the land group's agents, or by the fact that St. John had powerful friends in England. Whatever the reasons, some latter-day historians have, in general, followed possibility number one, with the result that St. John and his associates have been viewed in a favorable light, while Governor Johnson has been handed down to posterity in an undefined sort of purgatory.

A present-day observer, in examining the numerous charges and countercharges issuing from both, might well throw up his hands in disgust over the futility of ever trying to paint the true picture, and adopt the second possibility. To resolve the issue by calling it a fight between two groups of land speculators would be a convenient way to accommodate the opposing facts, but this conclusion might be incorrect.

This writer leans toward the third possibility, although with some qualifications. It seems likely that the Governor, Council, and Assembly, as members and representatives of the planter class, were not disinterested in lands and the acquisition of lands. However, they seemed more concerned with those lands for their own use rather than for speculative purposes, even though undoubtedly there were exceptions. Under provisions of the Quit Rent Act that they supported, they would be required to put those lands in productive use or keep them out of production at a considerable expense to themselves because of the quit rents.

Concerning Governor Johnson, except for the Purrysburg incident, which he explained, he seems completely to have been removed from any plot, plan or project to seize lands.

Despite continued research, it has not been possible to locate any portrait or likeness of Governor Johnson, other than a small woodcut showing his second arrival in America, accompanied by Cherokee Indians, whom he escorted back to America.

In any study of Governor Robert Johnson, the researcher is confronted with the lack of any known personal correspondence by the Governor. Such, fortunately, has presented no serious obstacle in the present work which is concerned with Johnson's direction and administration of the South Carolina government. Available are voluminous collections of official and semi-official correspondence by others, and documents by Johnson and numerous other officials during his administrations. A mass of correspondence between the Carolina government and various British agencies concerned with the Province is deposited in the Public Record Office, London, of which transcripts have been acquired for the South Carolina Archives Department and, to a more limited extent, the Library of Congress.

Also, extremely important sources of information are the journals of the South Carolina Council and Commons House of Assembly. These records contain the best information on the relationship of the two houses, and the Governor's transactions with both. Further, since the Council sat as both an executive and legislative body, its journal reveals the Governor's attitude and action on virtually all matters concerning the Province. Another pertinent collection consists of the records of the Society for the Propagation of the Gospel in Foreign Parts, containing some letters to and from Governor Johnson. The S.P.G. collection is most important for the large number of messages to the Society in England from its missionaries in South Carolina. These letters, in addition to their revelations of Society matters, provide insight into the problems confronting the Province and Governor Robert Johnson.

It will be noted that "Charleston" as a name place has been used in this work, instead of the early "Charles Town" and "Charlestown." The city was incorporated in 1783 as "Charleston."

In preparing this work, revised from a doctoral dissertation presented at the University of Southern California, the author acknowledges with deep appreciation the aid and assistance accorded him by many persons. First, I wish to thank these professors at the University of Southern California: Dr. Francis J. Bowman, Dr. Donald C. Cutter, Dr. A. R. Kooker, Dr. Carlton C. Rodee, Dr. Donald W. Rowland, and especially Dr. Russell L. Caldwell for his guidance. Next, gratitude is expressed to the University of Southern California Library; the Manuscripts Division and the Photo-duplication Service of the Library of Congress; the Huntington Library, San Marino, California; Mr. Wilbur J. Smith, head, Department of Special Collections, and Mr. Ralph Lyon, Jr., University of California at Los Angeles Library. Dr. J. H. Easterby, late director of the South Carolina Archives Department, showed unusual interest in this manuscript, gave helpful advice, and was the prime mover in getting it published.

In addition, I am deeply indebted to the Los Angeles-Pasadena Committee of the National Society of Colonial Dames of America for receipt of its 1955 award in American colonial history.

And finally, my thanks go to the former Director of the University of South Carolina Press, Mrs. Louise Jones DuBose, and her Assistant Editor, Mrs. Jane Roehrs, for valuable aid in revising and preparing the manuscript for publication; and to the two present members of the Press, Mrs. Kathleen Lewis Sloan, Assistant Editor, who brought this work to a completion, and Diane Long, for retyping the manuscript.

R.P.S.

Los Angeles, Calif.
October 1, 1966

CHAPTER I

Governor For The Proprietors

IN 1717, Robert Johnson, a son of Sir Nathaniel Johnson, a former chief executive, became governor of South Carolina as the Proprietors' choice.

Four years earlier, in April 1713, following Governor Charles Craven's voluntary request for retirement, the Lords Proprietors had informed the Queen in Council of this development and the need for a successor. They sought approbation for Robert Johnson, described as "a person of Integrity and Capacity well affected to her Majestys Government and every way qualified for that Trust."[1] The Council referred the request to the Lords Commissioners of Trade and Plantations, usually termed the Board of Trade, for consideration. In due course, the Board reported that it had no objection to the appointment, provided Johnson could qualify in the manner prescribed by law, that is, be able to give good and sufficient security in a bond of £2,000 sterling for observance of the acts of trade and navigation.[2] Johnson's appointment, however, was not put into effect, necessitating a further request by the Lords Proprietors after a considerable lapse of time.

In the meantime, two days after Governor Charles Craven had vacated the office, Robert Daniel, deputy governor of Carolina, proclaimed his commission on April 25, 1716.[3] Daniel's term ended between June 29 and October 29, 1717, when Johnson assumed the governorship for the first of his two separate terms.

Johnson's appointment had finally come after the Proprietors had again pursued the subject with the Prince of Wales; and the Board

---

[1] April 15, 1713, Records in the British Public Record Office Relating to South Carolina, transcripts in the South Carolina Archives, Columbia, (hereinafter cited as PR), Vol. VI, p. 54. The Proprietors perceiving the possibility of Craven's return, informed him that Johnson would be nominated as his successor, but no commission would be issued until Craven wrote them of his intentions. *See also,* A. S. Salley, *Commissions and Instructions from the Lords Proprietors of Carolina to Public Officials of South Carolina, 1685-1715,* (Columbia: Historical Commission of South Carolina, 1916,) p. 257.

[2] PR, p. 55.

[3] D. D. Wallace, *South Carolina: A Short History,* (Chapel Hill: University of North Carolina Press, 1951, reprinted by the University of South Carolina Press, Columbia, 1961 and 1966), p. 703.

of Trade had reported that it could find no cause why royal approval should not be forthcoming.[4] After consideration of the Board's report, the Prince thereupon declared his allowance and approbation of Johnson's appointment.[5]

At that time, Johnson put up the required bond, pledging that the acts of trade and navigation would be observed. Andrew Broughton and William Bonner had offered to be Johnson's surety in this matter.[6] Since inquiry showed Bonner was the owner of a considerable estate of about £600 per annum, and Broughton a merchant of undeniable character, bond was taken.[7]

Both Johnson's Commission and Instructions from the Proprietors bear the date of April 30, 1717, constituting him Governor of that part of the Province of Carolina which lay south and west of Cape Fear. In view of the subsequent, long-standing boundary dispute between North and South Carolina, it is of import that the Proprietors considered the dividing line to be Cape Fear.

The newly appointed Governor, who was to receive a salary of £400 per annum, paid quarterly, was required to subscribe to a number of oaths as specified by law. In turn, he was to administer oaths to members of his Council who, selected by the Proprietors, included Alexander Skene, Nicholas Trott, Thomas Broughton, Charles Hart, Francis Yonge, Samuel Wragg, and James Kinloch. Any four of these men would constitute a quorum, and the Governor, with the majority of the Council, could suspend other members, but only upon good and sufficient cause. In case of such suspension, the reasons for so doing were to be transmitted to the Proprietors, together with charges and proofs against the suspended member, and his answers to the accusations. However, the members of the Council were to hold the liberty to debate and vote in all matters determined in Council. As needed, from time to time, general assemblies of the inhabitants (i. e., freeholders and planters) were to be called in the manner and form then practiced in the Province.

---

[4] PR, Vol. VI, pp. 251-2, 254-5.

[5] December 6, 1716, PR., Vol. VI, p. 272.

[6] December 12-13, 1716, PR., Vol. VI, pp. 273-4.

[7] N. Blakiston to [Secretary of the Board of Trade], January 3, 1716/7, PR., Vol. VII, p. 2. [England did not adopt the Gregorian calendar until 1752. Before that time, March 25, rather than January 1, was observed as the first day of the year. Consequently, for the period January 1-March 24, the double date, such as 1716/7, was in frequent use.]

Full power to make laws for the public peace, welfare, and government of the Province was placed in the hands of the Governor, Council, and Assembly. The Governor was granted a specific negative voice over all ordinances, statutes, and laws, all of which were to be agreeable to the same in Great Britain. Additionally, the Governor was empowered "to execute and perform all other things necessary and proper" for the government of the Province. Governor Johnson was expressly commanded to transmit to the Proprietors copies of all laws, statutes, and ordinances then in force, and to send subsequent ones within six months of their passage, so they could either be confirmed or disallowed.

All possible assistance, he was instructed, was to be given to Colonel William Rhett, the receiver general, in obtaining fines, forfeitures, and forfeited estates. Also, an exact and full account was to be drawn up of the yearly rents due the Proprietors, specifying what each person owed, amounts paid, and by whom and what land had been sold.

To facilitate the defense of the Province, an inventory of all arms, ammunition, and stores belonging to the government was to be made, as well as an account of how any had been used. Storehouses were to be set up throughout the Province for receiving and keeping arms. Great care was to be taken that the Indians were not abused, and that justice was administered to them, idle words in view of the scant assistance the Proprietors provided during the Yamassee War. Besides, Johnson was to seek the Indians' "firm friendship" as they could serve as allies of the Province to aid in its protection and defense.

One other pertinent part of the Instructions had to do with the exorbitant rates of gold and silver and foreign coins in Carolina. Many complaints had been received in England concerning this condition, one the Proprietors declared as stemming from an act of Assembly called the "Bank Act." Governor Johnson was instructed to put this act into accordance with an act of Parliament, entitled "An Act for ascertaining the Rates of Foreign Coins in the Plantations," and to reduce as much as possible the paper credit that was "pretended" to be established by this Bank Act.[8]

Fortified with these Instructions, Johnson assumed the governorship, but at a rather inauspicious time; for the Province still suffered

[8] PR., Vol. VII, pp. 25-31, 35.

the effects of the Yamassee War, and Indian depredations were a common occurrence. A continuous fear prevailed of Spanish attack, either by land from St. Augustine, or by sea from Havana, or by a combined sea and land attack. This state of affairs wreaked havoc on colonial finances, while simultaneously, piratical attacks were wrecking the trade of the Province.

Two main factors were to shape Johnson's administration. One was the vulnerable situation of the Province, with the likelihood of attack. The other was the fact that Johnson was popular and respected in the Province, and had vital and real interests in South Carolina. Johnson's ties to the Province were close and of long duration. His father had been governor of Carolina in the trying period 1703-1709. The Johnson genealogical tree shows Nathaniel Johnson of Kibblesworth, "a scattered village one mile to the West of Lamesley,"[9] to be the son of William Johnson of Kibblesworth, and Margaret, daughter of William Sherwood, of Newcastle upon Tyne.[10] *Alumni Oxonienses* includes a Nathaniel Johnson matriculating March 10, 1656/7 in New College, with B.A., 1660, as "perhaps Sir Nathaniel Johnson: commissioner of hearth money . . ."[11]

Robert Johnson's father, listed as one of the seven freeholders of Kibblesworth in 1684,[12] was knighted by the King at Whitehall in 1680.[13] He served as "chief Farmer of the Chimney-money of his Majesty for the four Northern Counties." The Johnson coat-of-arms contained five cocks, three flaming towers or castles, and two spears.[14] In referring to this "loaded coat," along with Johnson's job as contractor of hearth money, Surtees speculated: "Do the flaming towers allude to his sooty profits, the *Denarii fumales?*"[15]

[9] Robert Surtees, *The History and Antiquities of the County Palatine of Durham* (4 vols., London: J. Nichols and Son; Durham: G. Andrews, 1816-1840), Vol. II, p. 216.

[10] *Ibid.*, Vol. II, p. 218. Among the collections of pedigrees presented by Brig. Gen. H. Conyers Surtees was that of Johnson of Kibblesworth. Society of Antiquaries of Newcastle-upon-Tyne, *Proceedings*, 4th series, Vol. I, no. 14 (1924), p. 203.

[11] John Foster, *Alumni Oxonienses: The Members of the University of Oxford, 1500-1714 . . . being the Matriculating Register of the University* (Oxford: James Parker and Co., 1891), Vol. II, p. 815.

[12] Surtees, *The History and Antiquities of the County Palatine of Durham*, Vol. II, p. 217.

[13] Presumably on Dec. 28. Wm. A. Shaw, *The Knights of England* (2 vols., London: Sherratt and Hughes, 1906), Vol. II, p. 255.

[14] John Guillim, *A Display of Heraldy*, 6th. ed. (London: R. and J. Bonwicke and R. Wilkin, 1724), p. 388.

[15] Surtees, *The History and Antiquities of the County Palatine of Durham*, Vol. II, p. 218.

Sir Nathaniel was mayor of Newcastle upon Tyne in 1680,[16] and was elected to Parliament that same year,[17] being returned in 1681 and again in 1685.[18] In 1686, he was appointed to succeed Sir William Stapleton as Governor of the Leeward Islands.[19] In that post, Johnson feared for the safety of the soldiers and moved his headquarters from Nevis to Antigua to improve his military position.[20]

In 1688 conditions were confounded by the Glorious Revolution, in which Johnson revealed his moral courage. While others changed allegiance without qualm or question, Johnson remained loyal to King James II who had originally commissioned him. Sir John Fortescue's remark is noteworthy: "Amid all the craven changes of that mean and pitiful time this man remained honest and patriotic, faithful to him whom he judged to be his lawful King, yet never unfaithful to his country."[21] Later, Sir Nathaniel was to lose a son, commander of a man-of-war in the East Indies, in King William's service.[22]

---

[16] William Wardell Bean, *The Parliamentary Representation of the Six Northern Counties of England* (Hull: C. H. Barnwell, 1890), p. 585. The translation of a Latin medical book is dedicated to "The Right Worshipful Sir Nathaniel Johnson, mayor," and to the aldermen and others. Society of Antiquaries of Newcastle-upon-Tyne, *Proceedings,* 4th series, Vol. II, no. 15 (1925), p. 113.

[17] On Dec. 1, following the death of the incumbent. Bean, *Parliamentary Representation,* p. 566.

[18] *Ibid.,* p. 567.

[19] *Ibid.,* p. 585; Alan Burns, *History of the British West Indies* (London: George Allen and Unwin, Ltd., 1954), p. 349.

[20] Burns, *History of the British West Indies,* pp. 349-51; J. W. Fortescue, *A History of the British Army* (13 vols. in 14, London: MacMillan and Co., Ltd., 1899-1930), Vol. II, p. 41.

[21] Quoted in Burns, *History of the British West Indies,* p. 374n. Unlike the near-legendary Vicar of Bray, Johnson put loyalty before the job. A verse from the famous song went:

When William was our King declar'd
To ease the nation's grievance;
With this new wind about I steer'd,
And swore to him allegiance:
Old principles I did revoke,
Set conscience at a distance;
Passive obedience was a joke,
A jest was non-resistance.
And this is law that I'll maintain
Until my dying day, Sir,
That whatsoever King shall reign,
Still I'll be Vicar of Bray, Sir.

W. Chappell, *The Ballad Literature and Popular Music of the Olden Time* (2 vols., London: Chappell and Co. [n.d.]), Vol. II, pp. 652-4, 787.

[22] "The Case of Robert Johnson," [c. 1724], PR, Vol. XIII, p. 393.

As the war hysteria mounted, charges were made against Nathaniel Johnson, and despite the Antigua legislature's affirmation of the governor's loyalty, it was felt that Johnson's voluntary retirement and decision to leave the colony were sagacious.[23]

Sir Nathaniel sailed for Carolina. His salary, reported to be £3,000 in arrears, still was unpaid to the executor of his estate in the 1720's. He had sent his family, including his wife[24] and son Robert [future Governor of Carolina], back to England, but they were captured by the French and were held prisoners for more than a year. The death of Mrs. Johnson is said to have resulted from the severity and harshness of the treatment she received.[25]

In Carolina, Nathaniel Johnson obtained a 1,940-acre grant of land on the Cooper River, where he experimented with silk culture, and which he named "Silk Hope." He also tried his hand at manufacturing salt and growing grapes for wine. In addition, Johnson, through his appointment as a cacique, had a right to two baronies of 12,000 acres each.

During Sir Nathaniel's tenure as governor, Queen Anne's War was in progress, and his acumen as a soldier was tested. He concentrated his efforts on building Charleston defenses, although he did permit James Moore to undertake, at Moore's expense, an attack on Spanish territory, which was a decided success. Johnson's defensive preparations proved their worth in 1706 when a joint French-Spanish attack was repulsed through the judicious use of land and sea forces. The Governor's courage and wisdom drew high praise.[26]

---

[23] Johnson's successor was Christopher Codrington. Burns, *History of the British West Indies,* pp. 375-6.

[24] In the Coleman deeds, there is recorded: "1671, Aug. 30. Settlement after marriage of Nathaniel Johnson (elder son of William Johnson) and Joanna, his now wife, daughter of Robert Overton. . . ." Society of Antiquaries of Newcastle-upon-Tyne, *Proceedings,* 3rd series, Vol. IX, no. 12 (1920), p. 161.

[25] "The Case of Robert Johnson," PR, Vol. XIII, pp. 392-3.

[26] Hayes Baker-Crothers, "Sir Nathaniel Johnson," in *Dictionary of American Biography,* ed. by Dumas Malone, Vol. X, p. 111; Mable L. Webber, "Sir Nathaniel Johnson and his son Robert, Governors of South Carolina," in *South Carolina Historical Magazine,* Vol. XXXVIII, No. 4 (October, 1937), pp. 109-110; David Duncan Wallace, *South Carolina: A Short History,* pp. 68-74; Herbert L. Osgood, *The American Colonies in the Eighteenth Century* (4 vols., New York: Columbia University Press, 1924), Vol. I, p. 203; Edward Channing, *A History of the United States* (6 vols., New York: The Macmillan Co., 1910-1925), Vol. II, pp. 346-7.

Sir Nathaniel also set up a police system used as protection against slave insurrection. He was instrumental in establishing the Anglican Church in South Carolina as the state church, for which he received severe criticism, including the charge of religious bigotry. Although Johnson's zeal for the Anglican Establishment may have been excessive, religious and political control were closely tied together after the Province had been divided into parishes. The religious issue, important as it was, may have been used to conceal a struggle between Anglicans and Dissenters for political control and its rewards.[27]

After Sir Nathaniel was replaced by Colonel Edward Tynte in 1709, he lived out the rest of his life in the Province, dying in 1712. His son Robert had become a freeman of Newcastle upon Tyne on January 19, 1702/3 or 1703/4[28] and was listed as a "merchant adventurer" and "mercer."[29]

Robert Johnson's experience as a merchant proved valuable. During this time, he closely associated himself with Carolina, keeping up with the bitter merchant-planter conflicts, and learned to understand the attitudes and problems of the merchant groups. Later, when he became Governor, he was able to moderate between the extremes of both parties.

Johnson also had become a large landholder in the Province. He was to be accepted in South Carolina, therefore, not as an outsider, but as a member of the Province who could be depended upon to reflect its interests. The question was whether Johnson's influence and exertions would be sufficient and effective enough to offset the melancholy condition of the Province, particularly in view of the rapidly increasing number of voices raised against proprietary rule. If the Proprietors recognized the true condition of affairs and

---

[27] Frederick P. Bowes, *The Culture of Early Charleston* (Chapel Hill: University of North Carolina Press, 1942), pp. 14-16; J. A. Doyle, *English Colonies in America* (5 vols., New York: Henry Holt and Co., 1882-1907), Vol. I, pp. 368-9; Charles M. Andrews, *The Colonial Period of American History* (4 vols., New Haven: Yale University Press, 1934-1938), Vol. III, pp. 241-5. Johnson was highly regarded by the Society for the Propagation of the Gospel. David Humphreys, *An Historical Account of the Incorporated Society for the Propagation of the Gospel in Foreign Parts* (London: Joseph Downing, 1730), pp. 81-83, 88-89, 103-4.

[28] *The Register of Freemen of Newcastle upon Tyne,* ed. by Madeleine Hope Dodds, in Newcastle upon Tyne Records Committee, *Publications,* Vol. III (1923), pp. 151, 200. For explanation of uncertainty about date, see *ibid.,* pp. ix-xiii.

[29] *Ibid.,* pp. 151, 200, and p. xv.

gave their full support to Governor Johnson, their ownership might still be preserved. Otherwise they stood in a very real danger of losing the Province.

Johnson arrived in South Carolina in 1717, between July 2 and October 10,[30] taking over the reins of government from Robert Daniel. In his opening address to the Commons House of Assembly, Johnson reminded the members, "I am not a stranger to you." He stressed his awareness over many years of public business, in England and the Province, and his efforts to promote South Carolina's prosperity and welfare while he was abroad. After this brief salutation, the new Governor then minced no words in chiding his listeners for the "disrespectful behaviour" shown the Lords Proprietors by their appeals to England.

Only a person with Johnson's kinship to Carolina would have dared open a new administration with such an attack on the Assembly.[31] Johnson, fully aware of the mounting discontent, then pointedly referred to the Commons' latest appeal several months before in which the King was asked that the Province be relieved from proprietary rule and taken under his protection.[32] With this approach, Johnson showed that he was prepared to take a strong stand to save proprietary rule.

After administering the reproof, the new Governor proceeded to make his recommendations to the Assembly on the need for repairing fortifications and taking further steps for defense. He urged the prevention of fraudulent practices in the packing of pitch and tar; requested improved methods of hulling and cleaning rice to raise the price of these commodities in England; and recommended the regulation of meat prices and the imposition of duties on all provisions exported (except rice), and the removal of duties on all imported provisions. He cited the need for the collection and printing of laws of the Province, and a statehouse and prison; and urged better support and encouragement for the clergy.

Johnson felt that such actions would enable the Province to lend assistance to Sir Robert Montgomery who wished to implant a colony in the southernmost part of the Province, beyond the Sa-

[30] Journal of the Commons House of Assembly of S. C. (hereinafter cited as JCHA), June 29, 1717, and notations following.

[31] JCHA, October 30, 1717.

[32] Ibid, June 29, 1717. "The humble address of the Representatives and inhabitants of South Carolina," to the King.

vannah River,[33] and to other prospective settlers. He called for prompt attention to the paper money problem. Because of the depreciation of the currency, the chief executive said he was forced to raise the price of land from three pounds per hundred acres to twelve pounds, in order to insure the Proprietors their former return on the sale of their lands.

Johnson made a point of stressing the beneficence of the Proprietors in their donative to the public of all arrears due for lands sold, and for quit rents.[34] This gift was to become, in short order, the subject of a dispute with the Commons House. But first the Commons, in customary fashion, congratulated the Governor on his safe arrival, echoed the words of his close association with the Province, and spoke with "hearty and unfeigned thanks" for his efforts in behalf of the Province while he was in Great Britain.

The Commons gave a favorable response to the Governor's recommendations, but took exception to his order raising the price of land, on grounds that the large amount of paper currency had been brought about by the Indian war. In defending its attitude toward the Proprietors, the Assembly said the actions had not stemmed from disrespect towards the Proprietors, explaining that "though the method we then took is now condemned, we thought it the best expedient to preserve ourselves from ruin; and is but what any British subjects in our circumstances would have done."[35]

Nor was it to take the Assembly long to reassert itself. The Commons House quickly started an argument with the Governor and Council over the site of the meeting place for a "grand conference." The meeting was called by Johnson to consider the important matter of peace with the Creeks, and although the Commons yielded on the place selected, the body had revealed its independent spirit.[36]

The dispute over the Proprietors' donative arose over the specific point of the terminating date of the gift. The discussion was to become prolonged and involve the important matters of raising the price of land and establishing a rent roll. Argument over the date could have served as a pretext for protesting the increased price of

---

[33] "Azilia: A Discourse by Sir Robert Montgomery, 1717," ed. by J. Max Patrick, in *Emory Sources and Reprints,* Series IV, No. 3 (Atlanta: Emory University Library, 1948).

[34] JCHA, October 30, 1717.

[35] JCHA, October 31, 1717.

[36] JCHA, October 31, November 1, 1717.

land and to hinder the drawing up of a rent roll, but the dispute centering around the date was genuine and significant.

The issue served to show the difficulties of proprietary government. Johnson and his Council asserted that the closing date of the donative was May 1, 1718. The Commons House maintained at first that the gift included rents only, later modifying its position to add purchase money for land sales, but only to November 3, 1716. The Governor and Council were forced to admit that this date was correct.[37] Johnson had received his instructions on the matter while still in England, but the Assembly, smarting under proprietary indignities, demanded to see such an order in writing under the seals of the Proprietors. During the dispute, Johnson found himself on the unsure ground of relying on spoken promises. Finally, in embarrassment, he had to retreat and refer the Assembly to Colonel William Rhett, a proprietary favorite, for confirmation of the new ground.[38]

An interesting byplay serves to contrast the attitudes of the Governor and the Commons House towards the Proprietors. In one of his messages urging the Assembly to accept the donative and establish a rent roll, Johnson spoke of the Proprietors as "our masters." The Commons, in answer, talked bitingly to Johnson of the Proprietors, "who are as you say your masters." Johnson's reply was telling: "You acknowledge [the Proprietors] are (as we say) our masters; and perhaps if you look over their charter you will find them to be your masters likewise." However, the Assembly had the last say, by tabling the matter.[39]

Another dispute between the Governor and Assembly involved the appointment of a gunner and powder receiver, an important position since that officer not only was in charge of collecting powder but also held the keys to the powder magazine. The Governor was willing to permit the Commons to nominate a collector of the powder tax but wanted to keep the magazine in his own hands as part of his military power as captain-general. The Assembly, nonetheless, had the keys delivered to its appointee with instructions to deliver to the Governor such powder as he should order. Johnson's protest was prophetic: "For if you can give such orders you

[37] JCHA, October 31, November 1, 5-6, 30, 1717.

[38] JCHA, November 5, 30, 1717.

[39] JCHA, December 5, 6, 9, 1717.

can also order him when you think fit, to deliver none and consequently you may wrest ye Government out of his hands."[40]

If Johnson had been inclined at this point to write off the Assembly as contentious, disagreeable, and uncooperative, he could have found plenty of evidence to justify his view. This quick appraisal would have been neither fair nor accurate. The Assembly was a hardworking group who penalized its members for missing meetings.[41] Like all legislative bodies, the Assembly had to spend time on trivial matters—such as deciding whether the members could use snuff, or regulating the tippling houses[42]—but it was primarily concerned with the welfare and interests of the Province, its own interpretation of those interests providing a special coloration, of course.

At the same time, the Assembly expressed open resentment toward the Lords Proprietors, and Johnson as the Proprietors' Governor was bound to be affected by that mounting hostility. There were reasons Johnson might expect to escape personal censure, however. He had close ties to the Province and was highly regarded there; furthermore, as a landholder of 25,000 acres, his personal and economic interests were not very different from those of many members of the Assembly. The ill-feeling of the Commons was aimed at the Proprietors, not against Governor Johnson. As long as the Assembly thought its rights and prerogatives were not infringed by proprietary usurpation, it was willing to cooperate and compromise with the Governor.

A good example was the controversy over the extension of the Indian Trading Act, during which two disputed points were compromised. The Governor and Council wanted to extend the Act for only three years, whereas the Commons favored a much longer period. Both sides agreed to a five-year extension. The other matter concerned payment to the Governor. Originally, all presents from the Indians went to the Governor as a perquisite of that office, but during the administration of Sir Nathaniel Johnson, a flat monetary gift to the Governor had been substituted. Afterwards, the presents went to the public. In 1717, the Assembly proposed to allow Robert Johnson £200 per annum in lieu of Indian presents.

---

[40] JCHA, November 28, December 4, 7, 9-11, 1717. Evarts B. Greene, *The Provincial Governor in the English Colonies of North America* (Cambridge: Harvard University Press, 1898), p. 187.

[41] JCHA, November 2, December 7, 1717.

[42] JCHA, April 11, October 30, December 5, 6, 1717.

The Governor and Council protested that, because of the weakened currency, the chief executive would be a "great loser"; thereupon the Assembly agreed to increase the payment of £400 per annum during the five-year extension period.[43]

To show further that there was no personal animosity, the Assembly readily appropriated £237-12s-9d to repair the Governor's house,[44] and followed his leadership on a number of important matters. It heeded Johnson's suggestion to increase the salaries of the clergy.[45] On the matter of collecting and organizing the laws of the Province, the Assembly agreed wholeheartedly, saying: "We think it a matter of so great a concern, that it ought no longer to be deferred, for we think it is of little use to us, to sit here and spend our time to pass laws, and at the same time no one can tell what is contained in them, and of consequence can not put them in execution. Neither indeed is it just to have a penalty of the law inflicted upon persons who can not reasonably be supposed to know them. And they are now so confused and multipled, that they are unintelligible to them that have the laws by them."[46]

In consequence, the Assembly provided funds to aid and encourage Chief Justice Nicholas Trott to prepare a collection of the laws for printing.[47]

In the matter of attracting new settlers, the Assembly also cooperated with Johnson, whose name some years later was to become associated with his township plan of settlement. The need for additional white inhabitants was recognized and means for acquiring them were suggested by other persons,[48] but Johnson was to be responsible for bringing about an effective plan of settlement. Soon after his arrival, his ideas upon this matter were being formulated. He urged the Assembly to make a present to Robert Wilson of Belfast for bringing settlers over from Ireland, and to provide a residence and provisions for the newcomers. Johnson suggested the Yamassee lands as the best place for their settlement. In response, the Commons House recommended that Wilson be given a grant of

---

[43] JCHA, November 22, December 6, 7, 10, 1717; D. D. Wallace, *South Carolina: A Short History,* pp. 78-79.

[44] JCHA, December 11, 1717.

[45] JCHA, December 5, 1717.

[46] JCHA, December 5, 1717.

[47] JCHA, December 11, 1717.

[48] E.g., Captain Patrick Traills, JCHA, January 17, 1716/17.

land. It approved offering incentives to new settlers by passing an additional bill to the Act for levying a tax of £95,000 on lands and Negroes. This measure provided £3,000 for paying the passage of those persons from Ireland, and for others who would arrive in the future, "in order to make them a free people." Of this sum, £837 was paid to Robert Wilson.[49]

In the vital matter of defense, the Assembly passed an Act to empower the Governor to raise forces for the defense of the Province, giving particular attention to the frontiers. The commissioners of the "Southern Rangers" were ordered to pay the soldiers and servants at the Savannah Town Garrison the sum of two shillings sixpence per bushel for Indian Corn, to encourage them to plant that crop. Payments were made to various persons for visits to the Indians, and for gifts, supplies and other expenses of entertaining them when they were in Charleston.[50]

Friendly tribes were considered an important aspect of defense. Proprietary government in South Carolina was not at a standstill at this time, and Governor Johnson held the confidence of the Assembly. It was believed that if the Proprietors would give their backing to Johnson and attune themselves to the needs of the Province, their government might be saved. But if proprietary rule remained unchanged, indifferent, the people of South Carolina were ready to take more drastic steps.

---

[49] JCHA, November 5, 28, 29, 30, December 11, 1717.

[50] JCHA, December 11, 1717.

Loyalty Not Interest

Courtesy South Carolina Historical Society

Coat of Arms of Sir Nathaniel Johnson

CHAPTER II

The Indian Menace

REASONS for the Carolinians' discontent with proprietary rule were varied, but behind them lay the fear of sudden, silent attack from the savage neighbor. There was, of course, another side to the picture, involving causes for the Indians' unfriendliness. It included the whole sordid tale of mistreatment that they had suffered at the hands of the traders. Despite these past indiscretions—and partly, in fact, because of them—the Indians were a very present danger in the Carolina of 1717. The Yamassee War was barely over, and the Indians lay close by, sullen and vengeful.

Another cause of Indian mischief was to be found in the three-power conflict for control of the Southeast. Viewed from Spanish eyes, this was a struggle to oust interlopers from their territory, or at least to prevent further expansion. Early in the struggle France had appeared as Spain's greatest enemy in the southern area,[1] but English pretensions soon made themselves felt. The English theme, like the French, was expansion, and in the vanguard were the Carolina traders, one of whom—Thomas Welch—as early as 1698 had reached the mouth of the Arkansas River.[2] The aggressive nature of English policy may be seen in a French report of 1708, when Sir Nathaniel Johnson was Governor. The French, believing the Carolinians were "sparing nothing to attract all our Indian allies to them," told of two English envoys sent by the Governor of Carolina to the Chickasaws. After visiting the Indians, one Englishman journeyed to the Choctaws, taking "a very big present." The Choctaws, according to the French report, were asked to join the English in destroying all the "little nations" in the French area, but they rejected the English plan. The other Englishman traveled to the

[1] William E. Dunn, *Spanish and French Rivalry in the Gulf Region of the United States,* 1678-1702, University of Texas *Bulletin,* 1705. Studies in history, 1 (Austin: University of Texas, 1917), pp. 6-9, 20-22, 147-8; J. G. Johnson, *The Spanish Period of Georgia and South Carolina History,* 1566-1702, University of Georgia *Bulletin,* Vol. XXIII, No. 9b, Special series: Studies, Vol. I, 9 (Athens: University of Georgia, 1923), pp. 1-2.

[2] Verner W. Crane, *The Southern Frontier,* 1670-1732 (Durham: Duke University Press, 1928), p. 46.

Mississippi country, carrying presents, and telling the Indians "his governor was sending him to tell them he wished peace with them and that in a short time he would be master of the country."[3]

Each of the three European nations hoped to use the Indians as allies, either in struggles against each other or as sources of trade, and sometimes both.

In contrast to Spain's mission-centered system of Indian control, with its emphasis on religious proselyting and instruction in agriculture and handicrafts, the English system was based solely upon trade.[4] In Carolina, as elsewhere, the system was subject to much corruption. Two of the most frequently repeated complaints were the traders' enslavement of free Indians, and their beatings and physical cruelty to Indians. Sometimes traders took Indian women as wives against their will.[5] Other abuses included the forcing of goods upon unwilling Indians; for example, forcing two hundred pounds of powder and five hundred pounds of bullets upon the Creek Indians.[6] Unfortunately for the Carolinians, the Creeks were to find use for such ammunition.

In an effort to control the multifarious abuses, South Carolina resorted to a license system for traders and sent agents among the various Indian tribes. They were sent to maintain friendly relations with the Indians, and also to keep an eye on Spanish and French activities, among the Indians or otherwise.[7]

A Board of Indian Commissioners was established who worked diligently and fined members for missing meetings.[8] These officials admitted it was "but a bare Board." It heard problems and abuses of the Indians of such a grievous nature that it felt these "might tend

[3] Sieur de Bienville to Pontchartrain, Minister of Marine, October 12, 1708, in *Mississippi Provincial Archives,* ed. by Dunbar Rowland and A. G. Sanders (3 vols., Jackson: Mississippi Department of Archives and History, 1927-1932), Vol. II, p. 39.

[4] Johnson, *Spanish Period,* p. 15; Crane, *Southern Frontier,* p. 7.

[5] A. S. Salley (ed.) *Journal of the Commissioners of the Indian Trade of South Carolina, September 20, 1710-April 12, 1715* (Columbia: Historical Commission of South Carolina, 1926), pp. 4 (September 21, 1710), 15 (August 1, 1711), 48 (October 25, 1712).

[6] *Ibid.,* p. 5 (October 28, 1710).

[7] *Ibid.,* pp. 42 (July 9, 1712), 46 (July 10, 1712). Indicatively enough, agents were instructed that when presents were given by the Indians, if they were of value worth sending to the Province, they should be sent to the Public Receiver for the use of the public. In return, the agents were authorized to make gifts to the Indians, but these were not to be more than half the value of the presents donated by the Indians.

[8] *Ibid.,* pp. 34 (June 20, 1712), 36 (June 27, 1712).

to the ruin and desolation of the Province" if no remedy could be found. The Yamassees in particular were frequent objectors to such practices as that of unauthorized white men settling among the Indians.[9]

A familiar complaint was the selling of rum to the Indians, and to solve the problem, the Yamassee and other Indians were told that their rum debts were forgiven and should not be paid. Because of the distance, the Board informed the Indians that it was impossible to prevent traders from carrying up rum, but urged the Indians to restrain their people from buying it.[10]

Another problem confronting the commissioners was the abduction and sale of free Indians.[11] The traders were warned that no Indian was deemed to be a slave, unless taken in war, or bought as such, and even those taken in war, if made free by their masters, were to be considered free men.[12]

As a further indignity, free Indians were forced to hoe crops and to carry packs for the traders, while the traders frequently took from the Indians their hogs, poultry, corn, and other provisions, paying them only what they thought fit. If the Indians protested, they were beaten and abused.[13]

Another grievance was that of debts, and at the time of the Indian defection it was estimated that Indians owed the traders about £50,000. It was believed by many Carolinians that one reason for the Indian uprising was the thought of thereby removing this large debt. The debts of Indians were often compounded, for sometimes they were required to pay debts on which their relatives and friends had defaulted.[14]

On top of these troubles, the licensing system gave all the appearances of breaking down. There were numerous reports of unlicensed traders; at one time, for example, eight traders among the Yamassees were reported without licenses. When Landgrave Thomas Smith was accused of having sent out several unlicensed traders, he answered the charge somewhat weakly by saying he traded outside

[9] *Ibid.*, pp. 9-10 (May 30, 1711).

[10] *Ibid.*, pp. 12-13 (July 27, 1711), 17 (August 3, 1711).

[11] *Ibid.*, pp. 13, 14 (July 28, 1711), 20 (August 15, 1711).

[12] *Ibid.*, pp. 18-20 (August 3, 1711).

[13] Board of Trade Journal, July 26, 1715, PR, Vol. VI, p. 140; Salley, *Journal of the Commissioners of the Indian Trade,* p. 4 (September 21, 1710).

[14] Board of Trade Journal, July 16, 1715, PR, Vol. VI, pp. 137-8.

the limits of the government. Former Indian Agent John Wright in 1712 reported that all the traders had traded without licenses. About two and one-half years later, the commissioners' secretary reported that most traders were then without licenses.[15]

The situation failed to improve, and in 1715 the Creek Indians were reported dissatisfied with English traders among them, as Spanish influence ascended. The Indians were distraught, for they had made several complaints without receiving redress. Upon a report that the Creeks intended to cut off the traders and then fall upon the settlements, agents were sent to the Yamassees, Pallachuccolas, and Creeks, to set up a conference at Savannah Town where grievances would be discussed.[16]

Governor Craven was en route with troops to attend the conference, but did not reach there in time. The attack came first to the agents at Pocotaligo, the Yamassee town, where they were trying to set up the conference, and to the traders among the Yamassees. Soon traders all over the Province were slain, and Indians of various tribes desolated most of the out-settlements. They then headed for the Edisto River settlements. So harassed was the Province that all women and children were sent to Charleston. Meanwhile, the men under arms, who were reported to number no more than 1,400, were defending the outlying plantations as well as they could, and endeavoring to keep the Indians away from Charleston.[17]

The Yamassees, Creeks, and their allies, had constituted the largest number of Indians to act in concert since the English had settled the Province. Governor Alexander Spotswood of Virginia feared the uprising might reach his state. He had received reports that there had been a greater than usual intercourse between the southern Indians and those to the northward.[18] Reports had also reached

---

[15] Salley, *Journal of the Commissioners of the Indian Trade,* pp. 6 (March 9, 1710/11), (March 22, 1710/11), 25 (March 21, 1711/12), 30 (May 14, 1712), 66 (October 6, 1713), 72 (May 6, 1714), 75 (May 20, 1714), 78 (August 31, 1714).

[16] Ibid., pp. 86, 110. (April 12, 1715). *See also,* Herbert E. Bolton, "Spanish Resistance to the Carolina Traders in Western Georgia," in *Georgia Historical Quarterly,* Vol. IX, No. 2 (June 1925), p. 129.

[17] "An Account of the . . . Yamassee War in South Carolina, Extracted from *The Boston News,* June 13, 1715." *Historical Collections of South Carolina,* ed. B. R. Carroll (New York: Harper & Brothers, 1836), Vol. II, pp. 570-572. Board of Trade Journal, July 28, 1715, PR, Vol. VI, pp. 140-141. For a French account, Bienville to Pontchartrain, September 1, 1715, in *Miss. Prov. Archives,* Vol. VIII, pp. 187-8.

[18] From A. Spotswood, May 27, 1715, PR, Vol. VI, pp. 89-91.

South Carolina from New England that Indians from Canada had gone to war at some distant place, possibly intending to join South Carolina's enemies. It was feared that the Indian War might spread northward and become general throughout the colonies.[19]

Nicholas Trott, the chief justice, described the plight of the Province in these words:

> One of the greatest Afflictions that could well be brought upon this Province the barbarous heathen Indians that are round about us from North to South and Five times our Number have all united themselves together & made War upon us Beginning with the Murder of our Traders and Several of the Inhabitants in the out Settlements And have since made further Incursions into the Settlements Killing all they meet destroying and laying wast ye Plantations where they came plundering & then burning the Houses Lying Sculking in the Bushes & Swamps that we know not where to find them nor could follow them if we did So that we may as well goe to War with the Wolfs & Bears.
>
> The whole Country is in Armes and nothing in it but hurry & Confusion. . . .[20]

The clergy of the Province reported:

> The melancholy circumstances this Province Lyes under by the Incursion of the Savages (to w[ho]m pity & compassion is unknown) who have no other notion or expression of Courage than the exquisiteness of their tortures & prolonging the Deaths they inflict upon their Captives, they seem to have nothing buy the shape of Men to distinguish them from Wolves & Tygars. The Southern parts w[hi]ch include a fifth of the Province are entirely depopulated. . . .[21]

South Carolina reacted to the disaster with an immediate declaration of martial law, while emigration was strictly forbidden. To bolster the Province's limited manpower, friendly Indians were recruited, and trusted Negroes were put under arms in organized battalions. Pleas for men were sent also to North Carolina and Virginia.[22] Appeals went to the Crown asking that orders be issued to

---

[19] PR, Vol. VI, pp. 119-120, from Sam Eveleigh, October 7, 1715.

[20] Nicholas Trott to Bishop of London, June 17, 1715, Society for the Propagation of the Gospel in Foreign Parts, London (hereinafter cited as SPG), Fulham Palace MSS, N. C., S. C., Ga., no. 6.

[21] Clergy of South Carolina to Bishop of London, October 18, 1715, SPG, Fulham Palace MSS, South Carolina, no. 231.

[22] Chapman J. Milling, *Red Carolinians* (Chapel Hill: University of North Carolina Press, 1940), pp. 145-6. Colonel Thomas Broughton, brother-in-law of Robert Johnson, received payment of £140 for a Negro killed in an action against the Indians. JCHA, December 11, 1717.

other colonies, especially Virginia, to give what assistance they could, and to declare war immediately against those Indians who had attacked South Carolina. Significantly, South Carolina asked that other American colonies be cautioned against furnishing the Indians with any of the munitions of war.[23]

The intimation that these colonies were trading with the unfriendly Indians later became a charge laid at Virginia's doorstep. The London Agents for South Carolina reported that most of the Province's troubles stemmed from Virginians who were trying to increase their Indian trade by supplying them with guns and ammunition. Virginia traders, it was charged, were found safe among the Carolina Indians after the Yamassee war had erupted, while Carolina traders were slain. The Carolinians pleaded that some regulation be placed upon Virginia traders less they undersell the Carolina traders, wrest all transactions, and turn the Indians against them.

Although South Carolina wanted the considerable profits from the Indian trade—despite the denial of the Assembly's Agents when they presented the State's case in London—a chief reason was the control of the Indians. The Agents warned that if the Indians were supplied entirely by Virginia, they would lose any dependence they felt on Carolina and would continue to insult the Province and its people. In that case, the Indians could never be brought to peace, the Agents said, adding that this was the desire of the Virginians and that it would be as long as they traded with them.[24]

Shortly before his appointment as Governor, Robert Johnson, along with other interested persons in England, appeared on several occasions[25] before the Board to report the serious straits in which Carolina found itself during the Yamassee War. The situation in the beginning was so dark it appeared that without additional sup-

---

[23] PR, Vol. VI, pp. 86-87, Address of the General Assembly of South Carolina to the King, *ca.,* May, 1715.

[24] Joseph Boone and Richard Beresford to the Board of Trade, December 5, 1716, PR, Vol. VI, pp. 261-9. The French, too, recognized the great importance of trade. When some Indians, formerly trading with Carolina, sought trade with Mobile, Bienville welcomed this new opportunity, promising the Indians the "same advantage" they had experienced with the English. However, in his report home he remarked: "These Indians will not find the same advantage with us that they had with the English who sold them merchandise very cheap and they took the peltries at a high price and here it is quite the contrary." Bienville to Pontchartrain, September 1, 1715, in *Miss. Prov. Archives,* Vol. III, p. 188.

[25] Robert Johnson's appearances, July 16, 28, December 20, 1715.

plies, the Province could not hold out for even six months. The Board asked what would be needed for an adequate defense. It was told that 500 men divided into fifty groups, each under a half-pay lieutenant, and located in small forts properly situated at the heads of rivers, would effectively prevent further Indian incursions.[26]

The South Carolina Assembly, convinced that the Proprietors were incapable of assisting them, appealed to the Crown and asked to be taken under the care and government of His Majesty.[27] This plea was to be heard with increasing frequency from that time onward.

Despite these entreaties, the immediate problem facing South Carolina was, bluntly, survival. Was it possible and by what means? The hopes of the settlers at the time seemed to rest on two advantageous possibilities; the Province might receive arms from England; and, the Cherokee Indians might give aid against the Creeks and Yamassees.

In due course some provisions of war were sent from England, and there was momentary expectation that the Cherokees, who had at first joined in the uprising but soon sued for peace, would now assist the settlers. Toward the close of 1715, Colonel George Chicken was sent to try to persuade the then peaceful Indians to become allies. They agreed to go against the Savannahs, Euchees, and Appallaches only.[28]

Later on, the Cherokees were influential with some of the smaller tribes in securing peace. Also, they promised to deliver up one of the chief mischief-makers, Wateree Jack, and all the white men's slaves, horses, and goods they had among them.[29]

While the Province was awaiting help from the Cherokees, the Proprietors in London, when questioned about the state of affairs in the Province, spoke of the Indian trouble as if it were a thing of the past. Any further disturbances, they claimed, would be met by the large shipment of war supplies sent over and the assistance

---

[26] Board of Trade Journal, July 16, 1715, PR, Vol. VI, pp. 137-9.

[27] Address of the South Carolina Commons House of Assembly to the King, August 1715, and interestingly enough, signed by the speaker, William Rhett, a proprietary favorite, PR, Vol. VI, pp. 116-7.

[28] George Chicken, "A Journal from Carolina in 1715," in *Year Book—1894, City of Charleston, S. C.* (Charleston: Walker, Evans & Cogswell Co., 1894), pp. 330-31, 334n; Clergy of South Carolina to Bishop of London, October 18, 1715, SPG, Fulham Palace MSS, South Carolina, no. 231.

[29] Committee of South Carolina Commons House, August 6, 1716, PR, Vol. VI, p. 241.

"they may constantly expect" from the Cherokees. In any great emergency, the Proprietors said, Carolinians could arm the slaves, and by this means, "they will be Impow[er]red to resist a greater Force than the Enemy will in all humane probability be able at any time to bring against them."[30]

With this pronouncement, the Proprietors decided to leave the safety of the Carolina settlers to themselves, their slaves, and friendly Indians. The danger of arming slaves had been proven and could only be resorted to in time of extremity, and even then not without the utmost anxiety. The price paid for Indian assistance was high.

At the beginning of 1717, the condition of the Province was described as "deplorable." On this "melancholy occasion" it was being defended "with a handful of Men, against numerous & Potent Nations, and We have no Allies of any Importance but the Cherikees, Whose Kings and Head Warriors are now with Us." The charge of maintaining these Indians, plus the expense of meeting their unreasonable demands, was purchasing friendship at too dear a rate, but the welfare of the Province was at stake. The country could not long bear the burden of tribute to the Indians. What South Carolina needed was more men. Instead, because of the lingering war and heavy tax burden, many inhabitants were choosing to abandon the Province, leaving their houses and lands, but taking slaves and other portable goods. This was done despite the most stringent laws of control. The Proprietors were told plainly that the fate of the Province depended upon their sending relief, or soliciting the Crown for help. Otherwise, South Carolina was in danger of being deserted and forsaken.[31]

There was much confusion on the eve of Johnson's assuming the reins of government. Many voices were now raised in support of the pleas for the King to take the Province under his royal protection. Some persons could not see an end yet to the Indian War "altho abundance of the people feeds themselves up with ye fancy that it is all over." On plantations and farms, at cowpens and on the trails and streams, people were still being killed by marauding Indian bands. Besides the terror this wrought, it also meant shortages in food crops. At Charleston, one distressed observer reported

---

[30] PR, Vol. VI, pp. 230-31, Lords Proprietors of Carolina to Board of Trade, July 27, 1716.

[31] Deputy Governor and Council of South Carolina to Proprietors, January 26, 1716/7, PR, Vol. VII, pp. 3-4.

that people were "ready to Eat up one another for Want of provisions," and the only food obtainable was of very poor quality. Beef, pork, mutton, butter and Indian corn were expensive, while the bread loaf had been drastically reduced in size. Rent was raised 100%. Pieces of eight sold for twenty-six shillings per ounce. Paper bills were diminishing in value, and fear was expressed that in a short time, no one would accept them. The high cost of living and inflation were coupled with taxation and it was said that "the taxes are so high that it is hard Living Especially for the poor." Once again it was asserted that suffering was being prolonged because Virginia kept furnishing the Indians with ammunition and other goods.[32]

Because of the continuous ravages of the Indians, it was not safe to attempt the resettlement of abandoned parts of the Province, some of which lay within eighteen miles of Charleston. The loss of citizens during the war was estimated at 400 killed, and fortunes depleted in the amount of £116,000, or more. In addition, because of large expenses in prosecuting the war, and in defending the people, debts in excess of £100,000 had been contracted.[33]

The peak of the crisis was reached at the time Johnson became governor, not a promising picture for the new leader. His future, however, depended upon the Province's survival; and its survival, in turn, rested on him.

It was evident that the proprietary policy of Indian control—the "buffer" policy—had broken down. The essence of this plan had been to protect the frontiers with friendly Indian nations who were supplied with arms, ammunition and goods unobtainable elsewhere, to make them dependent upon the Province. The Indians who were ordered not to give or to sell the arms and ammunition to other tribes were then used to awe others who might be disposed in an unfriendly manner toward South Carolina. Presumably, the Province was surrounded on its southern and western borders by powerful and friendly nations of Indians who offered a stout line of defense against hostile Indians, the French and Spanish.[34]

---

[32] Paragraphs and extracts of letters from South Carolina, February 6, 1716/7, April 27, 1717, PR, Vol. VII, pp. 17-21.

[33] Representation of the inhabitants of South Carolina to both houses of Parliament, PR, Vol. VII, pp. 45-46.

[34] Milling, *Red Carolinians,* pp. 84-85.

This policy became unrealistic with the alienation of the bordering Indians, and the increased activity of the French and Spanish who were accused of supplying arms and ammunition secretly to the Indians. The Province—the "Southern Frontier" of British America—facing these enemies was in deep trouble.[35] It was difficult to make peace with the various Indian tribes, because they were encouraged, it was believed, by the French and Spanish to continue harrassment and warfare.[36]

Further, the enormous amount of aid called for by the Cherokees was a yoke about the shoulders of the Province. Clearly, a new policy was needed. That opportunity arose as word was received that some of the Creek headmen were requesting permission to come to Charleston to treat for peace. Since the Creeks and the Cherokees, the two largest Indian nations, were mortal enemies, a plan was evolved to let them destroy each other. The policy was a dangerous one because of the large numbers in both tribes compared to the few fighting men left in Carolina, but the latter fact made it almost imperative to try. Of some comfort was the continuing Cherokee-Creek antagonism that might prevent a union of the two against the Province, so the campaign was begun "to hold both as our friends, for some time, and assist them in Cutting one another's throats w[i]thout offending Either."[37]

The means for working out this new policy successfully were laid in the lap of the Province, so to speak, because of the Indians' animosity to each other, but there were many Carolinians who opposed it. They felt great care must be taken in arranging a peace with the Creeks, for fear of disobliging the Cherokees, a friendly nation on the extremity of the Province. Forgetting the high price paid for Cherokee assistance, and the numerous insults suffered at their hands, some declared that neither in honor nor in justice could their friendship be abandoned.[38]

Fortunately, the new Governor paid no heed to such talk. He did not intend the Province to undergo continued blackmail at the hands of the Cherokees. Governor Johnson received kindly the

---

[35] Representation of the inhabitants of South Carolina to both Houses of Parliament, PR, Vol. VII, pp. 44-47.

[36] Committee of South Carolina Commons House to Joseph Boone, March 8, 1717/8, PR, Vol. VII, pp. 99-100.

[37] From Joseph Boone, April 25, 1717, PR, Vol. VII, pp. 15-16.

[38] Paragraphs and extracts of letters from South Carolina, PR, Vol. VII, pp. 18, 21.

headmen of the Creek nation who came to offer their overtures of peace. With notice of the Creek intention, Johnson called an immediate "grand conference of the Council and Commons House" to consider the terms of a peace settlement, saying that "no time may be lost in a matter of so great consequence."[39]

Charleston was selected as the site of the parley, and the Commissioners of the Indian Trade were instructed to order the Catawba Indians to remove themselves and see that none returned during the negotiations.[40] At the Governor's request, the Assembly commanded that steps be taken to receive and entertain the Indians at public expense.[41] Also, as suggested by the Governor, trade was opened with the Creeks during the treaty negotiations, although arms and ammunition were specifically excluded.[42]

Johnson worked feverishly to insure the success of the parley. He urged the Assembly to satisfy the desire of Emperor Brims' son for a fine suit of clothing for his appearance at Charleston, and prodded the Assembly on the matter of presents for the Indians. The Commons House responded by leaving the entire matter of gifts in the Governor's hands. Johnson pleased the Creeks in that respect and arranged to have their arms repaired. When he heard that ten young Indian men were displeased because they had received no presents, he saw that each was given a blanket and a clout.[43]

On the matter of the agreement, Johnson cheerfully communicated to the Commons that the Indians were "very well satisfied" with the proposals made them and were confident their head men would accept, including perhaps the Alabamas. The Governor quickly explained, however, that the Creeks held no authorization to act for that group.

Johnson thought it prudent to fulfill the Indian request for fifty men to accompany them home, "to show the French and Spaniards, that they do not want friends to assist them."[44] Johnson recom-

[39] JCHA, October 31, 1717.

[40] JCHA, November 1, 1717.

[41] JCHA, November 7, 1717. Several orders are found in the Commons House Journal for reimbursing various persons for housing, supplying, and entertaining the Creeks and other Indians. JCHA, December 11, 1717.

[42] JCHA, November 7-8, 1717.

[43] JCHA, November 13-14, December 9, 1717.

[44] JCHA, November 15, 1717. The French were worried about the Alabamas, especially since they had no goods there to use as presents to counteract those it was feared the English would offer, and since "the Indians are governed more by self-interest than any reason." Bienville to Hubert of St.

mended to the Commons that, (pursuant to the agreement), the number of slaves taken by the Cherokees be returned to the Creeks; and Colonel John Barnwell moved that an amount of powder and shot proportional to other trade goods be sent them.[45]

Despite the arrangements with the Creeks, Johnson realized that such treaties were always precarious. It was also believed that the French at Mobile, and the Spanish at St. Augustine, who had built forts among the Creeks, were continuing to live among them, providing them with presents and arms and ammunition, and buying the slaves and plunder they had taken in war against the English.

While busy with the Creeks, the Governor received a report of an attempt to win the Upper Cherokees over to French and Spanish interest.[46] He was also engaged in negotiations with a representation of Chickasaw Indians who wanted to send their skins to Savannah Town and trade with the Province. The Cherokees let it be known they were suspicious of the Chickasaw friendship, but Johnson could find no cause for their fear. Consequently the Assembly, in concurrence with the Governor and Council, agreed to present a coat and hat to the Chickasaw chiefs or head men, and the Commissioners of Indian Trade were ordered to open trade with them.[47] To salve Cherokee feelings, it was decided to lower the price of guns sold to them.[48] Additionally, Governor Johnson was urging the Assembly to prohibit trade and commerce with St. Augustine, Havana, and Mobile, and the indirect trade with Indian enemies.[49]

When a report was received from St. Augustine that the Creeks had made peace with the Cherokees, Johnson's courage may have sagged somewhat, but it is not recorded. Instead, in a masterful

---

Malo, Commissary General, September 19, 1717, *Miss. Prov. Archives,* Vol. III, pp. 222-3. The French in 1717 built Fort Toulouse among the Alabama Indians, near the confluence of the Talapoosa and Coosa rivers. *Miss Prov. Archives,* Vol. I, p. 243n; John R. Swanton, *The Indian Tribes of North America* (Smithsonian Institution, Bureau of American Ethnology, *Bulletin 145.* Washington: Government Printing Office, 1953), pp. 154-5; John Pitts Cory, *Indian Affairs in Georgia, 1732-1756* (Philadelphia: University of Pennsylvania, 1936), pp. 18-19; Andrés de Barcia, *Chronological History of the Continent of Florida,* translated by Anthony Kerrigan (Gainesville: University of Florida Press, 1951), pp. 358-9.

[45] JCHA, November 15, December 4, 11, 1717. The Commissioners of the Indian Trade had been ordered to open trade with the Creeks on December 4.

[46] JCHA, November 15, 1717.

[47] JCHA, November 30, December 4, 1717.

[48] No credit was to be extended. JCHA, December 4, 1717.

[49] JCHA, November 7, 22, December 9-10, 1717.

piece of understatement he remarked that if the report were true, "We are deeper ingaged than ever." He added that since the report was only conjecture, the Province could hope for the best.[50] Johnson was well aware of the long-standing enmity between Creek and Cherokee, and, as he suspected, the reported alliance failed to materialize. Instead, the Creeks and Cherokees were at war with each other, although both were avowedly friends of South Carolina. This was the very situation which Johnson and other Carolinians had been trying to bring about.

To protect the frontiers, now that the "buffers" were gone, the Province relied upon garrisons at Port Royal, Savannah Town (a few miles below the present-day town of Augusta but on the opposite bank of the river), and the Congarees (near the juncture of Congaree Creek with Congaree River, south of present-day Columbia), with an additional post later built on the Savannah River at the Pallachuccolas (about sixty miles from the mouth of the river), and Fort King George (built in 1721) at the mouth of the Altamaha. The frontiers were patrolled by ranger companies, while the inland passage between Port Royal and the Altamaha was guarded by two scout boats.[51]

Sometimes it was necessary for the Governor to prod the Assembly's memory about keeping this system operating. Once when the Savannah Town garrison was in great need of certain items, Johnson urged the Commons House to supply it immediately, stating that "the Lieutenant who has been in Town six weeks may be dispatched away and the Garrison not suffer."[52] Again, Johnson reminded the Assembly the Ranger Act was expiring and asked for a renewal. The Governor recommended that the new bill, which set forth the requisite number of Rangers for guarding the frontiers, should call for discharging from the service those failing in their duty. He said it should also "lay such a penalty on the persons who shall be drawn or otherwise serve the country as may oblige them to obey the same."[53]

---

[50] Extract of a letter from Robert Johnson to R. Shelton, secretary to the Lords Proprietors of Carolina, February 10, 1717/8, PR, Vol. VII, p. 120; Robert Johnson to Board of Trade, June 18, 1718, PR, Vol. VII, p. 135, and also in Public Record Office (hereinafter cited as PRO), Colonial Office (hereinafter cited as CO), 5:1293, p. 156 (Library of Congress transcript).

[51] Milling, *Red Carolinians,* pp. 151-2; Robert L. Meriwether, *The Expansion of South Carolina,* 1729-1765 (Kingsport, Tennessee: Southern Publishers, Inc., 1940), pp. 10-12, 32.

[52] JCHA, November 7, 1717.

[53] JCHA, November 5, 1717.

Inasmuch as the Yamassees had changed their loyalty before,[54] there was one last effort to alienate them from Spain and return them to English allegiance. Three Creek Indians, relations of the Huspaw King, proposed that if the English would send a small party of men with them to St. Mary's, near St. Augustine, the Huspaw King might be prevailed upon to desert his Spanish friends and to bring over the Yamassees once again to the side of Carolina. The Carolinians, therefore, authorized such a mission under command of Colonel John Barnwell who proceeded to St. Mary's. The three Creek Indians went to visit their relatives in St. Augustine but found the Huspaw King in such a temper that they dared not approach him about their mission; instead, at night, they fled from St. Augustine. Consequently it was reported that the Huspaw King was carried about the town in triumph, with drums and trumpets before him, and that the Spaniards had made him Chief General of 500 Indians who were being prepared to set out immediately against the inhabitants of South Carolina. The Spanish reportedly had promised the Indians that they would "buy our heads & horses at the same price." Colonel Barnwell feared that the southward parts of the Province would again be exposed to depredations and so made hurried plans to warn the Province of the impending danger.[55]

Alarm spread day by day within the government and among the inhabitants of Carolina over the impending arrival of 500 armed Indians; and the fear was expressed that the same wretchedness and distress would be suffered as had been during the Indian War.[56] This attitude was not without good foundation. In the outlying areas, inhabitants had been ambushed and killed, or taken prisoners. Traders reported that the Indians were dissatisfied and uneasy.[57] The attempt to bring Yamassees into alliance with Carolina had failed.

At this juncture the most adamant must have realized that the "buffer" policy in its old form could not be reinstituted. Governor Johnson went into action against the Indians, taking the offensive

---

[54] Johnson, *Spanish Period,* p. 21.

[55] John Barnwell to Governor Johnson, April 20, 1719, John Barnwell to Captain Beamour, April 21, 1719, Colonel William Rhett to his son William Rhett in London, April 25, 1719, PR, Vol. VII, pp. 186-9.

[56] Thomas Hasell, Gilbert Jones, and William Guy to the Secretary of the SPG. May 13, 1719, SPG, Series A, Vol. XIII.

[57] Thomas Hasell to the Secretary of the SPG, August 1, 1719, SPG, Series A, Vol. XIII.

immediately. He sent out a well-equipped expedition under Colonel Barnwell who attacked the Yamassee and other Indians in the vicinity of St. Augustine, doing much damage to their settlements, and bringing back Indian and Spanish prisoners.[58]

Three points in Governor Johnson's Indian policy now evolved:

1. Continuing the use of a number of strategically-located, garrisoned forts on the frontiers in conjunction with frontier patrols by the Carolina Rangers;

2. Encouraging the Indian nations to war among themselves;

3. Assuming the offensive against the Indians when it appeared that they were readying themselves for an attack.

The Governor never relaxed his support of this destructive phase of the Indian policy; and although it was not the most humane measure devisable, it was effective. Also, it protected the Province from surrounding natives, a most desirable wish. Any less realistic policy would probably have proved inadequate in the crisis.

Later, when Robert Johnson had returned to the Province as royal governor, he added a fourth, constructive point for protection against the Indians and European foes. His *township scheme* for settling the frontiers proved to be the most effective of all.

[58] John Barnwell to Governor Johnson [October 1719], PR, Vol. VIII, pp. 1-5.

Courtesy Carolina Art Association

Sir Nathaniel Johnson
AEtatis: 61/April: 7/1705

CHAPTER III

Victory Over The Pirates

CONFRONTED with the Indian menace on its southwestern frontiers, South Carolina had another serious problem on the Atlantic coast, where it faced the scourge of the sea—piracy. Unsavory characters had from time to time harassed shipping, and immediately preceding and during Johnson's administration there was an especially heavy concentration of pirates in the area. Trade plummeted as ships using Charleston harbor faced the probability of capture. Imports, exports, passengers, and the mail suffered severely, as captures became a daily occurrence.[1]

One notable example was an experience of one William Guy, missionary for the Society for the Propagation of the Gospel, who was returning to Charleston from Narragansett. The vessel in which he was sailing had arrived off Charleston harbor and lay off the bar of Ashley River, waiting for a pilot to bring it in safely. Hoping to obtain a pilot sooner, Guy went ashore in a small boat. During his absence, a pirate suddenly appeared and took the waiting ship, in which were Guy's wife, children and their possessions. After having kept them three days, the pirate sent his wife and children ashore, robbed of everything. Not only was his family destitute of clothing and household goods, but Guy had lost most of his books, papers, and other valuables. Upon hearing of his plight, the Society in London voted Guy a gratuity of £40 sterling beyond his regular allowance.[2] There were other victims, less fortunate than the Guy family, who had no place to turn for help or relief. Many even forfeited their lives.

---

1 Thomas Broughton to Secretary of the SPG, June 2, 1719, SPG, Series A, Vol. XIII; Board of Trade to Craggs, August 28, 1718, PR, Vol. VII, p. 150; Wm. Tredwell Bull to Bishop of London, November 18, 1718, SPG, Fulham Palace MSS, South Carolina, no. 17.

2 William Guy to Secretary of the SPG, November 20, 1718, SPG, Series A, Vol. XIII; Guy to Bishop of London, November 20, 1718, SPG, Fulham Palace MSS, South Carolina, no. 118; Wm. Tredwell Bull to Secretary of the SPG, November 24, 1718, SPG, Series A, Vol. XIII; Vestry of St. Philip's, Charleston, to Bishop of London, December 19, Secretary of SPG to Guy, April 1, 1719, SPG, Series A, Vol. XIII; C. F. Pascoe, *Two Hundred Years of the S. P. G.* (2 vols., London: The Society, 1901), Vol. II, p. 849.

Although the South Carolina government was exerting itself to the utmost, it seemed too weak to withstand the pirates. In a letter to the Board of Trade, Johnson informed the members that the Province was under a continuous alarm, and trade was at the stage of utter ruin. Twice within the preceding nine months, he wrote, pirates had stationed themselves off the bar and had captured all ships entering or leaving the port. Only about two weeks previous to his writing, four pirate vessels had appeared in sight of the town. This force, reported to be under the command of the pirate Edward Teach, or Thatch (best remembered as the notorious "Blackbeard"), consisted of a ship of forty-odd guns, three sloops, and more than 400 men. They took the pilot boat and captured eight or nine other vessels, aboard which were several of the chief inhabitants of the Province. The pirates were quick to realize their advantageous position: they sent a message that unless the Governor dispatched a chest of medicines, which they sorely needed, all the prisoners would be put to death. Left with no alternative, Johnson complied; whereupon the prisoners, already plundered of all they had, were sent ashore almost naked.[3]

To help abolish piracy, the British Government had issued a proclamation offering pardon to those pirates who would surrender and promise to stop their illegal activities. Johnson was given a commission to pardon pirates, but he did not feel that the proclamation had any good effect. He noted that a few had given themselves up and received a certificate of pardon, but several of these had already returned to their old ways. Johnson had received reliable information that on the seas between Carolina and New Providence there were more than twenty sail of pirates. Governor Johnson told the Board that unless ships were sent against them, the trade of this part of America would be entirely ruined. He asked particularly that a frigate or, better still, two frigates be sent to cruise in the vicinity of Charleston harbor. Concerning the assignment of Captain Woodes Rogers, then on his way to New Providence, Johnson wrote that he hoped that he had frigates with him and a good force of soldiers. Otherwise, Johnson said, he would run the risk of being attacked by the pirates, who were at that place

[3] Johnson to Board of Trade, June 18, 1718, PRO, CO 5:1293, pp. 154-5 (Library of Congress transcript). Samuel Wragg, a Council member, was one of the prisoners.

in numbers of 600 or 700. Since it was their "Nest & Rendezvous," Johnson felt that they would be unwilling to have the place settled.[4]

At this time—the summer of 1718—South Carolina enjoyed a brief respite from piratical mischief. While the pirates were on the coast that summer, they did not care to bother the few vessels then sailing, as the cargoes were of little value.[5] They preferred to wait for the fall season when the produce of the Province had been readied for shipment abroad; and when September and October came, pirate action reached its zenith.

Johnson again complained bitterly to England about the pirates who were blocking Charleston harbor for periods of eight to ten days, taking and plundering all vessels entering or departing, but soon was forced to use his own initiative. Two vessels commanded by Vane waited off the bar, one day taking a slave ship from Guinea and two other sloops, and the next assaulting four outbound ships. Disgusted with these continuing insults to the Province, and hearing that another pirate vessel careening at Cape Fear was likely to pay its respects to the Charleston port, Governor Johnson decided to attack. Two sloops and a force of 130 men were prepared and placed under command of Colonel William Rhett, who first steered in a southerly direction looking for Vane. Not finding him, and being unable to gain any information as to his whereabouts, Rhett changed course and headed north for Cape Fear. There he found a sloop of eight guns and fifty men, commanded by the notorious pirate Stede Bonnet, together with two of Bonnet's prizes.

Bonnet tried to escape the next day. Rhett followed, and in the chase, both Bonnet's sloop and the two from Carolina ran aground

---

[4] Johnson to Board of Trade, June 18, 1718, PRO CO 5:1293, pp. 155-7 (Library of Congress transcript); JCHA, December 3, 1717.

[5] Shirley Carter Hughson, *The Carolina Pirates and Colonial Commerce, 1670-1740,* in Johns Hopkins University *Studies in Historical and Political Science,* series 12, no. 5-7 (Baltimore: The Johns Hopkins Press, 1894), pp. 84-85. McCrady questioned the use of the term "Carolina Pirates," believing it to be misleading. He asserted that of forty-five pirates captured in 1699, none were Carolinians; among the thirty-eight taken in the 1716-18 period, only three, one of whom was acquitted, claimed to be from the Province. He maintained further that since the pirates came from the West Indies and the British Isles, it would have been proper to call them "British pirates on the coast of Carolina." Edward McCrady, *The History of South Carolina under the Proprietary Government, 1670-1719* (New York: The Macmillan Co., 1897), pp. 587-8. The audacious activity of the pirates on the Carolina coast in the fall of 1718 could only find its parallel in the previous century when the buccaneers, led by Henry Morgan, plied their trade at the expense of the Spanish fleets.

on the shoals. Rhett's vessel was within musket shot of the pirate sloop, and as the tide ebbed, his ship heeled toward the pirates'. Exposed to the fire from the pirate craft, the guns of Rhett's ship were pointing uselessly downward. After taking the pirate fire for six hours, Rhett's ship was freed by the incoming tide, while Bonnet's sloop was still held fast on the shoal. Seeing that Rhett was about to board his vessel, Bonnet sent out a white flag. He threw himself on Rhett's mercy, Rhett promised to intercede, and the pirate surrendered. Carolina casualties included ten men killed in the encounter and nineteen wounded, four of whom later died of their wounds. The captured pirates were taken to Charleston, where they were imprisoned while awaiting trial.

Bonnet, who was described as "a Gentleman of a Plentifull Fortune in Barbadoes, who turned Pyrate," escaped his confinement once but was recaptured, and sentenced to death. Twenty-two of his crew had already been executed.

Governor Johnson was naturally pleased at the turn of events, but he worried over the expense of the expedition, and he also feared that it had antagonized other pirates who infested the coast. Once again he urged the British government to send a frigate to protect Charleston harbor.[6]

His apprehension proved only too well founded, for soon the harbor was blocked by several pirate vessels, a menace compared by the Reverend William Tredwell Bull to the "Pestilential Fever" that had raged in Charleston during the fall. Hoping that the fever had finally passed, the minister remarked that "the greatest Plague to us now is by Piracy on our Coast."[7]

Since Governor Johnson's pleas to England for assistance in fighting the sea rovers had brought no response, he decided to enlarge his fighting force. His plan became especially imperative when it was learned that another pirate, the notorious Christopher Moody, was approaching the port, his ship carrying fifty guns and 200 men. The Province—now in an impoverished state—knew well

---

[6] Governor and Council of South Carolina to Board of Trade, October 21, 1718, PR, Vol. VII, pp. 164-6; W. T. Bull to Secretary of the SPG, November 24, 1718, SPG, Series A, Vol. XIII; Hughson, *Carolina Pirates,* pp. 100-102; *The Statutes at Large of South Carolina* (hereinafter cited as *Statutes),* edited by Thomas Cooper and David J. McCord (10 vols., Columbia: A. S. Johnston, 1836-1841), Vol. III, pp. 41-43.

[7] W. T. Bull to Secretary of the SPG, November 24, 1718, SPG, Series A. Vol. XIII.

the danger if the pirate should decide to turn his guns ashore. There was the further possibility that the town would be sacked, in keeping with other pirates' methods. There was no time to be lost. An embargo was placed on shipping; and the Governor sent scout boats to patrol the Charleston harbor entrance to resist any attempted landing. Meanwhile, he began assembling his fleet.

Before preparations were completed, an unidentified ship and sloop were sighted; but they made no hostile movements for three days. By then Johnson had readied four ships, and this time, the Governor sailed in person as the leader of the expedition. His fleet moved out into the harbor disguised as merchant ships. The pirates, completely deceived, prepared to intercept the vessels; the black flag was run up and the ships were called on to surrender. Johnson replied by raising the King's colors, opening the gun ports, and delivering a stinging broadside to the nearest pirate ship. Before the pirates could recover from their surprise, the Governor's fleet attacked them with unrelenting fury.

Through skillful maneuvering, and spurred on by its desperate plight, the pirate ship managed to escape, heading for the open sea. Johnson gave chase after ordering two of his vessels to remain to take care of the pirate sloop left in the harbor. The pirates on board, knowing what fate would be theirs if they were captured, put up a desperate fight to resist capture. After four hours, however, they were subdued by the Carolina forces.

On the seas, Governor Johnson's determined pursuit of the pirate ship caused the crew to throw overboard its boats and cannon in an effort to gain speed, but this was to no avail. Johnson sailed to within gunshot and opened fire. The pirates struck their flag and surrendered unconditionally. When the Governor's men boarded the craft, it was the Carolinians' turn for a surprise. Secluded in the hold was a crowd of women! The ship which the pirates had appropriated was on a routine trip from London bringing 106 convicts and indentured servants to the colonies of Virginia and Maryland. Thirty-six of this group were women. This was not the end of the surprise; the pirate commander slain in the struggle was not Moody, but the notorious and hunted Richard Worley.

Tally for the chase equalled "two vessels taken; twenty-six pirates, including Worley, killed in the struggle, and several others wounded." Nineteen captives were removed to Charleston where they were tried and received death sentences.[8]

The exultation of the Province over the extermination of the Worley gang was tempered by the realization that Moody was still at large and might at any moment swoop down upon the port. To prevent this occurrence, Johnson resolved to keep his ships mobilized until the immediate danger had passed. Some time afterward, the Province was relieved to learn that Moody, apprised of Charleston's preparations, had decided to take advantage of the royal proclamation of pardon. After plundering one last ship, he had set sail for New Providence to take pardon at the hands of the governor there.[9]

So far, the Province had achieved brilliant success against the pirates, but Johnson "was no dreamer."[10] He would not allow past victories to lull him into a false belief that all was secure, because he knew that the Province was still a prime target for other rovers sailing the seas.

Johnson persisted in trying to secure aid from England; but from the Lords Proprietors, he received only a letter of thanks for his judgment and conduct of actions against the pirates.[11] Johnson was not deterred. With the Council, he again plead to the Crown to supply a ship of war to protect the Province, citing to the Board of Trade the importance of South Carolina to Great Britain, especially to the King's navy. He pointed out that in the preceding year, the Province had produced for export to Britain 32,000 barrels of tar, 20,643 barrels of pitch, and 473 barrels of turpentine, "all Stores very useful for his Majesty's Navy."[12]

At last, action was taken in Great Britain on the repeated requests from Carolina. The Board of Trade requested the Lords Commissioners of the Admiralty to send such assistance as the public service

---

[8] Hughson, *Carolina Pirates,* pp. 113-120; Governor and Council of South Carolina to Board of Trade, December 12, 1718, PR, Vol. VII, p. 167; W. T. Bull to Secretary of the SPG, November 24, 1718, SPG, Series A, Vol. XIII; Harriott H. Ravenel, *Charleston, the Place and the People* (New York: The Macmillan Co., 1906), pp. 75-77.

[9] Hughson, *Carolina Pirates,* pp. 119-120; Ravenel, *Charleston,* p. 77.

[10] Hughson, *Carolina Pirates,* pp. 123-4.

[11] Lords Proprietors of Carolina to Governor Johnson, March 12, 1718/9, PR, Vol. VII, pp. 176-7.

[12] Governor and Council of South Carolina to Board of Trade, December 12, 1718, PR, Vol. VII, pp. 167-8.

would admit, and the Admiralty agreed to send a frigate there as soon as possible.[13]

Even without this assistance, however, the harbor had been reopened to commerce. In the hour of greatest need, the Lords Proprietors and the Crown had turned a deaf ear. The South Carolinians in time of peril had courageously banded together to relieve their beleaguered settlement, under the leadership of the Governor. Just as he had acted against the Indians, Johnson had also taken the offensive against the pirates, refusing to allow insidious individuals, whether pirates or Indians, to overcome his people.

Nor did he tolerate any "neutralist" position, such as the Creeks had attempted in their effort to hold the balance of power between the French, Spanish, and English colonies. The Governor was equally unrelenting in action against the pirates, despite the fact that some prominent persons, including Colonel William Rhett, tried to intercede on behalf of Stede Bonnet. Bonnet paid the price his crimes demanded.

Despite these accomplishments, Johnson recognized the fact that the Province had not reached a satisfactory level of security, because criminals still sailed the ocean, with reports flowing in of their piratical invasions.

There were no further steps that the Governor could take because the treasury was depleted; and still no word had come that the Admiralty intended to send any assistance. No longer did Johnson lend hope that outside help would come, but instead insisted that Carolinians must provide for themselves. The Assembly was induced to pass a bill providing funds for the payment of debts contracted in the fitting out of the two expeditions.[14]

In one of South Carolina's darkest hours, when pirates ravaged the coastline, as Indians attacked the settlements and the Spanish and French invasion loomed as imminent threats, many citizens were ready to flee the Province. Johnson influenced them to stay, convincing them that they could save themselves, showing them how it could be done.

Johnson applied the same firm hand in his dealings with South Carolina's European rivals, the Spanish and the French, for the

[13] Board of Trade Journal, April 7, 21, 1719, PR, Vol. VII, p. 180; William Popple to Josiah Burchett, April 7, 1719, PRO, CO 5:1293, p. 168 (Library of Congress transcript); Burchett to Popple, April 20, 1719, PRO, CO 5:1293, p. 169 (Library of Congress transcript).

[14] McCrady, *Proprietary Govt.,* pp. 621-2.

domination of the Southwest. Although wars among European powers were usually reflected in struggles between their American colonies, these nations would not be drawn into war by the activities of their colonials, or because of the abuse of their colonists by representatives of another European power. Thus, repeatedly, the Carolinians found themselves left to their own devices in dealing with the Spaniard and the Frenchman, with no help from England even though the Province was the British southern outpost of mainland colonies.

French influence with the Indians continued to grow and become more important as the settlement at Mobile was enlarged. French traders had been sent to replace English traders who were killed at the outbreak of the Yamassee War, and afterwards, the French were busy building forts among the Creeks and other Indian nations in an effort to consolidate their gains.[15]

One informed observer commented early in 1720 that, if the French—located so conveniently for dealing with the southwest Indians—could obtain British trading goods, they would soon have all those Indians at their command. He estimated that the tribes numbered 15,000 to 20,000 fighting men, and said he feared that, if a war were to break out with the French, Carolina would have to expect the first victories to be in the enemy's hands.[16] Others, including Johnson, took an even dimmer view. As the consequence of any French war, they felt Carolina would fall into enemy hands, and Virginia and other of His Majesty's dominions would be exposed to the gravest dangers.[17]

Johnson reported that France had 5,000 to 6,000 fighting men in the area, and the number was being bolstered daily by new recruits from the home country. The French had seized Pensacola from Spain and were growing ever more dangerous and powerful. They had constantly encroached on what was considered to be English territory, and were preparing to build a fort 100 miles nearer to Carolina. The Governor warned that these encroachments must be prevented.[18]

---

[15] Committee of S. C. Commons House to Boone, March 8, 1717/8, PR, Vol. VII, pp. 99-100; Johnson to Board of Trade, January 12, 1719/20, PR, Vol. VII, p. 237.

[16] From Thomas Smith, February 22, 1719/20, PR, Vol. VII, pp. 305-6.

[17] S. C. Assembly to Board of Trade, December 24, 1719, PR, Vol. VII, p. 225.

[18] Robert Johnson to Board of Trade, January 12, 1719, PR, Vol. VII, pp. 244-6.

Similar complaints were issued against the Spaniards. Besides manipulation of the Indians, they provided a haven for escaped servants and slaves, for robbers and for debtors from South Carolina. Governor Johnson deplored the fact that, although return of these persons had been demanded on several occasions, no satisfaction had ever been forthcoming. Despite the Florida Governor's repeated reply that he was writing to learn what was his sovereign's pleasure in the matter, the escapees were always kept and protected.[19]

Although the French were becoming more aggressive in their Indian policy, the gravest foreign danger to South Carolina came from Spain. In Europe, in late summer 1718, the formation of the Quadruple Alliance, to constrain Philip V to observe the treaties of Utrecht (1713) and Rastadt (1714), had led to military action. Stanhope, the British minister, had dispatched Admiral George Byng to the Mediterranean Sea, where he destroyed a Spanish fleet at Cape Passaro. Afterwards, England declared war on Spain, despite a brisk dissenting debate in the House of Commons over the King's war message. Some members believed that the war was caused by merchants' grievances which could have been satisfied without hostilities, while Robert Walpole denounced the fact that the attack on the Spanish fleet had taken place prior to the war declaration.[20]

As usual, there was a mirroring of these affairs in the New World, and in 1719-20, the threat of a Spanish attack on South Carolina was recognized. Carolina spies in St. Augustine had sent back information that preparations were being made there for an attack on the southern parts of Carolina. Upon receiving this news, Governor Johnson quickly assembled a body of troops and marched to the expected landing spot of the enemy, waiting almost two weeks for the onslaught. During this time, scouts reconnoitered the water and land areas, but found no signs of the Spanish. Johnson, deciding that the information he had received was false, disbanded the troops.

Unknown to him, the Spanish fleet, under the command of Don Alfonso Carrascosa, had begun its journey to Carolina. Shortly after sailing from Havana, the fleet had intercepted two French ships, the

---

[19] Johnson to Board of Trade, June 18, 1718, PR, Vol. VII, pp. 135-6.

[20] *The Parliamentary History of England* (London: T. C. Hansard, 1811), Vol. VII, columns 581-3; Basil Williams, *The Whig Supremacy* (Oxford: Clarendon Press, 1939), pp. 165-7. A Spanish fleet sailing against England was disabled by a violent storm off Cape Finistere. *Parliamentary History,* Vol. VII, columns 596-7n.

Marechal Duc de Villars and the *Comte de Toulouse,* which had sailed from Pensacola, a port recently captured by the French. The vessels were taking Spanish prisoners to Havana, according to the terms of the capitulation agreement. Following their meeting with the French, the Spanish changed their minds and shifted their interests from Carolina to the task of recapturing Pensacola. Because of these happenings Carolinians were spared an attack.[21]

This news in Charleston was followed later by word that the Spaniards were preparing a more grandiose scheme. A stockpiling of armaments had been taking place at Vera Cruz, and the Viceroy in Mexico had ordered the Governor of Havana to raise whatever forces he could on the island of Cuba to join in the attack against Carolina. The King of Spain had also sent the Viceroy orders to raise large numbers of men in an effort to recapture from the French and English those places formerly belonging to Spain or claimed by it. The circumstances were "Very Mellancholly" and could not be represented "in much Darker Colours" than they appeared. The Board of Trade was requested by Johnson to ask the King to send 500 or 600 regular troops and one or two frigates to save the lives and the estates of the Carolina inhabitants, as there was a foreboding that all would be lost.[22]

The fears and doubts of the distraught people were very real, as the Proprietors had never supplied adequate military assistance, and none appeared to be forthcoming from the Crown. The courage that they were able to summon during this trying period can be attributed to the determined leadership and exemplary conduct of a few individuals in official capacity. Foremost among these was Governor Robert Johnson. Just as his father had done in 1706, Johnson assembled what equipment and troops he could muster to defend the Province against the expected Spanish assault, one that did not materialize.

The direction of South Carolina affairs, however, was taken out of Johnson's hands by a change in the chief executive's office. The

---

[21] Barcia, *Chronological History of the Continent of Florida,* pp. 381-5; Governor and Council of S. C. to Board of Trade, November 6, 1719, PR, Vol. VII, pp. 208-10; "Narrative of Events after the Spaniards Recaptured Pensacola," *Miss. Prov. Archives,* Vol. III, pp. 242-4. Henry Folmer, *Franco-Spanish Rivalry in North America, 1524-1763,* in *Spain in the West* series, Vol. VII (Glendale, Calif.: Arthur H. Clark Co., 1953), p. 225.

[22] Governor and Council of S. C., to Board of Trade, November 6, 1719, PR, Vol. VII, pp. 208-10.

Spanish danger had been the catalytic agent in a turn of events that involved more than a change of governors.

Before he left office, Governor Johnson tallied up the defensive forces and fortifications that were in existence in South Carolina. His computation showed that there were 1,600 fighting men between the ages of sixteen and sixty, all of whom were required to bear arms. This number was one-fourth of the estimated 6,400 white population in the Province, an increase after 1715 of approximately 100 persons. (Of the 500 newcomers sailing to Carolina from England, Ireland, and elsewhere, 400 had been lost in the Indian war in which the Province became engaged.)[23]

In an official report before the Board of Trade, two of the Lords Proprietors and their secretary, Richard Shelton, reported that there were in Carolina between 1,500 and 2,000 fighting men, and about 2,000 families of white people. Also, they named other losses as a result of the settlement of the French at Mobile, and the Indian war. Negro slaves in the Province were estimated at between 14,000 and 15,000.[24]

Concerning fortifications, Governor Johnson said that "to awe the Indians and prevent their comeing with us and to inspect ye better what their designs are and to Secure our People and goods whilst we trade with them," garrisons were maintained on the outskirts of the Province, as follows:

1. At the Congarees, about 130 miles north of Charleston [near the present City of Columbia], a captain and twenty men were stationed.

2. About forty miles westward and 140 miles from Charleston, at the Savannah garrison, there was also a captain with twenty men.

3. On Port Royal Island, to keep the inland waterway from St. Augustine under surveillance, and to prevent white persons and slaves deserting to that Spanish post,[25] two scout boats of ten men each were stationed. The men were provided small forts in which they could secure themselves if retreat became necessary.

---

[23] Johnson to Board of Trade, January 12, 1719/20, PR, Vol. VII, p. 234.

[24] Board of Trade Journal, July 28, 1720, PR, Vol. VIII, pp. 253-4.

[25] Charges against the Spaniards in this connection may be found in "Statements Made in the Introduction to the Report [1741] on General Oglethorpe's Expedition to St. Augustine," in B. R. Carroll (ed.), *Historical Collections of South Carolina* (2 vols., New York: Harper and Brothers, 1836), Vol. II, pp. 347-59.

4. A captain, a lieutenant, and twelve men were on James Island in Johnson's Fort (named for Robert Johnson's father), which commanded the ships coming up the bay to Charleston.

All of these forces were paid from public funds. None of the posts had great strength except Fort Johnson, which was described as a "Regular Tryangle with Draw Bridges, a dry ditch and a Platform below of about 12 Guns of 12 pound Ball, and ab[ou]t 10 from 6 to 9 Pounders in the upper works." The other forts were described as strong enough to withstand the Indians, since they "know nothing of beseiging [nor] will [they] Fight against walls."[26]

As early as the administration of Sir Nathaniel Johnson, Charleston had been enclosed by a regular fortification, which a violent hurricane had blown down in 1713. The heavy debt incurred in fighting the Indian War had not left sufficient funds to rebuild the fortification, but under the Spanish threat, the town had been provided with reasonably good defenses.[27]

The danger from Spain continued well into 1720. Early in March, word arrived that a Spanish force of 1,200 men in four ships were en route to St. Augustine; from there the troops were expected to invade South Carolina by land.[28]

By then, as result of Johnson's prodding, defense had reached such a state of preparedness, that the Province was ready to "give them a much Warmer Recepcon (and smarter repulse) than they expect."[29]

---

[26] Johnson to Board of Trade, January 12, 1719/20, PR, Vol. VII, pp. 234-5.

[27] *Ibid.*, p. 235.

[28] Jonathan Shrine to Samuel Wragg, March 3, 1719/20, PR, Vol. VII, pp. 314-6.

[29] Othniel Beale to Samuel Waldo, March 4, 1719/20, PR, Vol. VII, pp. 317-8.

CHAPTER IV

Johnson and the Charleston Revolution

THE OMINOUS threat of Spanish attack brought forth defensive preparations on the part of South Carolina, and that same danger provided the opportunity for a momentous change in the government.

After Governor Johnson had put the town in readiness, he called out the militia to meet the expected Spanish invasion. As he had ordered, the officers mustered their regiments at the appointed time.

During this excitement, anti-Proprietary leaders took the opportunity for action by circulating their secretly-prepared Articles of an association. They were presented to members of the militia and signed by nearly everyone present.

Governor Johnson had been at his plantation [possibly at Belvidere] some miles from Charleston and knew nothing of this development of a conspiracy against the Lords Proprietors. It was made known to him later in a letter from some of the plotters to the Proprietors' overthrow.[1]

Johnson soon found that he was a chief executive without a government. The opposing, revolutionary party had declared the Province free of proprietary rule and subject only to the King's command. Johnson, in the transition, was asked to become a royal governor and thereby renounce the authority of the Proprietors, a request in which he could not acquiesce.

Johnson knew how true were many of the complaints against the Proprietors. He had witnessed the Lords' inability or unwillingness in times of great need to aid the Province against the Indians and pirates, or to supply help against the French and Spanish. He had himself felt the wrath of proprietary disapproval, and had seen the Proprietors correspond secretively with their favorites in the Province, while reprimanding their Governor, or plainly ignoring him.

[1] McCrady, *Proprietary Govt.,* p. 646; Alexander Hewat, *An Historical Account of the Rise and Progress of the Colonies of South Carolina and Georgia* (London, 1779), reprinted in Carroll, *Historical Collections,* Vol. I, pp. 222-6; William J. Rivers, *A Sketch of the History of South Carolina to the Close of the Proprietary Government by the Revolution of 1719* (Charleston: McCarter and Co., 1856), pp. 295-8.

Johnson's expenses in taking over the government and serving as chief executive had been large. He had not been in the governor's chair long enough for the salary and fees of his office to increase in line with his liabilities—not to mention that his salary was in arrears. He had, in fact, lost a considerable fortune while holding office. All of the factors were present that might have led him to desire the retention of the office under any circumstances.

The grievances of both the Governor and the inhabitants against the Proprietors were unquestionably real. But Johnson wondered if they justified a revolution? As for the people, they had made their choice, that revolution was necessary. The Governor's decision was much more difficult.

To his credit, Johnson never hesitated. He saw clearly—just as when there had been pirate, Indian, Frenchman or Spaniard to battle—the direction in which his duty and honor led. After having met all of the other challenges of his hectic administration, he was not the man to fall prey to the fear of unpopularity or even unemployment. Johnson, therefore, in doing his duty, upheld the trust placed in him by the Proprietors, feeling that as their legally constituted governor, there was no middle ground and that there could be no surrender.

He rebuffed the approaches of the popular [revolutionary] party, saying:

> I am obliged to your good opinion of me, but I hold my Commission from the true and absolute Lords and Proprietors of this Province who Recommended me to his Majesty and I have his approbation, and Itts by that Commission I act and I know of no Power or Authority that can disposses me of the same, but those Powers only that gave itt [to] me in Subordination to that Authority.
>
> I shall allways act and to my uttermost Maintain their Lordship's Just Powers and Perogatives without encroaching uppon the Peoples Rights and Priviledges.
>
> I do not expect or desire any favour from you, only that of Seriously taking into your Consideration, The Aproaching danger of a Foreign Enemy and the Steps you are taking to Envolve yourselves and the whole Country in Confusion.[2]

---

[2] PR, Vol. XII, pp. 188-9; Francis Yonge, *A Narrative of the Proceedings of the People of South Carolina, in the Year 1719* (London, 1726), reprinted in Carroll, *Historical Collections,* Vol. II, pp. 164-80.

In these few words, Johnson had set himself at odds with the revolutionary party. He refused to consider their plea for him to act as their Governor; instead, he asserted that he *was* the Governor, and that it was without their power to remove him. The revolutionists were well aware of the action they were taking, but he left it to them to discover what his removal would mean and how that action might be interpreted. Acknowledging that mutiny and revolution were serious crimes, they were quick to present their case before the British Government, hoping their declared adherence to the Crown of Great Britain would erase the stigma of their offense against the Proprietors.

Whatever their reasons, Johnson felt that the people were seeking redress by a remedy that was incorrect, illegal and unwise. The revolutionaries, however, did not "plead *Law,* but *Necessity.*"[3]

Several years afterward, when seeking the appointment from the Crown as royal governor, Johnson virtually defended the revolution in these words:

> "A Warr breaking out with Spaine, the Province was threatened with an Invasion from them and the Indians their Allyes, and the Inhabitants of Carolina believing they could never be secure in their Lives and Fortunes without his Majesty's Immediate assistance and Protection [,] did unanimously renounce all Obediance to the Lords Proprietors Authoritys and humbly implored his most Sacred Majesty to take them into his immediate Government and Protection."[4]

Johnson also mentioned that at the time it had been desired that he continue as governor. He also made it clear that the revolt had been directed against the Proprietors and not against the chief executive or the administration.[5]

Even at the time of the revolt, Johnson was not unsympathetic to the popular cause. In reporting the overturn to the Board of Trade, he spoke of the Province's heavy debts and taxes, the Spanish design to attack it, the French build-up, the continual danger of another Indian War, and differences between the Proprietors and the people over the overlords' privileges. He reported that these matters had "Stirred up the Minds of Severall of the Richest In-

---

[3] Yonge, *Proceedings,* in Carroll, *Historical Collections,* Vol. II, 142.

[4] Memorial of Robert Johnson [c. 1726], PR, Vol. XII, p. 183.

[5] Memorial of Robert Johnson [c. 1726], PR, Vol. XII, pp. 183-4; Yonge, *Proceedings,* in Carroll, *Historical Collections,* Vol. II, p. 142.

habitants" who had convinced the "Commonallity" that neither the people nor their estates would ever be safe, nor would the Province much longer exist unless it received the immediate protection of the Crown. One step led to another—he recalled—until finally "with one Accord [they] disclaimed any Obediance to the Lords Prop[rie]t[o]rs."[6]

Different contemporaries had different reasons to offer for the overthrow of proprietary rule. One thing was certain: the revolutionary Assembly, in its appeal to the King, was not a believer in a single causation theory. A multitude of charges was leveled against the Proprietors, all of which added up to the fact that proprietary rule could no longer be tolerated. Among the Assembly's reasons was the charge that the Proprietors had failed to comply with their pledges to teach Christianity to the Indians. Additionally, it was said that they had made no effort to transport people to the Province, but, instead, had hindered and impeded settlement. They had built neither churches nor schools, and had made no contribution toward the establishment of forts and fortifications.

Absenteeism from proprietary meetings was another complaint. Quite often, important decisions affecting the security and prosperity of the Province had been made by only two or three of the Proprietors, it was charged.[7] Those few who attended pretended that they had proxies from their absent colleagues, or from the guardians of those Proprietors who were minors. The situation, it was further charged, was particularly irksome in view of the frequent veto of colonial legislation.

In fact, it was declared that the Proprietors' uncertain methods in handling their government "have put us under Unspeakable hard-

---

[6] Johnson to Board of Trade, December 27, 1719, PR, Vol. VII, pp. 227-8. In the same letter Johnson asked that, if the king took over the Province, he be recommended for the governor's office. *Ibid.*, p. 228.

[7] Petition and Representation of S. C. Assembly, February 3, 1719/20, PR, Vol. VII, pp. 271-99. Carteret, the palatine, left England in June 1719 for the post of ambassador to Sweden. W. Baring Pemberton, *Carteret: The Brilliant Failure of the Eighteenth Century* (London: Longmans, Green and Co., 1936), pp. 29-30. There were four possible ways in which the proprietary veto power could be exercised: by the Proprietors' deputies serving as a council, by the Governor, by another person (sometimes appointed) with a veto over the Governor, and by the Proprietors themselves, who "Suffer noe Law to pass or if passed to be of any longer force than suites with their Private views & Designes to the great Confusion and entire loss of all Public Credit soe necessary in the Frontier Collony and destructive to the Liberties & Propertes and Violation of the free Constitution of his Majesties free born Subjects." Petition and Representation of S. C. Assembly, Feb. 3, 1719/20, PR, Vol. VII, pp. 284-5.

ships never knowing our Constitucon, Destroy all Public Credit Soe necessary in this Frontier Province to Defend our Selves against our Enemys And defeat[in]g all Measures taken for our Safety and Preservation and good Government of the Province."[8]

The list of vetoed and repealed laws was long; but the Carolinians were particularly angered at the repeal of a law laying duties on Negroes imported from Africa. The Assembly had planned to use this revenue to repair fortifications, to keep troops on the frontiers, and to maintain the clergy. Because of the numerous expenses the Province had been under, all taxes and other funds had been anticipated for many years. The Proprietors' veto had, therefore, deprived the clergymen of their maintenance and had left the colony in a position to be an "Easy Conquest" to the Spaniards who were well aware of South Carolina's weak defenses.[9]

Another, particularly obnoxious veto had been the repeal of an act setting forth the method of selecting representatives for the Assembly. The Carolinians felt their law corresponded to the laws of England and had established a mode of election similar to that in other American colonies. Under the law, members were to be chosen by ballot in the various parishes, with the number of representatives corresponding to the size of the election district. The repeal meant a return to the method of summoning all the free-men of the Province who were divided into two groups, to choose their representatives, by subscribing their names to lists of candidates. Most of the candidates were strangers to the freemen, and this method made an opening for "Faction, Corruption and Tumultuous Meetings." It caused the freemen to expend time and money for the trip to Charleston, if they were determined to participate in the election.[10]

The Court System—if it may be called that—of the Proprietors came in for an especially bitter denunciation. The Assembly's wrath in this instance was directed at Chief Justice Nicholas Trott as well as the Proprietors. It was charged that the Proprietors had failed to set up the required number and types of courts . . . "have Abandoned all to an Unaccountable disorder and Confusion under

[8] *Ibid,* pp. 280-1.

[9] *Ibid.,* p. 282.

[10] Petition and Representation of S. C. Assembly, February 3, 1719/20, PR, Vol. VII, pp. 271-99.

the Administracon and Underhand Management of a Single Person."[11]

The Province had often sought to have the Proprietors remove Trott, but always without success. At every attempt, the Chief Justice was able to convince the Proprietors that within the Province, he was the only person who could serve their interests, "Tho no person has been ever more prejudicial to them."[12]

South Carolinians were also incensed that the Proprietors had practically abandoned them during the Yamassee war. From England had come only 150 small arms, although the Proprietors told the Board of Trade that they had furnished the Province with large supplies of arms and ammunition. In an effort to forestall inquiry into the condition of the Province, the Proprietors had made another misrepresentation: that they had ordered the Receiver General to appropriate all funds at his disposal to the use of the Province. This was not true, the Assembly asserted, saying that the Receiver General had been ordered to transmit to the Proprietors every cent of the money held in his hands. It added that the Proprietors had left the Province to struggle alone with its difficulties, not even corresponding with their Governor, nor "took noe more Notice of us than if they had Abandoned the Province."[13]

These complaints reinforced their grievances against the Lords Proprietors, and while one may have been no more vital than the other, self-preservation was a major reason in promoting the revolt. A contemporary felt that the chief cause was the orders of the Proprietors repealing the acts of Assembly, and the fear that the French were rapidly expanding their activities.[14]

The political climate in England may have made such a revolt possible, although it was not a cause. Certain influential elements in the British Government, particularly the Board of Trade, were interested in seeing all of the colonies placed under the direct rule of the Crown. They were, therefore, already oriented to South Carolina's pleas for royal rule which arose from the Indian war, the continued depredations afterward, and the Proprietors' indifference

---

[11] *Ibid.*, p. 285.

[12] Ibid., pp. 285-6; Anne King Gregorie (ed.), *Records of the Court of Chancery of South Carolina, 1671-1779* (Washington: American Historical Association, 1950), pp. 6-7.

[13] Petition and Representation of S. C. Assembly, PR, Vol. VII, pp. 287-90.

[14] W. T. Bull to Secretary of the SPG, January 27, 1719/20, SPG, Series A, Vol. XIV.

to the Province's welfare. The Assembly had applied vainly to the Proprietors for aid, and seeing that none was forthcoming, directed its Agents to make no more approaches, but appeal for the protection of the King.[15]

This and later requests were warmly received by the Board of Trade, which had been in consultation with the Proprietors and several others well acquainted with affairs in Carolina. The Board reported that the Proprietors were either unable, or disinclined, to send necessary aid during the Indian war. It said the situation would be the same in any similar exigencies that might occur in the future. Because of this, the Board suggested that the Proprietors surrender their charter to the Crown, as the best means of protecting the inhabitants. In return, they could retain their property rights to the soil of Carolina. The overlords would not accept the Board's advice; thereupon the Board recommended that the Crown take measures for securing the Province to His Majesty.[16]

Nearly three years after the outbreak of the Indian war, it was reported: "Our Indians continue Comitting so many Hostilities and Infest our Settlements and Plantations to such a Degree that not only those estates which were deserted att the breaking out of the War Cannot be resettled but are likewise dayly thrown up to the Mercy of the Enemy to the Ruin and Impovishm[en]t of Severall Numerous Families." The inactivity of the Proprietors, and their efforts to stigmatize the request for the Crown to take over the protection of the Province as the action only of a party or faction, resulted in an "Address of the Representatives and Inhabitants of S. C., to the King."[17]

The Board of Trade again felt it incumbent upon itself to suggest that "proper methods should be taken for resuming of this & all other Proprietary Governm[en]ts into the hands of His Majesty." It declared that such action was necessary because any misfortune befalling the Carolina Province would consequently affect others of His Majesty's colonies on the American continent.[18]

---

[15] Board of Trade Journal, June 28, 1716, PR, Vol. VI, p. 288.

[16] From Board of Trade, July 19, 1715, PR, Vol. VI, pp. 98-99.

[17] Memorial of Joseph Boone to Board of Trade, May 13, 1718, PR, Vol. VII, pp. 126-7; *ibid.*, pp. 128-30, February 24, 1718.

[18] Board of Trade to Secretary Craggs, May 6, 1718, PR, Vol. VII, p. 125. Suggestions that the King take the Province under his protection had been made as early as 1706.

The Yamassee war, plus the continued Indian hostilities and depredations, had led the people of South Carolina to press intensely for royal government, to remove themselves from proprietary rule. When the Board of Trade expressed its wishes to terminate the proprietary government by judicial[19] (not revolutionary) means, this gave Carolinians hope that indirectly their "revolt" had received royal sanction.

The Assembly of the Province, meanwhile, passed a law to regularize its actions.[20] The "inhabitants taking into their consideration their calamitous circumstances, and for the preservation of their lives and estates, according to the supreme law of Nature," renounced proprietary rule.[21] Since Robert Johnson had refused to continue as Governor, they elected James Moore[22] to the difficult task of guiding the Province until the King's desire was made known. Because Moore was then Governor did not mean that serious problems were automatically ended. The change in governorship had added some problems and intensified others, under the declaration of independence from the Proprietors.

The change placed Robert Johnson in an unenviable position. A majority of the inhabitants, including influential persons, were in favor of the proprietary overthrow, and some were planning to leave the Province if the Proprietors were reinstated.[23] Those not engaged in the revolution, some of the inhabitants in "best repute," were looked upon with an "evill Eye" when they were not willing to join the movement.[24] Besides, nearly all of the militia had gone over to the revolutionary camp, giving the appearance that Johnson was acquiescing in the proceedings of the popular party.

The established clergy was also in an uncomfortable, delicate situation. The ministers were fond of Governor Johnson whom they spoke of as "a Gent[leman] worthy of all esteem," a good friend of the church; and said they had "more discretion than to be concerned any ways in ye deposition of a Lawful Govern[o]r." Most of the

---

[19] The more immediate issue was that a Proprietary Charter was a legal contract between the King and the Proprietors. It could not be terminated without due process of law.

[20] *Statutes at Large of S. C.,* Vol. I, p. 57 (ed. Thomas Cooper). Act of December 23, 1719.

[21] *Statutes,* Vol. I, pp. 58-59.

[22] *Ibid.*

[23] Richard Splatt to Samuel Barons, July 20, 1720, PR, Vol. VIII, p. 34.

[24] W. T. Bull to the Society, May 12, 1720, SPG, Series A, Vol. XIV.

clergy chose to remain aloof and wait until word had come from England on how the crisis was to be resolved. Said they: "Since the people can never be supposed to be ye proper Judges in such a Case, but in matters of difficulty & grievance have ye liberty & ought therefore to appeal to his Majesty who alone hath power and authority to Judge of ym & remedy them as he sees fitt."[25]

Unfortunately for the clergy, its plans for prudence and caution were upset by a nonpolitical matter. Governor Moore published an order strictly forbidding marriage except by licenses signed by him. Johnson, on the other hand, forbade the clergy to obey that order. The clergy was in a quandary. Upon reflection that Johnson was the legally appointed Governor with approval from His Majesty, and any untoward acts might tend to dispossess the Lords Proprietors of their just rights, they decided to obey Governor Johnson and perform no marriages without his license. This led to their being rudely insulted by some of the "inferior sort" and lowered their standing with the new government which threatened to discontinue their salaries. It was proposed in the Assembly that such an action be taken, but the matter was dropped,[26] after it had been suggested unsuccessfully that the Anglican clergy be deported from the Province and replaced by a "better Sett." Despite resentment, it had been feared that any measures taken against the clergy would prejudice the revolutionary cause in England; therefore no drastic action was taken.

The clergy was soon again to place itself in the fire of criticism. This time it was a drought—another nonpolitical issue. Scarcely a drop of rain had fallen on the Province for five months. People had planted and replanted their crops several times, droves of cattle had been lost, and food prices had been greatly increased.[27] Because of the calamity, it was decided to proclaim a day of fasting and humiliation.

---

[25] W. T. Bull to Secretary of the SPG, January 27, 1719/20, SPG, Series A. Vol. XIV.

[26] W. T. Bull to the Society, May 12, 1720, SPG, Series A, Vol. XIV; Bull to Secretary of the SPG, August 12, 1720, SPG, Series A, Vol. XV. The clergy complained: "The dissenting Teachers have invaded the rights of the Church by Publishing the Banns of Marriage in their Meetings & joyning people in Marriage contrary to the prescribed form." Clergy in South Carolina to the Society, October 10, 1721, SPG, Series A, Vol. XV.

[27] Richard Splatt to Samuel Barons, July 20, 1720, PR, Vol. VIII, pp. 34-35.

Colonel Moore issued an order setting aside Wednesday, July 20, for the fast, but Johnson proclaimed that it would be held on Friday, July 22. The clergy decided to observe the date proclaimed by Johnson, much to the disgust of some citizens, a few of whom became violent and abusive in their language.

Indicative of Johnson's influence, however, was the fact that the churches were fuller than usual on the special day set aside for observance by him.[28] This showed also the support for Johnson, some of which was passive and could not be utilized effectively. Colonel Moore even charged that Johnson was responsible for preventing one-third of the people from paying their taxes.[29] There were some dissatisfied with the revolutionary government but saw no advantage in returning to proprietary rule. These provided slight comfort for the deposed Governor. But active aid soon arrived as ships of the King's navy sailed into Charleston harbor, including the *Flamborough,* commanded by Captain Hildesley. The vessels had come belatedly in answer to Johnson's pleas for help in fighting the pirates.

Until their arrival, Johnson had moved with discretion, protesting the revolution, but not causing any serious disturbance. Hildesley, on his arrival, became Johnson's ally, and soon let it be known that he greatly disapproved of what had transpired in the Province. He railed openly against the new government and succeeded in making himself *persona non grata* to the Carolina regime, and many people of the Province. Besides, he engaged in a duel with New Providence's Governor Rogers, a visitor in Charleston, over some disagreement they had in the West Indies. Both participants were slightly wounded, but Rogers soon returned to his country, while Hildesley remained to encourage Johnson to resume control of the Carolina government, offering his aid.[30]

Johnson then commissioned Hildesley colonel of the Berkeley county regiment. Soon Colonel Moore accused Hildesley of having very nearly occasioned a great amount of bloodshed.[31] To strike back at the Captain, the new government authorized its Agent in

---

[28] W. T. Bull to Bishop of London, August 12, 1720, SPG, Fulham Palace MSS, South Carolina, No. 252.

[29] JCHA, July 13, 1720.

[30] John Loyd to Secretary Craggs, February 2, 1720/21, PR, Vol. IX, pp. 12-18.

[31] From James Moore, March 21, 1720/21, PR, Vol. IX, p. 22.

London, Joseph Boone, to make the charge that Hildesley had been trading with the Spaniards at St. Augustine, and furnishing them with arms and ammunition. On being questioned, Boone was unable to produce affidavits or other proofs of Hildesley's guilt.[32]

Influenced by the Captain—and with the knowledge that there were five warships in Charleston harbor to support him—Johnson decided to make a move. On May 9, 1721, he called his Council together to propose methods for his restoration. A message was sent to Colonel Moore, complaining of the difficulties the Province had suffered as a result of the unjust usurpation of the government, and announcing Johnson's intention to resume the reins of South Carolina. Johnson promised complete safety to person and estate, and announced that he would deliver the government in good faith into the hands of any governor appointed by the King. Johnson added that his action was designed to preserve the peace and tranquility of the Province, as well as to assert his own right.[33] Moore answered abruptly that he was determined to keep the government until the King's pleasure was signified, adding a warning that his government was in a good position for that purpose.[34]

Upon receipt of this message, Johnson drew up his troops before the town, a force consisting of about 120 men, eighty of whom were sailors from the *Flamborough*. Promptly from the fort three guns were fired at Johnson's troops, resulting in the request from him that Captain Pearce of the *Phoenix* be allowed to act as mediator.

When Captain Pearce, accompanied by a member of Johnson's Council, approached Governor Moore about surrendering the South Carolina revolutionary government, he replied in the negative, saying that no terms could induce him to do so.

Later, when the request was made that Johnson be permitted to see the Orders of Regency,[35] Moore complied, showing him also some other letters. After having read these, and given due consideration to the whole problem, Johnson ordered his men, including some South Carolinians, to disband, and promised that he "never

---

[32] W. Popple to Joseph Boone, April 18, 1721, PR, Vol. IX, p. 26; Popple to Josiah Burchett, April 20, 1721, PR, Vol. IX, p. 27.

[33] Johnson to Moore, May 9, 1721, PR, Vol. IX, p. 28.

[34] Moore to Johnson, May 9, 1721, PR, Vol. IX, p. 29.

[35] Moore to Boone, May 11, 1721, PR, Vol. IX, pp. 30-31.

would trouble his head with the present Governm[en]t anymore."[36] Johnson wisely realized that any other action on his part would result in bloodshed and involve the Province in further confusion and uncertainty. Captain Hildesley, on the other hand, was not satisfied with the turn the proposed reconquest had taken. The morning following Johnson's capitulation, Hildesley so insulted the captain of the main guard that he was placed under arrest to protect him from the enraged inhabitants. Later he was released on the application of Captain Pearce, and was accompanied by a heavy guard to the dock.[37]

Meanwhile, the wheels of the government in London had begun to turn. In Council, the Lords Justices had taken the Carolina question under consideration. They at last had discovered that the Province was of great importance because of its products and its strategic location as a frontier to the British colonies in America. It was also evident that the Province was in imminent danger of being lost at this critical time by the current state of confusion. The Lords Justices ordered that the government of the Province be taken provisionally into the hands of the Crown, and that the Board of Trade be requested to prepare a commission for a governor to be appointed by the King.[38] The man commissioned as provisional governor, Francis Nicholson,[39] was no stranger to America. Nicholson arrived in Charleston May 22, 1721,[40] less than two weeks after Johnson wisely had decided to forego attempts to regain the government.

Within the Province, Governor Nicholson proved himself a staunch supporter of education[41] and a great friend of the established church. The clergy had eagerly awaited his arrival,[42] and he did not disap-

---

[36] *Ibid.* For more information, *see also* the recount by William J. Rivers, *A Chapter in the Early History of South Carolina* (Charleston: Walker, Evans, and Cogswell, 1874), pp. 11-12.

[37] Moore to Boone, May 11, 1721, PR, Vol. IX, p. 31.

[38] August 11, 1720, PR, Vol. VIII, p. 36.

[39] August 16, 1720, PR, Vol. VIII, pp. 42-57. Nicholson had served as deputy governor of New York, governor of Maryland, and governor of Virginia.

[40] From Richard Waddon, May 28, 1721, PR, Vol. IX, p. 32.

[41] Edward McCrady, "Education in South Carolina prior to and during the Revolution," in *Collections of the South Carolina Historical Society* (5 vols., Charleston: The Society, 1857-1897), Vol. IV, p. 10; Francis Nicholson to Secretary of the SPG, November 6, 1721, SPG, Series A, Vol. XV.

[42] Secretary of SPG to Nicholson, October 29, 1720, SPG, Series A, Vol. XIV; W. T. Bull to Secretary of the SPG, December 19, 1720, SPG, Series A, Vol. XV; William Guy to Secretary of the SPG, January 24, 1720/21, SPG, Series A, Vol. XIV.

point them in their expectations. Nicholson supported the building of churches, and it was through his urging that the Assembly fixed a suitable salary for the clergy.[43]

An aggressive Assembly who had overthrown one governor and a government could be expected to quarrel with a man like Nicholson in view of his previous American career, even though he held his commission as governor from the King.

During Governor Nicholson's tenure, there was considerable disagreement between the Commons House on one side and the chief executive and his Council on the other. Nicholson was hurt by what he termed the strange and arbitrary, if not illegal, actions of the legislators, some of which he found to be inconsistent with the best interests of the King's government. This was difficult for him to bear, especially since he felt that he and the Council were carrying out the royal Instructions loyally and dutifully, or at least trying to. Adding to his dismay was the Assembly's making resolutions on every occasion without the consent or even the advice of the Governor and Council, and the lower house's insisting on what it chose to call its "Old Privileges" that went back to proprietary times. Governor Nicholson said he found the "Spirit of Commonwealth Principles both in Church and State" daily increasing, and he felt this stemmed partly from the influence of the New Englanders.[44]

Nicholson complained that State and Church politics of many of the people on the American Continent were variable. He felt that this instability might be related to "the Uncertainty of ye Weather both in Respect of heat and Cold."[45]

Before long, a money bill dispute broke out between the Governor (supported by the Council), and the Assembly. According to Nicholson's Instructions, the Council had the power to frame, alter and

[43] W. T. Bull to Secretary of the SPG, August 20, 1721, SPG, Series A, Vol. XV; Clergy of South Carolina to Secretary of the SPG, October 10, 1721; SPG, Series A, Vol. XV; Clergy of South Carolina to Secretary of the SPG, July 12, 1722, SPG, Series B, Vol. IV, Part 1; W. T. Bull to Secretary of the SPG, October 10, 1722, Series B, Vol. IV, Part 1.

[44] It might be recalled that during the existence of the Dominion of New England, Nicholson served under Andros as deputy governor in New York, but lost this government as a result of Leisler's rebellion. Also, Nicholson was a high churchman, and was accused groundlessly of having a strong leaning toward Catholicism.

[45] Francis Nicholson to Board of Trade, June 18, 1724, PR, Vol. XI, pp. 134-5; Nicholson to Board of Trade, August 5, 1724, PR, Vol. XI, pp. 152-3.

amend money bills. The Commons House refuted this right and voted in favor of denying the Council this power.[46]

During the period of provisional royal government there was continual strife over the question of popular right versus royal prerogative. Under the former government there had been many complaints about proprietary overlordship, but the government had been based on a Charter that was as binding on the Proprietors as it was on the South Carolinians. In effect, it served as a written constitution to which the people could appeal when they thought the Proprietors had exceeded the bounds of their authority or had violated the rights of the people. It was charged that the people had but changed masters, that the Board of Trade was now assuming a role even more arbitrary and negligent than the Proprietors, and there was no Charter to which to appeal for immunity.[47] The Carolinians later developed such forms of appeal in defense of their rights and privileges, as reference to the British Constitution or to natural rights theories, but none of these had the tangible feel of a charter in which obligations and privileges were stated in writing. This was a lesson Americans later put to good use.

Neither had the elimination of proprietary rule removed the external dangers facing the Province. Indians still surrounded the frontiers and the French remained at their bases, eager for expansion. France and Spain were reported to have furnished the Indians with 3,000 muskets to use against the British Province, in an attempt to win the redmen's friendship. The Indians continued their sporadic attacks on the Province,[48] necessitating the people to go to great expense and raise their taxes to maintain garrisons and scout boats on the frontiers. Ships from New York had begun trading with the French at Mobile,[49] and Carolina was losing the

---

[46] Ralph Izard (for the S. C. Council) to Duke of Newcastle, December 20, 1725, PR, Vol. XI, p. 362; David Duncan Wallace, *Constitutional History of South Carolina from 1725 to 1775* (Abbeville, S. C.: Hugh Wilson, 1899), p. 49.

[47] Edward McCrady, *The History of South Carolina under the Royal Government, 1719-1776* (New York: The MacMillan Co., 1899), pp. 92-93. McCrady questioned what rights and liberties the Carolinians gained by the overthrow of the Proprietors.

[48] Brian Hunt to Bishop of London, November 12, 1723, SPG, Fulham Palace MSS, South Carolina, no. 235; Letter from Francis Nicholson, August 25, 1724, PR, Vol. XI, p. 185; Representation and Petition of S. C. General Assembly to the King, March 11, 1726/7, PR, Vol. XII, pp. 233-4.

[49] Arthur Middleton to Nicholson, July 21, 1724, PR, Vol. XI, p. 145.

advantage of English trading goods, one of its chief means of Indian control.

A problem which caused great inconvenience was the closing of the Proprietors' Land Office in the Province. This, in effect, prohibited land sales. The Proprietors, although no longer in control of the government, retained ownership of the land, and people now hesitated in taking up lands on the frontiers. Immigration was also hindered and delayed. Frontier settlement eventually would provide the ultimate solution to the problem of defense, but as long as the Land Office was closed, this defensive measure was held in abeyance.[50]

Final disposition of the Province was a matter which weighed heavily on the minds of the Carolinians. As long as the Proprietors owned the land, there was the fear that the government might be restored to their hands, and it was rumored that such would be the case. The Rhett-Trott faction tried to use this talk to its own advantage.[51] Meanwhile, in England it was thought that the Province might be sold to the South Sea Company, and overtures were made in that direction.[52]

[50] Arthur Middleton to Nicholson, July 21, 1724, PR, Vol. XI, pp. 144-5; Letter from Nicholson, August 25, 1724, PR, Vol. XI, p. 185; Charles Hart (for governor and council) to Board of Trade, September 4, 1724, PR, Vol. XI, p. 208.

[51] Nicholson to Board of Trade, June 18, 1724, PR, Vol. XI, p. 135; Letter from Nicholson, August 25, 1724, PR, Vol. XI, p. 185.

[52] Abel Kettelby to Nicholson, January 17, 1720/21, SPG, Series B, Vol. IV, Part 1.

Courtesy Gibbes Art Gallery

LADY ANNE (JOANNA) OVERTON JOHNSON
—by an Unknown Artist

CHAPTER V

English Decisions; Carolina Deadlock

IN THE midst of the uncertainty over the disposition of the Province, Governor Francis Nicholson decided to return to England.[1] The reins of government were left in the hands of Council President Arthur Middleton who became acting governor. Nicholson was thanked by the Council for his services and requested to try to counteract the malicious and false impressions cast upon the Province by Richard Shelton, the Proprietors' secretary. Both Council and the Commons House asked him to aid them in keeping the Province under the King's government.[2] Nicholson duly conducted himself in London as the friend of the Province.

Another friend, Robert Johnson, was also in England. He presumably had left Carolina in the latter part of 1723, as he carried a letter which Nicholson had written on November 12, prior to his own departure from the Province. The letter was addressed to David Humphreys, secretary of the Society for the Propagation of the Gospel in foreign parts.[3] In England, Johnson worked for the benefit of the Province, particularly in trying to have rice removed from the enumerated list, and to have the bounty on pitch and tar reinstated. The Commons House took note of this work and sent him its thanks.[4]

The Proprietors in England also were busily at work, making a last-ditch effort to retain ownership of their Carolina lands and to regain the government. They maintained that neither the turbulence of the inhabitants, the mistakes of the Governor, nor anything else in any way affected their proprietary rights. Besides, they said that

---

[1] Address of Inhabitants of St. Andrew's Parish to Governor Nicholson, May 13, 1723. Among the ninety-two signatures is that of "Robt. Johnson." SPG, Series B, Vol. IV, Part 1.

[2] R. Izard to Nicholson, May 21, 1726, PR, Vol. XII, pp. 58-59; Thomas Broughton, Speaker, to Nicholson (May, 1726), PR, Vol. XII, pp. 59-60.

[3] Nicholson described Johnson as follows: "He is a Gent. of Universal Good Character in all respects he is a very great Friend of the Church and Clergy," SPG, Series B, Vol. IV, Part 2.

[4] March 23, 1724/5. A. S. Salley (ed.), *Journal of the Commons House of Assembly of South Carolina, for the session beginning February 23, 1724/5 and ending June 1, 1725* ([Columbia]: Joint Committee on Printing, General Assembly of S. C., 1945), p. 66.

they were sure the revolt had been brought about by persons who were greatly in arrears in quit rents. The displeasure at repeal of Assembly laws was in no wise their fault, for they had been so commanded by His Majesty, they averred. In any case, they claimed an "Indisputable Right" to the Province. The Proprietors also took this opportunity to lash out at Nicholson, saying that many of the Carolinians had been so intimidated by his actions that they were prepared to leave the Province if he should return as governor. In another communication, the Proprietors announced that since the trouble which had led His Majesty to appoint a provisional governor was over, they had appointed Samuel Horsey as their governor, and asked the King for the royal approbation.[5]

In the interim, Johnson had appealed to the government in his own behalf. He claimed that as a result of the expense of going to Carolina and using private funds that had been expended in fighting the pirates, his circumstances were £1,000 the worse for having held the office of governor. Johnson also recited the uncollected funds owed his late father, who, while governor of Carolina, had defended Charleston from a combined French-Spanish attack; he also mentioned back pay owed to his father from his service in the Leeward Islands. His salary as general of the Islands, and as captain of an Independent Company were in arrears, and due from the Crown to Robert Johnson, executor of his father's estate. Because of these considerations, and in view of Governor Nicholson's desire to quit the government, Johnson asked that the King commission him Governor of South Carolina.[6]

While Johnson was seeking the office, the Proprietors were working to regain by diplomacy what they had lost by force. Seeing that the case was going more and more against them, they found it necessary to shift their tactics. Five of them (all except Carteret) memorialized the Privy Council, setting forth their new "popular front" policy. In this, they asked that the King take control of the South Carolina government instead of appointing a provisional governor. It was their observation that neither the grievances of the Proprietors nor the difficulties of the Province would be served by another provisional governor, alleging that appointments of such a temporary nature made the official vulnerable. It was their contention that a

[5] Representation of Richard Shelton (on behalf of proprietors) to Privy Council; Proprietors to King [May 1726], PR, Vol. XII, pp. 29, 66-71.

[6] "The Case of Robert Johnson" [c. 1724]. PR, Vol. XIII, pp. 391-3.

provisional governor came too easily under the influence of the planters, who felt it was cheaper to make friends with him than to do justice to the Lords Proprietors. This accusation besmirched the character of the one provisional governor who had served, Francis Nicholson.

In surrendering their claim to the government, the Proprietors requested that their right in the land and quit rents (those in arrears, and those current) be secured to them. By admitting that the reins of government were no longer rightfully theirs, the Proprietors hoped to salvage a major financial profit.[7]

The Proprietors had quite naturally learned that Johnson was seeking the governorship. It might have been expected that they would look more favorably upon the cause of their former representative, who had defended their interests under pressure as best he could. He had refused all pleas to join the revolutionary party. When the opportunity arose, he had made plans for retaking the government, desisting only to prevent unnecessary bloodshed. His loyalty to the Proprietors had persisted despite their slighting him and showing favoritism for Justice Trott and Colonel Rhett. The Proprietors rewarded Johnson for his loyalty by writing the Privy Council that he was not properly qualified to be governor, and sought in other ways to hinder his appointment. They hoped to leave the government no choice in appointing him, saying:

> For if Mr. Johnson acted with that ardour and duty as he ought when he was the Proprietors Governor he will necessarily behave with resentment towards those persons who deposed him and if he was remiss and faulty in discharge of his duty the subscribing Proprietors are confident such a behavior will not at the least recommend him to His Majesty's Royal Favor.[8]

To strengthen their case, they made a number of charges against Johnson. He was, they said, governor of a province in which the capital town was strongly fortified; and yet when the revolution came, he made not the least struggle—not one gun was fired—but quietly turned the government over to the people.

Johnson accidentally procured a copy of the Proprietors' charges against him. He petitioned the Privy Council to be heard in his own defense. When his request was refused, he answered the charges in writing to the Duke of Newcastle.

[7] Proprietors to Privy Council, October 12, 1727, PR, Vol. XII, p. 253.
[8] Proprietors to Privy Council, October 12, 1721, PR, Vol. XII, pp. 253-4.

Johnson stated that he had performed his duties while governor to the best of his abilities, showing justice alike to Proprietors and inhabitants. He said, "When the subscribing Propriet[o]rs shall think fitt to give any one Instance of his Failure therein, he is ready to give an answer thereto." Johnson insisted that periodically he had given the Proprietors accounts of affairs in the Province and had made proposals on what he thought proper for the Proprietors and the peoples' needs. The ex-governor suggested that these communications had not been laid before the Proprietors by their secretary, Richard Shelton. Johnson reminded the Duke that Carolinians felt the highest enmity toward Shelton, whom they considered to be the "chief author of all the Hardships they complained of."[9]

Johnson defended his action at the time of the revolution in Charleston, maintaining that he had done all he could to prevent it, and afterwards, to suppress it. As to the fortifications, he said those manning them around the town were in conspiracy with the revolutionaries. When Johnson had called out the militia, it went over to the opposition, and there was no organized armed force on which to call. He said that the people had proffered him not only the government in the King's name, but after his refusal, they still continued to treat him with respect and civility.[10]

Johnson did not mention that following the victories over the pirates—which naturally increased his popularity—the Assembly had worked in harmony with the proprietary government. To promote the welfare of the Province, the Assembly at that time had created a special fund to meet expenses of government and had also made plans for sinking and cancelling the bills of credit. The Proprietors, however, took that occasion to order the dissolution of the Assembly and the election of a new one, in order to bolster the Trott-Rhett faction. The result was the election of a legislature more hostile to the Proprietors.[11]

---

[9] Proprietors to Privy Council, October 12, 1727, PR, Vol. XII, pp. 253-6; "The Answer of Robt. Johnson," November 7, 1727, PR, Vol. XII, pp. 258-65.

[10] "The Answer of Robt. Johnson," November 7, 1727, PR, Vol. XII, pp. 258-65.

[11] Yates Snowden, *History of South Carolina* (5 vols., Chicago: Lewis Publishing Co., 1920), Vol. I, pp. 183-4; Yonge, *Proceedings,* in Carroll, *Historical Collections,* Vol. II, pp. 148-51; David Ramsay, *History of South Carolina* (2 vols. in one, Newberry, S. C.: W. J. Duffie, 1858), Vol. I, pp. 34-36.

Another objection made by the Proprietors against Johnson's appointment was that they despaired of having their rights and quit rents taken care of by Johnson. They described him as a very large planter holding more than 19,000 acres of land, and said he and his relatives, who were among the largest landowners in the Province, were in arrears with their quit rents.

Johnson denied he was in arrears; he claimed the proprietors owed him more than £500, and this was after the quit rents had been subtracted. His relatives, he said, had never refused to pay what they owed, and if their quit rents were in arrears, it was probably due to the Proprietors' failure to appoint a receiver for the past several years. Johnson thought "the reason is very new" that he ought not be appointed governor because he had an estate in the Province. Such an arrangement, he felt, had never before been considered a disqualification, "for who is more likely to promote the true Interest of a Collony than he whose Personal Interest it is so to doe?"

To a third objection, Johnson admitted that he had consented to the passage of a law laying a duty on all British goods entering Carolina, but this was a duty he hoped to use for repairing fortifications. Upon representation of the Commissioners of the Customs, however, the law was made void. Johnson in no way felt responsible for the law, because similar legislation had been passed before his time, with no criticism. Similar laws had also been passed in some colonies of the Crown. The result of this argument was a general Instruction to all governments to pass no such laws in the future.

At the final charge that paper money had been greatly increased during his administration to hurt trade, Johnson lashed back, saying that this was not true. Johnson had secured the passage of a law for sinking and destroying all paper money within three years, a measure greatly pleasing to the merchants. At the same time, he attacked the contradiction in the position of Shelton, who had appeared before the Board of Trade, citing Johnson's refusal to consent to the issuance of paper money as a reason for popular displeasure.[12]

The Proprietors' plot was obvious. In order to reserve the lands in the Province for themselves, they sought to downgrade Johnson

[12] Proprietors to Privy Council, October 12, 1727, PR, Vol. XII, pp. 253-4; "The Answer of Rob[er]t Johnson," November 7, 1727, PR, Vol. XII, pp. 258-65. Both the three-year paper money law and Shelton's statement were matters of public record. The Proprietors had admitted this previously, when it suited their purpose.

and shift the blame for their loss to his shoulders. The former governor stoutly refused to accept the responsibility for the revolt, observing that the Proprietors' actions "were done directly contrary to the opinion and advice given them by Mr. Johnson."[13] He questioned their motives for surrendering the sovereignty of the Province to the King, and doubted that they sought "the peace and prosperity of the Colony and the pleasure they shall always have to enlarge His Majesty's Dominion and prerogative."[14] Others besides Johnson had become skeptical of the suddenly pious and altruistic mouthings of the Proprietors, the overlords who soon shifted their position.

The Proprietors at that point decided to relinquish not only their claim to the government of the Province but also their lands in Carolina. They petitioned the King to pay each of them the sum of £2,500, out of which no fees or deductions were to be taken, and assist them in collecting quit rents and other fees which were due them.[15] This amount, they said, was £9,500. On the other hand, there were claims against the Proprietors for salaries and the like, amounting to £824-7s-1d.[16]

To protect their still considerable interests in the Province, the Proprietors asked the King to appoint Colonel Horsey governor. The opportunity to smear Johnson again was not neglected; he was referred to as a person "of whose Conduct & disability we have had such wofull Experience."[17]

Despite these charges, Johnson's stature increased, and his loyalty to the Proprietors in a hopeless situation appealed to the British authorities. Neither could the authorities have failed to note that, through his course of moderation, he had retained the admiration and respect of the people of the Province. A new Governor would have to hold the support of the Assembly, so that royal Instructions for Carolina might be carried out successfully. He would have to be flexible but firm.

Johnson appeared to be the one man who could be counted on to maintain royal prerogative without causing the people to feel that he was depriving them of their rights and privileges. Further, it was altogether possible that there would be further conflicts arising in a

---

[13] *Ibid.,* p. 265.

[14] Proprietors to Privy Council, October 12, 1727, PR, Vol. XII, p. 255.

[15] Proprietors to the King, March 5, 1728, PR, Vol. XIII, pp. 1-2.

[16] Proprietors to Privy Council, 1728, PR, Vol. XIII, p. 8.

[17] Craven to [Duke of Newcastle], April 3, 1728, PR, Vol. XIII, pp. 16-17.

Province which had just ended a revolution. In the future, it would be necessary for the new Governor to inhibit such actions. He would also have to solve other problems that arose without surrendering royal prerogative.

Governor Nicholson, with his absolutist views, had failed in his administration in South Carolina, just as he had failed elsewhere in the American Colonies. Governor Johnson was an exception to this type of appointed Governor, most of whom were failures. Whether or not the British authorities recognized his unique qualifications for the governorship, there were conventional reasons for his appointment: the past service of his family, and the fact that he was not without influential friends in England.[18]

In England, negotiations over the ultimate disposition of the Province, and the appointment of a Governor, were nearing the climactic and decisive stage; in South Carolina, affairs were approaching a hopeless deadlock. Nicholson's departure had left the government in the hands of Arthur Middleton, whose administration was even less satisfactory than Nicholson's.[19]

As speaker of the Assembly, Middleton had made the formal act of setting in motion the revolt, but as Governor he soon found that it was one thing to be a leader in a revolution and quite another to try to govern the revolutionaries in harmony. His burden was not lightened by the uncertainties concerning the disposal of the Province, which in turn encouraged increased activity among the Trott-Rhett faction. William Rhett was dead but his son and his two sons-in-law, together with Joseph Blake, were carrying on in the same tradition. Others, such as Benjamin Whitaker, were causing Middleton trouble.[20]

The paper money problem which had led to such a vexing controversy under Nicholson continued under Middleton. Problems of

---

[18] Colonial patronage was mainly in the hands of the Duke of Newcastle. Mark A. Thomson, *The Secretaries of State, 1681-1782* (Oxford: Clarendon Press, 1932), p. 48; Stebelton H. Nulle, *Thomas Pelham-Holles, Duke of Newcastle: His Early Political Career, 1693-1724* (Philadelphia: University of Pennsylvania Press, 1931), p. 41; Basil Williams, *Carteret & Newcastle: A Contrast in Contemporaries* (Cambridge: Cambridge University Press, 1943), p. 20; and the interesting comment on Newcastle by Sir Lewis Namier, *The Structure of Politics at the Accession of George III*, 2nd ed. (London: Macmillan and Co., Ltd., 1957), p. 234.

[19] McCrady, *Royal Government*, pp. 69-74.

[20] Nicholson to Board of Trade, June 18, 1724, PR, Vol. XI, p. 135; Middleton to Nicholson, April 1727, PR, Vol. XII, p. 194.

defense and Indian struggles, which had been largely responsible for issuance of paper money, generated a planter-merchant rift. Planters favored increasing quantities of the bills and worked to prevent their redemption, but merchants, constituting a creditor group, opposed them. The Bank Act of 1712 had provided more money by an arrangement that was classified as a typical land bank scheme of the period. The bank scheme, however, had proven to be unfeasible, because of the rapid depreciation of the bills, when the Yamassee War necessitated more issues of paper.[21]

In the 1720's, Governor Nicholson consented to a bill providing for a new issue of £120,000. Through the influence of British merchants, the measure was disallowed, but not before much of the paper had been issued. The law was later amended by provisions of a new act that promised rapid redemption.

Under Middleton's government, the Commons House began demanding more paper money, but the Council refused. Before long, though, the need to put down Indian hostilities forced Middleton and the Council to agree on reissuing £20,000 due for retirement. As soon as the danger had passed, the squabbles began again, threatening violence, and virtually paralyzing the administration of the government.[22]

Middleton found the people riotous and tumultous, insulting the Council and other officers. The acting Governor repeatedly called on the Assembly for legislation, but it passed only those bills that Middleton felt were directly in conflict with the King's Instructions and made no provision for raising taxes. Middleton—the former revolutionist—bemoaned the fate of the Province and concluded that he might as well order the Assembly's dissolution. He said:

> And if such a Petty Collony as this, are suffered to run out, at this Rate, and are permitted to take such boundless Libertyes, daily affronting the Royal Authority and his Representative and Ministers here, as will appeare they have done, and

---

[21] Osgood, *American Colonies in the Eighteenth Century,* Vol. II, pp. 371-3.

[22] Wallace, *South Carolina: A Short History,* pp. 134-9; McCrady, *Royal Government,* pp. 80-82; Leila Sellers, *Charleston Business on the Eve of the American Revolution* (Chapel Hill: University of North Carolina Press, 1934, pp. 70-71; Richard M. Jellison, "Paper Currency in Colonial South Carolina: A Reappraisal," *South Carolina Historical Magazine,* Vol. LXII, No. 3 (July 1961), pp. 134-47, gives a concise account of the paper money struggle of the 1720's. He upholds the viewpoint of the Commons House on the need for an expanded paper currency.

> that without the least Censure or Resentment from home, I know not where will be the end of these things.[23]

During this period the Assembly had made no provisions for the security of the Province. The situation, it was said, was caused by restless people "who seem to have abandoned all Rule for Maintaining of Civil power."[24]

The attitude of the Commons House was illustrated by an incident involving Landgrave Smith which foreboded the type of trouble in store for Johnson. Smith had been confined on the charge of high treason, but was never prosecuted. However, during his confinement Chief Justice Richard Allein refused to grant him a writ of habeas corpus out of term, and Smith complained to the Commons House. It appointed a committee to examine his grievances and resolved to hear him despite the objections of the Council.[25] A copy of its report was sent to the Chief Justice who was told to appear before the House with his answer to the complaints, in writing. Allein, however, refused to appear, noting that the affair was outside the concern of the Assembly, and said that if he were accused of misbehaving in office, he was accountable to the King or to the President and Council; and if he had violated the Habeas Corpus Act, then he was liable to the penalties mentioned in that Act. In previous cases where judges had been called before the lower house, it was for the breach of privilege of that house. Smith's complaint failed to fit into that category, therefore the Chief Justice could not be called upon to answer to the Commons House, "without derogating from the Power and Authority he was entrusted with."[26]

Angered by this reply, the Commons resolved that Allein's message was an affront, constituted contempt, and that the Chief Justice should be taken into the custody of their messenger immediately. At the time, the Chief Justice was attending a session of Council. The messenger entered the Council chamber, and without making known to the President and the Council the nature of his errand, attempted to arrest Allein. The President forthwith ordered the messenger out.

---

[23] Middleton to [Duke of Newcastle], May 17, 1728, PR, Vol. XIII, pp. 44-46; JCHA, March 1, 6, 1727/8.

[24] Council of S. C. to the King [n.d.], PR, Vol. VIII, pp. 267-8.

[25] JCHA, August 2-4, 1727.

[26] Council of S. C. to the King [n.d.], PR, Vol. XIII, pp. 326-30.

On hearing of these developments, the Commons passed another resolution terming the President's handling of its messenger, as "arbitrary and unprecedented & an Infringement on the liberties and privileges" of their House. In return, Middleton dissolved the Assembly.[27]

More friction soon arose. The Council having rejected a number of measures passed by the Commons, the lower House decided to request a long-term adjournment. The stated reason was the difficulty of keeping enough members together to conduct business, due to their illness and the excessive heat of the season. Because the House had not performed the necessary functions, the president refused its request; thereupon, the Commons—as was permissible—adjourned itself, to meet again the following week. The body never met again, except for two or three members, who soon absented themselves.[28]

Apprehension of attack from one source or another continued during the administration of Middleton. There was the constant fear that if war between England and Spain should break out, Carolina would be in danger of invasion from St. Augustine and of attack by the Spanish Indians.[29]

Another vexing problem, especially to the established church, was that of dissenters. One clergyman described the situation this way:

> Sectaries of all kinds, my Lord, swarm here, 'Tis a country of almost Polish liberty.
>
> Every man taking ye liberty of doing whats right in his own eyes as to religion, it may without help of a figure be truly said —there's no King in Carolina. Schismaticks, yea unbaptized persons have been admitted, before my time, Church officers; as Vestrymen & Church-wardens.[30]

The narrator, who found personal and ecclesiastical trouble in Carolina, returned to England in the fall of 1729, and reported that "Carolina is now in a distracted condition: government despised: property invaded: justice perverted: malice, villanous calumny defended: tricking in trade is universal."[31]

[27] *Ibid.*

[28] *Ibid.*, pp. 333-4.

[29] Clergy of S. C. to the King [*1727?*], SPG, Fulham Palace MSS, South Carolina, no. 152.

[30] Brian Hunt to Bishop of London, December 18, 1727, SPG, Fulham Palace MSS, South Carolina, no. 139.

[31] Brian Hunt to Bishop of London, September 8, 1729, SPG, Fulham Palace MSS, South Carolina, no. 139.

A few months later, in December, Sir Alexander Cuming said that he found "the whole Province Complaining of want of Government, and that Every Person did what he himself thought fitt, which threw the Country into Such Confusion, that no Person had any Security either for Life or Property."[32]

Even if witnesses had exaggerated, it was clear that the Province of South Carolina was in a rapidly deteriorating condition. Fortunately, however, its future was about to be determined.

In 1729 an agreement was reached, to be fulfilled by September 29, in which seven of the eight Lords Proprietors agreed to surrender their title and interest in Carolina. The Crown was to pay the seven the sum of £17,500, free and clear of all deductions, plus an additional £5,000 for quit rents that were in arrears and due, to June 1, 1729.[33] Lord Carteret was not a party to the agreement and retained his one-eighth interest, thereby sharing with the King revenues from land sales and quit rents.[34]

---

[32] Cuming to Newcastle [received by Board of Trade, July 14, 1730], PR, Vol. XIV, p. 220.

[33] *Statutes,* Vol. I, pp. 60-71.

[34] McCrady, *Proprietary Govt.,* pp. 678-680. Such an "anomalous condition," comments McCrady, "was only put to an end by a change scarcely less anomalous," when Carteret in 1744 was given as his portion a large tract of land in North Carolina south of the Virginia border.

37 And Be it further Enacted by the Authority aforesd. that this Act and every thing therein Contained shall be in force from and after the Ratification hereof untill the full term and time of five years, and from thence to the end of the next Sessions of the General Assembly after, and no longer.

Robt. Johnson

[illegible]

Read three times & Ratified in Open Assembly the 20th day of March 1718/9

Tho: Broughton

Char: Hart

Fran: Yonge

Courtesy S. C. Archives Department

Signature of Robert Johnson, *et al,* on an Act to Regulate Indian Trade. March 20, 1718/1719, included in Engrossed Acts of the General Assembly.

CHAPTER VI

The First Royal Governor

SOUTH CAROLINA had become a royal colony, fulfilling the fervent wishes of its people. The Proprietors had been compensated with a generous settlement, and the Province awaited the appointment of the Crown's governor.

In England, on November 22, 1729, the Board of Trade received notification that Robert Johnson would be the Carolina Governor, and that the King wished it to draw up drafts of a Commission and Instructions for him.[1]

The draft of the Commission was subsequently approved by the Privy Council which ordered that a warrant be drawn for the King's Seal.[2] Johnson's Commission was then sealed December 13, 1729 as Captain General and Commander in Chief in and over the Province.[3]

Prior to, and following his appointment, Johnson was consulted concerning affairs in Carolina,[4] and made recommendations to the Board of Trade. Johnson asked for detailed Instructions, especially in regard to security and defense, quit rents, land regulations, absentee overlordship, office holding in absentia, boundary troubles, the economic foundation of the Province, and all points of contention between popular and prerogative interests.

Johnson's Instructions were completed September 7, 1730.[5]

A number of the Instructions dealt with such purely administrative matters as the taking and administering of oaths, the quorum for the Council, and suspension of its members.

Other instructions included:

---

1 Board of Trade Journal, December 2, 1729, PR, Vol. XIII, p. 245.

2 December 11, 1729, PRO CO 5:192, p. 47 (Library of Congress transcript).

3 PRO CO 5:192, pp. 48-63; Hardwicke Papers: Add. MSS, 36128, fo. 335-42 (Library of Congress transcript).

4 Board of Trade Journal, May 16, 28, 1728, PR, Vol. XIII, pp. 37-38; November 29, 1728, PR, Vol. XIII, p. 41; PR, Vol. XIV, p. 31.

5 PRO, CO 5:192, pp. 65-71 (Library of Congress transcript).

(1) The Assembly was not to be allowed to adjourn except by the Governor's consent; nor were its members to have any powers or privileges denied members of the English House of Commons.

(2) Council and the lower house would be given the power to frame money bills.

(3) No law was to be passed lessening or impairing the royal revenue without special permission from the Crown.

A significant provision concerned quit rents, resulting from the purchase of the Province. In buying the Proprietors' seven-eighths interest in the lands, The Crown had paid £5,000 in consideration of quit rents that were due and in arrears. The Crown said it was now willing to remit the rents, provided the Assembly would repeal legislation, formerly approved by the Proprietors, entitled "An Act to Ascertain the prices of land, the forms of conveyances and the manner of recovering of Rents for Lands, and the prices of the several commodities the same shall be paid in."

The Crown also specified that it wanted legislation enacted to require registration of all land grants; to deny grants to any persons who were unable to cultivate them,[6] and annual quit rents to be paid by those possessing lands grants from the Proprietors.

Further, Johnson was instructed that the Crown was to be kept fully informed of affairs in the Province; that the Governor was not to consent to any bill without first submitting a draft for approval or disapproval, to prevent prejudice to the royal prerogative or the property of the inhabitants, or would in any way affect trade and shipping of the British kingdom. In the event that such a bill was passed, it was decreed that it must include a provision suspending execution until the royal pleasure had been made known.

The Crown, concerned about limited-time laws which might expire before assent or refusal was given, instructed Johnson that no laws could be enacted to be in force for less than two years; and that no law once disproved by the King could be re-enacted.

Governor Johnson was ordered to transmit a copy of the laws in force in the Province upon his arrival in Carolina, together with his suggestions for changes; and that within three months after passage, he was to send copies of new laws, statutes and ordinances, including an explanation of the need for passage. Failure to do so, he was

[6] PRO, CO 5:192, pp. 72-73 (Library of Congress transcript).

advised, would place him under "Pain of our Highest Displeasure, and of the forfeiture of that years Salary."

Johnson was directed to obtain legislation for raising and settling funds, money to defray the necessary expenses of the government, and for salaries for the Governor and other officers, and to send copies of the journals of the Council and Assembly.[7]

Johnson was specifically forbidden to create any new courts or judicial offices, or to disband any in existence; no officers of the courts were to be removed except for good and sufficient cause, and this transmitted to the home government; judges and justices of the peace were not to have any time limitation placed upon their Commissions, in order to prevent arbitrary removal; no court of judicature was to be adjourned except upon sufficient cause; justice was to be administered without delay and impartially; appeals were to be permitted in cases of errors from courts, to Governor and Council, and appeals were to be allowed to the Privy Council in cases involving over £300 sterling.[8]

If no law was in existence restraining "Inhumane Severity," toward servants or slaves, Johnson was instructed to try to secure one, with the provision included that the willful killing of Indians and Negroes could be punished by death, and penalties would be imposed for maiming. The Crown also wanted a law passed to place duties on the importation of Negroes to discourage the traffic, and to provide that duties be paid by the purchaser rather than the importer.

A final Instruction said that, except for papists, liberty of conscience was to be permitted to all persons "So as they [may] be contented with a quiet and peaceable enjoyment of the same, not giving offense or Scandal to the Government."[9]

Johnson was pleased that the suggestions he had made in writing and in personal appearances before the Board of Trade had been incorporated into the Instructions. But from his familiarity with the Province, he realized how difficult it would be to carry out all of them.

Meanwhile, high hopes attended the arrival in South Carolina of its first Governor since the Crown's purchase from the Lords Proprietors. Robert Johnson was a former proprietary Governor and

[7] PRO, CO 5:192, pp. 75-80.
[8] PRO, CO 5:192, pp. 88-98.
[9] PRO, CO 5:192, pp. 95, 101, 114.

personal friend of many Carolinians and, coming from England, had numbered among his party on the way over a peculiarly American group. In his care were the seven Cherokee Indians who had been taken on a visit to England by Sir Alexander Cuming, where they were received by King George II. While there, the Indians were entertained at the Mermaid Tavern and in private homes. They had created a sensation wherever they went, thereby promoting America and especially the Province of South Carolina.[10]

Johnson had been present at a conference between the visiting Cherokees and the Board of Trade when the Indians were asked to sign a Treaty of Friendship.[11] One provision of the Treaty would permit the British exclusively to build forts within Cherokee territory, and to trade exclusively with the Indians. The treaty, although signed by the Indians, was not binding because, of those in England, only two were chieftains and were not authorized to sign for their tribe. Despite this fact, the cause of the colonials was furthered, and an era of friendship between the British and the Cherokees seemed about to begin.

The new Governor of South Carolina, who had received £700 to defray expenses of the Cherokees in London and for the journey home, arrived in Charleston December 15, 1730, with 124 articles of Instructions from the Crown.[12] One article specified that he use all possible means for regaining the Indians to the English interests and try to secure a law regulating the Indian trade.[13]

Johnson's first important consideration was to set in motion the long idle wheels of the Assembly that had already been called by a Proclamation from Middleton.[14] The Governor found that the

---

[10] Chapman J. Milling, *Red Carolinians,* (Chapel Hill: The University of North Carolina Press, 1940), pp. 275-77; Crane, *Southern Frontier,* pp. 294-7; Ramsay, *History of S. C.,* Vol. I, pp. 55-57; J. B. O. Landrum, *Colonial and Revolutionary History of Upper South Carolina,* (Greenville, S. C.: Shannon and Co., 1897), pp. 16-17.

[11] *Ibid.;* Board of Trade to Duke of Newcastle, August 20, 1730, PR, Vol. XIV, pp. 257-9; Board of Trade Journal, August 18, September 7, 9, 1730, PR, Vol. XIV, pp. 17, 19-24.

[12] September 9, 1730 (received by Johnson September 16), British Museum, Additional MS, 24322 (Library of Congress photostat); A. Garden to Bishop of London, April 20, 1731, SPG, Fulham Palace MSS, South Carolina, no. 74; PRO, CO 5:192, (Library of Congress transcript), pp. 65-120; Johnson's Commission as governor, signed December 13, 1729, is found in Hardwicke Papers: Add. MSS, 36128, fo. 335-42 (Library of Congress transcript).

[13] PRO, CO 5:192, pp. 105-6.

[14] Journal of the Council of S. C. (hereinafter cited as JC), Vol. V, pp. 10-11 (December 17, 1730).

newly elected members had not met to transact any business, and there was little time for a session before they would wish to return home to tend their plantations. Legislation was needed and a long delay would ensue if a new election had to be held. After advice from Council, the Governor decided to meet with the existing group, saying: "Trusting Intirely in the Good Disposition you would meet in, to Do what should be found necessary for Setling and promoting the Good of the province." He felt confident that they would justify his good opinion of them.[15]

In his first address to the Assembly, Johnson made certain recommendations, but primarily he emphasized the favors of the Crown toward the Province, such as the purchase of seven-eighths of its charter from the Lords Proprietors. He held out the olive branch to the Assembly, hoping for co-operation, but he was determined to fulfill his Instructions and to maintain the Crown's prerogative.[16]

The question of royal prerogative versus assembly privilege soon arose. John Lloyd, who was elected Commons House speaker, made the customary claim for lower house members for freedom of debate, easy access to the Governor, and protection from arrest, to which traditional rights Johnson agreed. Johnson then said that if the Assembly would recommend a well-qualified person to serve as its clerk, he would appoint him to that office. The following day, the Commons House decided to show its independence by choosing a clerk and a messenger and sending them to the Governor to take the oath of office. Instead of swearing them in, Johnson returned the legislative body a message expressing his regret over the disagreement, and repeating his offer to appoint as clerk any qualified person recommended by the Assembly. He stated his determination that the royal Instructions would be the rules of his government, regardless of the rights the lower house had assumed during the proprietary period.[17]

In mentioning his Instructions, Johnson was following Article 14, which read in part: "And you are hereby expressly enjoyned not to

---

[15] JC, Vol. V, p. 23 (January 21, 1730/31).

[16] Johnson's speech was reported and summarized in the new English periodical, *Gentleman's Magazine,* Vol. I, no. 5 (May 1731), pp. 218-9. About that magazine, see Walter Graham, *English Literary Periodicals* (New York: Thomas Nelson and Sons, 1930), Chapter V; and C. Lennart Carlson, *The First Magazine: A History of the Gentleman's Magazine* (Providence, R. I.: Brown University, 1938).

[17] JCHA, pp. 605, 608 (January 21, 1730/31); JC, Vol. V, pp. 22-23, 26-27 (January 21, 22, 1730/31).

allow the said Assembly or any of the Members thereof any Power or Privilege whatsoever, which is not allowed by Us to the House of Commons or the Members thereof in Great Britain."[18]

Johnson was reasonably sure that the English House of Commons did not appoint its clerk and he therefore insisted that the Carolina Commons could claim no such right. Expressing uncertainty concerning the messenger, the Governor conceded that perhaps the English House of Commons exercised that right, and he would be willing to allow the Commons House of Carolina the privilege. Its messenger, he said, would be permitted to qualify when he presented himself to the Governor.[19] This arrangement was an attempt at compromise; Johnson would appoint the clerk, the Commons could select its messenger.

The lower house acceded to this offer and sent the messenger to the Council chamber where he was sworn in. Simultaneously, the Assembly informed the Governor that a similar situation to that involving the clerk had been a point of controversy between Middleton and a previous Assembly, resulting in the public business being retarded. For that reason, the Assembly notified Johnson that it had chosen John Baily as clerk and had sent him up to qualify.

Once again Johnson refused and expressed surprise that the lower house still insisted on such a right. He stated firmly that in England the clerk was an officer not chosen by the House of Commons and the election law of the Province specifically removed any such right the Assembly might have formerly claimed. Furthermore, said Johnson, if the lower house did not accept his offer to recommend a proper person to him, he would forthwith choose and commission a clerk himself.[20]

The Commons House, undeterred by this threat, referred again to the deadlock in Middleton's time and said it would not retreat or surrender a point in a case so concerned with Assembly privilege.

At this juncture, the Governor tried a new tactic. He asked the Commons House to send up Baily, which was done. Johnson thereupon informed Baily that he felt inclined to give him a commission as the clerk, but asked him if he would act by virtue of his commission alone and not by reason of any other authority. After receiving

---

[18] PRO, CO 5:192, pp. 70-71 (Library of Congress transcript).

[19] JC, Vol. V, p. 27 (January 22, 1730/31).

[20] JC, Vol. V, pp. 28-29 (January 22, 1730/31).

permission to acquaint the lower house with this turn of events, Baily returned and offered to accept the Governor's commission. That afternoon he was sworn in, "by Virtue of his Majesties Commission now Given me by his Excellency the Governor and not by any other Authority whatsoever."[21]

The case seemed closed, when matters took a new turn. Either Baily had misunderstood the Assembly or the body had changed its mind, for it refused to accept Baily as clerk on the basis of the Governor's commission. At this development, the Governor, on the advice of the Council, prorogued the Assembly until the following month.[22]

Upon reconvening, the Commons informed the Governor of its choice of Eleazer Allen as clerk and sent him to be sworn in. Johnson replied that he was of a strong disposition to agree with the legislative body so that the public business would be impeded no longer.[23] Nevertheless, he consulted the Council. Afterwards Johnson reported that he and Council were in complete accord that the right of appointing a clerk rested with the Crown. They realized, he said, "that it is vain to Dispute about a Right you [the Assembly] Seem Determined not to be Convinced in." To prevent further delays, the Governor advised the Commons House to send Allen to take the oaths, so that he could serve pending receipt of a ruling from England that he hoped would remove the question from any future dispute. Allen was then sworn in.[24]

In a letter to the Board of Trade explaining the situation, Johnson presented fairly the case of the lower house. He observed that the Assembly pleaded custom, claiming it had exercised the privilege of appointment in the Proprietors' time and during Governor Nicholson's administration. It also had maintained, he said, that such was the legislative privilege in Barbados and some other British colonies. The Governor concluded by saying that he had insisted that the appointment was His Majesty's prerogative.[25]

In time, the Board sent a reply informing Johnson that, in England, the King always appointed the clerks in the House of Commons. It instructed him to disallow the Carolina Assembly this

[21] JC, Vol. V, pp. 30-32 (January 22-23, 1730-31).

[22] JC, Vol. V, p. 33 (January 23, 1730/31).

[23] JC, Vol. V, p. 38 (February 18, 1730/31).

[24] JC, Vol. V, pp. 39-40 (February 18, 1730/31).

[25] Johnson to Board of Trade, March 26, 1731, PR, Vol. XV, p. 20.

greater privilege than that claimed by the British. Johnson, therefore, insisting on the royal prerogative, said that he must name the clerk himself,[26] and showed the King's order to commission Isaac Amyand clerk of the Assembly.[27]

Although he was supported by the royal authorities and a definite order on the appointment, Johnson did not flaunt his victory in the Assembly's face. He remained silent, wisely waiting for an opportune moment.

After a lengthy recess, the Assembly met. When Johnson proceeded to appoint the said Isaac Amyand as clerk,[28] the Commons replied that it could not give up its privilege until it had addressed the King. It advised the Governor that it had instructed its agent in England to exert himself to the utmost to save the long-standing privilege. Meanwhile, the Assembly said it hoped that the Governor would not obstruct business by insisting upon Amyand's immediate admittance as clerk.

Johnson found himself in a much firmer position than when the difference of opinions first arose. The Assembly at this time was embroiled in an argument with the Surveyor General and others over the land problem, a dispute that was becoming more involved and more fervid. The legislative body was hardly in a position to antagonize the Governor on this occasion when it was greatly in need of his support.

Johnson skillfully took advantage of this crucial state of affairs by stating that he would not depart from His Majesty's positive command. One reason for Johnson's new, unconditional attitude, was his order from the Board of Trade; but he was motivated in part by the strategic situation then existing. Timing was important because his object was to have the Assembly bow to royal command and to accept the order with grace, so that future business would not be obstructed by contrary legislators.

His attitude, although conciliatory, was firm. He readily granted the Commons his permission to make further application to England, after he had restated the facts in the case. Johnson left the legislative body to ponder whether it would "obey the King, & pro-

[26] A. Popple to Johnson, November 18, 1731, PR, Vol. XV, p. 55.

[27] Johnson to Board of Trade, June 26, 1732, PR, Vol. XV, p. 135; Greene, *Provincial Governor,* p. 151n.

[28] From Johnson, June 25, 1732, PR, Vol. XV, p. 134; Johnson to Board of Trade, December 15, 1732, PR, Vol. XVI, p. 4.

vide for the Safety of the Country, or not, for the Consequence of the refusal must lye at Your Door."[29]

There was little the lower house could do but acquiesce. It informed Johnson that upon consideration of his message, it had decided to accept Amyand as clerk.[30]

Johnson had won a minor victory for the royal prerogative, by knowing when and how to retreat, while at the same time recognizing the proper juncture for firmness and authority. Above all, he had accomplished an object lessen without alienating the Assembly.

The scope of the problem in South Carolina—and other colonies — was illustrated by another incident in the prerogative-versus-privilege conflict. This question involved the Crown's desire for the establishment of a civil list. On this point, Governor Johnson's Instructions were specific. He was to obtain passage of a law providing for the necessary charges of government and for the salaries of the Governor and other officers.[31] Johnson, in his first formal speech to the Assembly, had recommended such a plan and sent the body a copy of his Instructions[32] on the subject.

A few months later he inquired specifically what had been done to provide adequate salaries for the chief justice and the attorney general. At this prodding, the Assembly resolved that the chief justice be given the sum of £600 as his salary for one year, and that the attorney general, in lieu of salary, be provided monies from fines and forfeitures, as was customary.[33]

Johnson answered the Assembly three days later, supported by the unanimous opinion of the Council, that the specified salary for the chief justice was not adequate to maintain the dignity and honor of the office. The King had ordered that there be granted a suitable and honorable provision for that officer, and Johnson requested compliance with His Majesty's command. Johnson added that the case involved a point affecting the honor of the Crown, the welfare and happiness of the people, and the necessary and impartial administration of justice, "without which no State can be happy or Subsist."[34]

---

[29] JC, Vol. V, pp. 337, 339 (December 13, 1732).
[30] JC, Vol. V, p. 340 (December 14, 1732).
[31] PRO, CO 5:192, pp. 79-80 (Library of Congress transcript).
[32] JC, Vol. V, pp. 25-26 (January 21-22, 1730/31).
[33] JC, Vol. V, p. 115 (July 17, 1731).
[34] JC, Vol. V, pp. 118-9 (July 20, 1731).

The lower house accepted this recommendation favorably, and increased the salary to £700, a sum, considering the condition of the Province, it felt to be in keeping with the dignity of the office.[35] Johnson, in turn, expressed pleasure at the house's deference to the King's Instructions and to his own recommendation; yet he was not wholly satisfied. Although the salary had been raised, he countered that it was still insufficient. The amount fell short of what had been given at previous times, and, in proportion, was much less than was allowed many persons in less responsible and less time-consuming offices.[36] The £700, in Carolina money, was at that time equal to only £100 sterling. Despite Johnson's protests, the Assembly could not be induced to increase the amount.[37]

Nothing more was said about placing the chief justice's salary on a fixed, rather than an annual appropriation. The chief justice would shortly experience the disadvantage of such a system.

The inconveniences caused by the lack of a civil list for royal officials must have been plainly evident to the Governor and the Council, for at that time the Council was trying to include a provision in the Tax Bill to pay Arthur Middleton for his service as acting governor. When Middleton held office, he was at such odds with the Assembly that the body had not voted him any salary. As late as 1731, the Assembly was still resisting the attempt to pay him for his services, although the Council insisted on it.[38]

Meanwhile, the lower house was providing for Governor Johnson's salary. It decided to allow him £3,500 for the year, which was equivalent to £500 sterling. This amount satisfied the Council, which, however, was displeased that the King's desire for a settled salary had not been met. It requested that the same amount be fixed as an annual salary for the Governor during the length of his administration.[39] Johnson, himself, felt it necessary to take a hand in the matter and reminded the Commons of the King's Instructions. He seemed to feel some awkwardness in discussing his own salary, and was quick to say he did not fear that the Assembly would forego granting him the same salary as long as he remained governor. He said he acted only in obedience to his orders and commands.[40]

---

35 JC, Vol. V, pp. 120-1 (July 22, 1731).
36 JC, Vol. V, pp. 122-3 (July 23, 1731).
37 Johnson to Board of Trade, November 14, 1731, PR, Vol. XV, p. 39.
38 JC, Vol. V, pp. 134-6, 138-9 (August 12, 14, 1731).
39 JC, Vol. V, p. 126 (July 28, 1731).
40 JC, Vol. V, pp. 140-1 (August 17, 1731).

Until the session ended, the lower house tried to stall, on this point and a proposal for a civil list, the latter needing extensive consideration as it was an innovation. At the same time that the Assembly was declining to act on these matters, it was not remiss in expressing high regard for the Governor and gratitude to the King for his appointment.[41] These statements were not mere platitudes, for in all probability the Commons would have been quite willing to see that Johnson received a salary on a fixed basis, provided the danger of establishing a precedent were not evident. From past experience, the members were aware of the possibility that some future governor might not be as acceptable to them as was Johnson.

The Council agreed with the Commons House that, because the session was so near an end, it would be difficult to provide an establishment for all officers. It held, however, that the fixed salary for the Governor should be settled without delay. Despite this appeal, the lower house still declined to act.[42]

Johnson again felt called upon to intervene. He thought his Instructions might imply that he could not accept the salary as proffered by the lower house. Therefore, he decided that he would maintain the office at his own expense until he had received permission from the Crown to accept a salary for one year only, as enacted by the Assembly. Johnson warned the Assembly that its action in the affair did not entitle it to the favor of His Majesty, and the Governor added that so "neither ought it to Induce me to pass the Quit Rent and Appropriation Bills now before me."[43]

Although plainly insistent, Johnson was not obdurate in the matter. He was careful not to say that he would not assent to these measures. He was aware of their importance to the Province, and, as later events illustrated, probably had no intention of vetoing them. The Assembly recognized the threat in the Governor's message, but knew that it held the upper hand. It had decided that if Johnson refused to approve the Quit Rent and Appropriation Bills, his

---

[41] JC, Vol. V, pp. 141-2 (August 17, 1731).

[42] JC, Vol. V, pp. 142-3 (August 17, 1731).

[43] JC, Vol. V, p. 143 (August 17, 1731). Percival, in July, 1732, recorded hearing the Queen remark about the need to curb the colonists who had become so insolent, particularly in New England, as to refuse to pay their governors, "unless he be subject to their pleasure." Another speaker commented that the opportunity for curbing the New England people had been lost "by not bringing their refusal of granting a salary for life on Governor [Jonathan] Belcher of Massachusetts the last year into Parliament." *Percival Diary*, Vol. I, p. 288.

actions would destroy hopes and plans for discharging the public debts, and "Consequently Conclude this Session much more to the General Dissatisfaction than was expected.[44]

Meanwhile, the Council had drafted and presented to the lower house a bill "for Settling a Salary on his Excellency during his Administration."[45] The bill was not approved by the Commons,[46] but strangely was turned down by the narrowest margin. The Governor, because of this, was left with some hope that such a measure might receive approval at the next meeting of the Assembly "notwithstanding the aversion all America shew to precedents of this nature which influences our people very much." As finally presented by the Assembly, Johnson's salary was established as £500 sterling for the year, plus £114 to cover the rent on his residence. In addition, the Assembly made him a present of £500 sterling, in consideration of the attention he had given the public affairs of South Carolina in England, particularly his efforts on behalf of the Province's being placed directly under the Crown. This unsought gift was an indication of the Assembly's esteem for the Governor.[47]

Despite these manifestations of good will, the Assembly had won an important victory in maintaining its rights and privileges. The lack of a civil list was never an impediment to Johnson's administering the government. His private fortune had made it unnecessary for him to rely upon the salary of his office, although with Johnson's skillful handling of the Assembly, he never had to worry about threats of his salary being stopped. Apparent were the possibilities of future hardship for some governor who was not in Johnson's favorable position and other royal officials who had to depend on the good will of an Assembly for their salaries. Some of these were to learn in time how readily legislators would refuse to appropriate funds for their offices.

In justice to Johnson, it should be noted that he did intend to press this issue of salaries in the future. Unfortunately, his plans became lost in the struggle over lands which soon beset the Province.

Despite the failure of the civil list proposal, Johnson was well pleased with the accomplishments of the Assembly in its first year. In contrast to the deadlock existing before his return to Carolina,

---

[44] JC, Vol. V, pp. 144-5 (August 18, 1731).

[45] JC, Vol. V, pp. 144 (August 17, 1731).

[46] JCHA, pp. 796-7 (August 18, 1731).

[47] Johnson to Board of Trade, November 14, 1731, PR, Vol. XV, p. 39.

much was accomplished. When bills passed and were presented to him, he readily signed them into law. Among necessary measures enacted were an appropriations bill, tax bill, those relating to quit rents, to drawing juries, and for improving the regulation of the Indian trade.[48]

As in the conduct of any government, minor problems, administrative and otherwise, frequently arose. For instance, at the time of the signing of the bills of the Assembly, the Council and Commons disagreed on the proper form for formal ratification. The lower house said that the laws should be countersigned by its Speaker, a practice which was begun during Nicholson's administration. The Council did not agree, and at the very end of the session a dispute was on the verge of erupting. Johnson prevented further disagreements by suspending consideration of the affair until the next meeting of the Assembly.[49]

Another difficulty confronting the Governor in the early days of his administration was the conflict with the persistent troublemaker Nicholas Trott, who insisted upon a renewal of his commission as chief justice.

Trott, who had received his commission[50] for the office from the Lords Proprietors, maintained through a curious argument that he had as much right to his office as anyone in the Province had to his lands. The Proprietors, he said, had appointed him to the office during *good behavior* and not during *pleasure*. Surrendering of the Province to the King, he argued, could not void a grant made while the Proprietors were indisputably in possession of the Province, because if the contrary were so, then all the people's grants to their lands would be null and void, which was not the case.

Trott cited the act by which the Proprietors surrendered the Province to the King and specifically the clause reserving to every person his estate and interest in the Province. The former chief justice maintained that this clause protected the rights of those lawfully claiming offices by grants from the Proprietors.

Originally, Trott had made his appeal to Middleton and his Council, who denied the request because Trott's actions had been one of the causes leading to the overthrow of the Proprietors. However, to

[48] JC, Vol. V, pp. 148-9 (August 20, 1731).

[49] JC, Vol. V, pp. 147-8 (August 20, 1731).

[50] A copy of the commission may be found in SPG, Fulham Palace MSS, South Carolina, no. 82.

Trott, the Council stated that its reason was lack of Instructions from the King. This failed to satisfy Trott, who claimed that an act of Parliament carried its own authority with it, and needed no particular direction for enforcement.[51] Upon hearing rumors that Robert Wright had been appointed chief justice in his place, Trott insisted that the action was invalid because of his prior claim.[52]

Among Governor Johnson's Instructions from the King was an article directing him upon his arrival to determine what offices were claimed under the common seal of the Proprietors, under what terms they were granted, and of what value they were. After this information had been sent to the Crown, and consideration given the claims, further Instructions were provided. The Governor was ordered to allow no one to hold office except by a Commission granted by the Crown or by the Governor under the provincial seal.[53] Upon receiving these Instructions, Johnson reported that Trott was the only person claiming office by virtue of a commission from the Proprietors. He added that Trott, out of office since Nicholson's term, had acknowledged that his authority had ended then, and that he had made no claim to the position until after the passage of the purchase law turning the Province over to the Crown.[54]

Nevertheless, Trott had memorialized the Governor and Council, but was flatly informed that Robert Wright was the new chief justice.[55]

Thus Johnson's government had to concern itself with other vexing problems, in addition to those involving prosperity or even survival of the Province.

---

[51] Trott to Bishop of London, January 10, 1729/30, SPG, Fulham Palace MSS, South Carolina, no. 85; Statutes, Vol. I, p. 70.

[52] Trott to Bishop of London, March 28, 1730, SPG, Fulham Palace MSS, South Carolina, no. 86.

[53] PRO, CO 5:192, pp. 89-90 (Library of Congress transcript).

[54] Johnson to Board of Trade, November 14, 1731, PR, Vol. XV, p. 38.

[55] Copy of Memorial and Council minutes, received by Board of Trade, January 26, 1731/2, PR, Vol. XV, pp. 45-49. The King's warrant to Johnson for Wright's appointment was dated November 30, 1730, PRO, CO 324:50, pp. 89-90 (Library of Congress transcript).

CHAPTER VII

Indians: Friend And Foe

DEFENSE, with its varied facets, was one of the urgent difficulties facing the new royal government in South Carolina. There was need for defense against European foes and Indian enemies alike.

Shortly after his arrival, Johnson informed his Council of the treaty made between the Indians and the Crown in Great Britain.[1] At the same time, word had reached the Governor and Council of some disturbances between the Cherokees and the Lower Creeks.[2] A debate arose on the best way to send home the Cherokees who had returned from Great Britain with Johnson, to prevent their falling prey to their enemies. Finally, it was decided to call the Indians before the Council for a conference. Upon their appearance, the Cherokee chiefs, after expressing gratitude for the many kindnesses extended, said they would rely on the Governor's wisdom for their safe return.

But the Indians balked at the Governor's suggestion that they stay in Charleston until he could send for headmen of their Nation to act as an escort for them and their presents. The Indians expressed fear that their people might be waylaid coming to Charleston, and asked that one white man be sent to their Nation to give notice of their impending arrival. The Governor agreed and offered to send two white men. The Indians replied that they were willing to go by themselves as long as a white runner went in advance to the Nation.

The Indians were then asked if they would travel light, carrying their arms but leaving their presents in the city until they could be accompanied home with greater security. After consulting among themselves for some time, the Indians announced they would carry the treaty and the presents, for they felt their people would not be pleased if they came without them. Governor Johnson then prom-

---

[1] JC, Vol. V, pp. 11-12 (December 18, 1730).

[2] JC, Vol. V, p. 11 (December 18, 1730).

ised to have white men go, with packhorses and other necessaries for transporting all their goods.[3]

Robert Bunning, who had been interpreter for the Cherokees while the Indians were in Great Britain, was engaged to escort them to their Nation. The public treasurer, Colonel Alexander Parris, was ordered to assist Bunning in providing the necessary supplies for the journey and to prepare an estimate of the cost.[4] This expense amounting to £457-10s-0d was later approved by the Council.[5]

Before the Cherokees left, word reached Charleston that the Creeks and some other Indians had taken a parcel of goods from a trader in the Cherokee settlements, and that the Cherokees had sent out parties to intercept the goods going to Creek towns.

The Governor and Council resolved that restitution must be made to the Cherokees for the goods taken by the Creeks, and that an interpretation of the peace terms of the treaty should be given to the Cherokees. For this reason, Bunning received additional instructions on how the treaty might be enforced adequately by the Indians.

Mapmaker George Hunter[6] also offered to go with the seven Cherokees to their Nation, and he was accepted and approved by the Council. On arrival, Hunter was authorized to swear in Eleazer Wiggan as an additional interpreter and enforcement officer for the treaty's peace instructions.[7]

On January 1, Bunning and Hunter were sworn.[8] They left Charleston before the 21st, for on that day Johnson, in his speech to the Assembly, noted that the Cherokees were on their way home with their presents.[9] Later, Johnson reported that he had received word that the Indians and their presents had arrived safely.[10]

Throughout Johnson's administrations as proprietary and royal Governor, good relations with Indians were of prime consideration because of the importance of the fur trade to the Carolina economy

---

[3] JC, Vol. V, pp. 12-13 (December 18, 1730).

[4] JC, Vol. V, p. 13 (December 18, 1730).

[5] JC, Vol. V, p. 14 (December 18, 1730).

[6] Hunter's map is reproduced in A. S. Salley, *George Hunter's Map of the Cherokee Country and the Path thereto in 1730,* in *Bulletins* of the Historical Commission of South Carolina, No. 4 (Columbia: The State Co., 1917).

[7] JC, Vol. V, p. 16 (January 1, 1730/31).

[8] JC, Vol. V, p. 17 (January 1, 1730/31).

[9] JC, Vol. V, p. 25 (January 21, 1730/31).

[10] JC, Vol. V, p. 79 (May 12, 1731).

and the necessity for keeping them as friends. The constant struggle among the three European nations for control over the Indians continued during Johnson's final term and made it more necessary than ever to cultivate their friendship as protection for the Province.

The usual method to win Indians over to their side was the presentation of gifts. In 1730 when one of the Indian "kings" visited Charleston, the public treasurer was ordered to give him a laced hat, a jacket, breeches, two shirts, a pair of shoes, and a pair of red stockings.[11] Such a policy did not evolve from British magnanimity but from bribery and threat. Once the Indians were bound to the English cause, the threat was held over their heads that any mischief on their part would cause the presents to cease.

This system was good in theory; but in practice it was difficult to make it work because the Indians were too canny. They soon learned that they could obtain gifts from the other two European powers, also. This tended to break the system down, and often it was the Indians more than the English who used it effectively, suggesting that they might change their allegiance for better terms.[12]

Another policy tried was that of entertaining the Indian chiefs who came to the capital, or, as in the case of the seven Cherokees, to London. Effort was also made to impress the Indians with English might and splendor. They were well entertained, and sometimes these affairs were climaxed by the signing of treaties.

In one case, when several Creek headmen came to Charleston, the Governor ordered the colonel of the troop of horse and captains of the two town companies with their men to march some distance from the city to meet the Indians. After the exchange of greetings on both sides, the headmen with their attendants—about sixty-three in all—were escorted into Charleston. Once there, they were taken immediately to the Council chamber, where they were received by the Governor and several members of the Council.[13]

---

[11] JC, Vol. V, p. 14 (December 18, 1730).

[12] The other European powers were affected in the same way; e.g., Barcia mentioned that Don Juan Pedro Matamoros (governor of Pensacola), "wanted to inquire in the provinces about the condition of those nations, but he was without means to do so, for no officer of the garrison could venture out without bringing the kind of gifts the Indians are known to like; otherwise he risked certain danger. If the Spaniards do not bring gifts when they go to their villages, the Indians accuse them of being basehearted, as they consider good only the man who freely gives them what they want." *Chronological History of the Continent of Florida,* p. 375.

[13] *South Carolina Gazette* (hereinafter cited as *SCG),* May 27-June 3, 1732.

After the ceremonies and formalities were over, the Indians, provided with suitable lodging and entertainment, were permitted to remain in town several days.

An interesting sidelight on an Indian visit was provided by the *South Carolina Gazette,* which reported that before the headmen left the meeting, they were introduced to some ladies who had been in an adjoining room observing the ceremonies. Stated the *Gazette:* "When to shew the awe that Beauty strikes, even upon Savages, one of these Kings advancing to take the Ladies by the Hand, according to the Indian Custom, made a Sort of Retreat and expressed himself so particularly as to say: That *he was sensible he was not made to touch such Things as those.*"[14] Such reporting was in no way designed to harm the paper's circulation among feminine readers.

Of much more significance was a notice printed the following week that Samuel Eveleigh had splendidly entertained the Indians at his house for dinner. The *Gazette* reported that afterwards he took them aboard the *Fox* man-of-war in the harbor for a tour greatly pleasing to the headmen. Later, voices were raised questioning Eveleigh's motives, hinting that he was treating the Indians kindly because of his own interests. The *Gazette* editor wrote, however, that the motive of the former Indian commissioner and councilman was not for private gain but for good understanding between the Indians and Carolina, to promote trade. Eveleigh was following the trend of the day and the editor added significantly, "It being the known Artifice of the French and Spaniards, who have Dealings with the same Persons, to trick us out of our Trade, by Excelling in smooth faced Stratagems of this Kind."[15]

About two months later, another party of Indians, the Chickasaws, wanted to visit the Governor at Charleston. But between the time of the Creek departure and receipt of the Chickasaws' request, the town had been visited by "great Sickness and Mortality." One report described the malady, saying, "The Distemper was a violent Fever, not without Symptoms of Malignancy, & w[hi]ch killed the 2d or 3d or at farthest the 4th Day . . . . It raged in such manner, & proved so mortal, that every House almost looked like a Hospital, & the whole Town as one Single House of Mourning. The Buryings

[14] *SCG,* May 27-June 3, 1732.
[15] *SCG,* June 3-10, 1732.

were from 5 to 10, and once 11 of a Day."[16] Few escaped this "vilent malignant fever," Governor Johnson decried. He reported that one hundred thirty white people and a great many slaves died, a sizeable loss to the town of about 3,000 people.

Those who could, left town for their plantations. Governor Johnson felt it necessary to remain, and his devotion to duty during the epidemic ended in personal tragedy, for he suffered the loss of "the best of wives," a son, and three servants. He observed also that almost no one who came into town from the country escaped the fever, and nearly everyone who contracted it, died.[17]

Because of the fever, the Chickasaws were forbidden to visit the town; instead the Governor went out to meet them. The Indians made their speech, paid their compliments to him and, in turn, were given presents, starting their homeward journey the same day.[18] The Governor of the Province did not want the Indians to see the sad situation in Charleston, nor did he wish to risk the danger of their contracting the illness which would do nothing toward improving Indian relations.[19] But he invited them to come again.

Some of the Chickasaw and other Indian headmen came to Charleston the following year to pay their compliments to the Governor. They had traveled nearly 900 miles to make the visit, it was reported. While there, they were taken aboard the ship *Squirrel,* which saluted them with its mighty guns, a display delighting the Indians.[20]

---

[16] A. Garden to Bishop of London, November 8, 1732, SPG, Fulham Palace MSS, South Carolina, no. 31.

[17] Johnson to A. Popple, September 28, 1732, PR, Vol. XV, p. 235; Johnson to Board of Trade, September 28, 1732, PR, Vol. XV, p. 229. Mrs. Johnson's obituary is in *SCG,* July 1-8, 1732, and her death is reported in *Gentleman's Magazine,* Vol. II (September 1732), p. 979.

[18] *SCG,* August 5-12, 1732.

[19] Later, in the year 1738, when Charleston was suffering from a dreadful smallpox attack, that disease was transmitted to the Cherokee Indians, who were reported to have lost almost half their nation. The Indians claimed they had been poisoned and some of their towns began trafficking with the French, although Oglethorpe endeavored to heal the breach. Other tribes, such as the Catawbas, suffered similar disasters at various times. James Adair, *The History of the American Indians* (London: Edward and Charles Dilly, 1775), pp. 232-3; Newton D. Mereness (ed.), *Travels in the American Colonies* (New York: The Macmillan Co., 1916), p. 239; "A Treaty Between Virginia and the Catawbas and Cherokees, 1756," in *Virginia Magazine of History and Biography,* Vol. XIII, No. 3 (January, 1906), pp. 227-8n. *See also,* Douglas Summers Brown, *The Catawba Indians: The People of the River* (Columbia: University of South Carolina Press, 1966) 16 ff.

[20] *SCG,* July 7-14, 1733.

On another occasion, some headmen of the Upper Cherokees visited Charleston to renew their treaties. Among these were three of the seven Indians who had gone to England with Sir Alexander Cuming and returned with Johnson.[21]

A drawback to this policy of Indian visits was the embarrassment resulting from their frequent unruliness when they came in large numbers, uninvited. Charleston had no regular police force, so it was sometimes necessary to call out the militia to insure order and protect the town. This was extremely inconvenient for the citizens, especially at planting time, or when they were trying to escape the rigors of the season. In 1733 upon the arrival of a contingent of Cherokees, the Governor was equal to the situation; he issued a Proclamation prohibiting trade with the Cherokees anywhere except in their own Nation.[22] Johnson's action had further been made necessary by the outbreak of smallpox in Charleston, and it was his wish to keep the Indians away from the town and the disease,[23] one that proved deadly to the Indians.[24]

Once when word came from the Pallachuccola garrison that the Dog King and a large contingent of his followers wanted to come down, the Governor replied that he did not expect anyone from the Indian Nations unless he sent for them. Nevertheless, he said that he held the Dog King in such high esteem that he would permit him and three or four of his headmen to make the trip. To the garrison commander the Governor wrote that if the Dog King showed any resentment upon receiving this message that he be permitted to bring the whole group. He asked the Commander to say that the Governor had no wish to offend the King, and if he would accept the offer to come with a small party of Indians, rum would be sent up to satisfy those left behind. In either case, the Governor ordered Captain James McPherson's scouts to conduct the Indians down to the settlement.[25]

Not all of the relations with Indians struck a friendly tone but, fortunately sometimes disagreements were speedily resolved, as that

---

[21] *SCG,* May 5-12, 1733.

[22] *SCG,* January 27-February 3, 1732/3.

[23] JC, Vol. V., pp. 358-9 (January 26, 1732/3).

[24] St. Julien Ravenel Childs, "Notes on the History of Public Health in South Carolina, 1670-1800," in *Proceedings* of the South Carolina Historical Association, 1932, pp. 15-16.

[25] JC, Vol. V, pp. 116-7 (July 20, 1731).

of the runaway Indian slave who had been shot by the Waccamaw Indians. Hearing of this affair, the Commons House observed that it would be of the "utmost ill consequence" unless retaliatory measures were taken.[26] Because this event had occurred while some of the Waccamaw Indians were in Charleston, Governor Johnson met with three of the Waccamaw headmen and demanded reparation. The Indians submitted and promised to bring 150 heavy deerskins to the Governor within three months.[27]

While such situations as these were irritating and disagreeable, they were not nearly as alarming as reports of Indian hostilities. It soon became evident that in view of the tri-power struggle for Indian control, for South Carolina to reply upon a gifts' program for retaining their friendship would be placing the balance of power in the aboriginals' hands. Clearly something else was needed and something had to be done.

Governor Johnson's usual policy on hearing of Indian uprisings was to make the best preparations he could, and then wait. But in one instance, when word was received from Fort Moore of expected hostilities from the Chickasaws, he recommended sending a party of scouts to reinforce the fort and learn the intentions of the Indians.[28]

He had no wish to excite the Province which had not forgotten the recent Creek trouble, the populace becoming upset whenever a recurrence was imminent. Because of this, the Governor kept still when he heard about hostilities, only reporting such information to the Commons House. After he had once made a report on Creek affairs, the Commons House voted to send a commissioner immediately to inspect the nation and regulate matters between the Indians and the Province.[29]

Later, the commander of the Savannah garrison sent word that two Carolina traders had been found murdered on the path leading to the upper Creek country, and it was thought that the Creeks were responsible. The man who found the bodies appeared before Council, and under oath recounted the tragedy.

To prevent further trouble, Governor Johnson moved quickly into action. He ordered the following:

---

[26] JCHA, p. 648 (March 19, 1730/31).
[27] JC, Vol. V, p. 61 (March 19, 1730/31).
[28] JC, Vol. V, p. 82 (May 14, 1731).
[29] JC, Vol. V, pp. 110-11 (July 10, 14, 1731).

The commanding officer of each militia company and regiment muster and arm his men immediately;

Those who would volunteer to march against the Indians to protect the frontier be taken out for that purpose;

A lieutenant and twenty men be added to the Rangers under Captain James McPherson's command; the Rangers be divided into parties of twenty to patrol the frontier alternately and visit the out settlements of Pon Pon to encourage the people to stay where they were; also find two particular Indians, a Yamassee and a Creek, long in the Province, and encourage them to stay, as they might prove useful;

At all times, latest news of proceedings be sent to the Governor.

To help guard the frontier farther northward, a commission was issued to Charles Russell to enlist twenty men and a sergeant. Russell, too, was instructed to encourage the people in that area to be on their guard but to remain in their settlements. Since Captain Rowland Evans of the Pallachuccola garrison was ill, a commission was sent to the fort's lieutenant, Phillman Parmiter, to command the fort. Colonel Charlesworth Glover, who was departing on a mission designed to hold the Yuchi Indians to the Carolina interest, was ordered first to take an inventory of all arms, ammunition, and other war weapons at the fort. Glover was ordered to furnish a duplicate list to Commander Parmiter and to inform him that he would be held accountable to the public for every article in the inventory. Colonel Glover was also empowered to present gifts to the Yuchi in an amount not to exceed £200 Carolina currency.[30]

Another act of hostility was reported soon afterwards. A Mr. Cattell informed the governor that some Creek Indians who had resided in the Province for a number of years had been at his cowpen. They had driven away his overseer and slaves, robbed his house, destroyed his corn, and broken down his fences. In retaliation, the Governor ordered Captain McPherson and Captain Russell to take detachments of their men and try to capture or kill the Indians, with captives under sufficient guard to be sent down to the Governor.[31] Although these various reports seemed ominous at the time, they were independent actions, rather than a part of any organized Creek plot against South Carolina.

---

[30] JC, Vol. V, pp. 203-5 (August 16, 1732).
[31] JC, Vol. V, p. 205 (August 30, 1732).

Subsequently, it became known that the Carolina traders among the Creeks were safe and being treated civilly, and the Indians were reported to be "in perfect Amity with this Government." The Creeks denied any knowledge of the murder of the two traders, the event which had stirred the Province to action. Upon confirmation of this news, it was decided to discharge the extra men who had been enlisted as frontier rangers.[32]

The slaying was attributed instead to some Spanish Indians, whose action was instigated at St. Augustine. Johnson believed the Spaniards wanted to so terrify the Carolina traders that they would leave the Creek nation, and not be in a position to influence the Creeks in opposing a Spanish plan of building a fort to resettle the Province of Apalache there. The Spaniards had been driven out of the vicinity during Sir Nathaniel Johnson's administration, but in the 1730's, were reported in the process of building a fort. Robert Johnson strongly asserted that the area belonged to the British Crown by right of conquest, but he wondered "how far the not having kept possession will make it not so." Johnson reported to the Board of Trade that he was doing all in his power, by his agents among the Creeks, to convince the Indians that they should not allow the Spaniards to remain there. At the same time, he realized that the Spaniards had agents among the Creeks, which made the outcome doubtful.[33] The Creeks, located near settlements of all three European powers, were unpredictable; they could not be relied upon as a firm ally, either militarily or as a source of trade.

A more effective means of Indian control that had been formulated during Johnson's administration as proprietary governor was again applied. This was the policy of stopping all trade with an unruly Indian tribe to bring it in line until behavior improved. Cited was an example of the past, the misbehavior on the part of the Cusseta and Coweta tribes that had brought a suspension of trade with them. When they were again peaceable, the ban was lifted and once more traders were permitted to visit their towns.[34] This policy proved effective provided Indians were not supplied by

[32] Johnson to Board of Trade, September 28, 1732, PR, Vol. XV, p. 229; JC, Vol. V, p. 206 (September 6, 1732).

[33] Johnson to Board of Trade, September 28, 1732, PR, Vol. XV, pp. 229-30.

[34] JC, Vol. V. p. 263.

traders from other English colonies, or if the Spanish and French were not in a position to furnish them with equivalent items.

As in the proprietary period, Carolina was once again having difficulty with the Virginia traders, this trouble arising through the Cherokee Indians. Some of the "young ungovernable fellows," a minority among the Cherokees, had been extremely insolent toward Carolina. They had threatened the lives of several of the traders if they did not sell them goods for a lower price, although prices had been decided by agreement between the Indians and the Province. The Cherokees went so far as to seize a store of goods valued at from £400 to £500 Carolina money. This caused all of the Carolina traders to leave the Nation, coming down to Charleston, and none thought it safe to return. Governor Johnson, on receiving this information, called the General Assembly into session.[35]

The insolence was brought to the members' attention and a memorial was sent to the King on the matter, stating that the event had occurred despite the kindnesses shown the Cherokee's party in Great Britain, and "besides a Considerable Expence which . . . [the] Subjects of this Province have been at in making them presents."

The Commons House agreed that the traders would not be permitted to carry goods to the Cherokees until the Indians had made restitution for the goods they had taken, and had submitted themselves to the South Carolina government. The Governor then issued a proclamation to that effect.[36] Although trade with South Carolina ceased, it was soon noticed that Virginia traders were on their way to the Cherokee Nation, carrying a large quantity of goods, including ammunition. Johnson decided to stop the Virginia trade until the Cherokees had submitted, as a "prudent Act of self preservation, and [it is] commendable in us not to Suffer people to be Supplied with Arms and Ammunition that had given us such cause to believe they designed mischief to the Province." Johnson believed that the Virginians were solely responsible for the Indians' insolence toward Carolina. They could undersell the Carolina traders, and on an open market, the Carolinians would have to trade at a loss or abandon it altogether. But despite this, Johnson said the Province would be willing to give up the trade to Virginia, if thereby South Carolina

[35] Johnson to Board of Trade, November 9, 1734, PR, Vol. XVII, pp. 189-90; *SCG,* May 4-11, 1734.

[36] *SCG,* June 1-8, 1734.

could be freed from Indian attack, but he well knew that the best control was through trade.

By stopping the Virginia trade temporarily, Johnson achieved results. A contingent of sixty or seventy Cherokees made their way to Charleston to sue for peace. The Governor during their visit was in ill health, so he sent Colonel Parris, the public treasurer, to meet them. Parris joined up with the Indians about a mile from Charleston, and finding that they wanted to make peace, allowed them to come into town. Once there, the Indians acknowledged their error, promised restitution, and made their submission to the government. At this, the Governor agreed to reopen trade between the Province of South Carolina and the Cherokee Indians.[37] The effectiveness of trade control in regulating the Indians was demonstrated, and in such instances where external factors could be managed, this policy served its purpose well. Yet, the real success of Johnson's Indian policy was the fact that it combined several stratagems.

The gift-giving system as an isolated measure, although approved by the Board of Trade and other governmental agencies, could not serve effectively as a long-range program. Presents could win over the Indians temporarily, but they could not purchase their full allegiance. Besides, once having tasted British beneficence, they called for more and more presents at frequent intervals. As for past favors, the Indians found it very convenient to acquire short memories.

In dealing with the Creeks, Governor Johnson found that more was involved than the Indians. The French had built a fortification, known to the English as the Alabama Fort (Fort Toulouse), in the middle of the Upper Creek Country, that was kept garrisoned and mounted with fourteen pieces of cannon. The French had been impeded, at least for the time being, from building another fort nearer the South Carolina border. The Creeks, "a Nation, very bold, active and daring, consisting of about thirteen hundred fighting men," were temporarily in alliance with South Carolina and trading with the Province. However, the French were trying constantly to win them over, and, in fact, had been successful with some of the Indian towns.

---

[37] Johnson to Board of Trade, November 9, 1734, PR, Vol. VXII, pp. 191-2; *SGC,* October 26-November 2, 1734.

Reasons for the French success were varied, including the strategic location of their fort in the midst of the Indian Nation. Another was the fact that the French could provide more liberal gifts to the Indians than could the Carolinians. To counteract these plus factors, the General Assembly of South Carolina recommended giving more presents to the Creeks to withdraw their interest from the French, resulting in a "gifts race"[38] between the two. The Carolinians were also disturbed because they thought the French were attempting to induce the Cherokees to join a French-Cherokee alliance; and to ward off such a danger, they decided the Province must build its own forts among the Indians.[39]

The French, on the other hand, realized that they could not hold the Indians to their interest without purchasing deerskins, for which there was no market in France. Therefore, they found ways of encouraging vessels from New York and other ports to trade the skins for British woolens, which helped greatly to alienate the Indians from the English interest.[40] From South Carolina's viewpoint, it was believed that if this trade could be halted, and the Creeks made dependent chiefly upon the English, the Choctaws, whose lands adjoined the Creeks, would soon see the advantages the Creeks enjoyed in the Carolina trade and might want to follow. In this way, French influence over the Choctaws would be measurably weakened, and the Indians might become attached gradually to the English interest.

The necessity for some English forts among the Creeks and the Cherokees grew stronger, although the establishment of Georgia was expected to offer some protection to South Carolina.[41]

---

[38] Memorial and Representation of Governor, Council, and Assembly of S. C., to the King, April 9, 1734, PR, Vol. XVI, pp. 391-4. On French presents, Bienville's Report, May 15, 1733, in *Miss. Prov. Archives,* Vol. I, pp. 194-5.

[39] Memorial and Representation of Governor, Council, and Assembly of S. C., to the King, April 9, 1734, PR, Vol. XVI, pp. 395-6. Meanwhile the French, busy fighting the Natchez and Chickasaw, expressed deep concern over English efforts among the Choctaws, particularly about the visit of Red Shoe to Carolina. Bienville to Maurepas, August 26, 1734, September 30, 1734, October 4, 1734, April 14, 1735, in *Miss. Prov. Archives,* Vol. I, pp. 233-6, 242-3, 254-6, Vol. III, pp. 672-3; Corry, *Indian Affairs in Georgia,* pp. 18-19, 36.

[40] PR, Vol. XVI, pp. 391-4. There were also French objections to this trade. Bienville to Maurepas, July 26, 1733, in *Miss. Prov. Archives,* Vol. I, pp. 209-10.

[41] PR, Vol. XVI, pp. 391-4. Historical Manuscripts Commission, *Manuscripts of the Earl of Egmont: Diary of Viscount Percival, afterwards First*

It had become apparent that all Indian policies—even in combination—had their shortcomings. Johnson, however, had another stratagem to use, that of encouraging the Indians to war among themselves. This was put to good use at a time when some Tuscaroras from North Carolina converged on the Catawba Indians of South Carolina seeking revenge against their enemies. In carrying out their mission, they committed some acts of aggression against white settlers which brought the matter to the Governor's attention. He warned them in strongest language to avoid any future damage to the people and told them they would be required to make restitution for past mischief.[42]

When Governor George Burrington of North Carolina heard about the incident, he became concerned. He hastily communicated the news to England that the South Carolina Indians were expected to attack the Tuscarora, and that the Five Nations of the Iroquois League had promised to send 1,000 men to aid the latter.[43] The message, in turn, alarmed the Board of Trade. The agency wrote the Governor of South Carolina expressing surprise that it had heard nothing from Johnson about the whole affair. The Board remarked that it did not doubt "but [that] you will use all possible pr[e]caution to pr[e]vent so great an Evil." Also written at the same time were the governors of North Carolina and New York "to use their Endeav[o]rs to put an End to these misunderstandings."[44]

Johnson's reply was revealing. It illustrated his keen understanding of the Indian problem, and set forth one of the main issues in his Indian policy. In his letter, Johnson expressed wonderment that Governor Burrington should be so uneasy at the thought of the Catawbas attacking the Indians of North Carolina, especially since Burrington himself had felt that the Tuscaroras needed chastisement. He added that nothing further had happened in the affair, and Johnson assured the Board that if it had, it would have been

---

Earl of Egmont (hereinafter cited as *Percival Diary)* (3 vols., London: His Majesty's Stationery Office, 1920-1923), Vol. II, p. 120. The British Government was also reported to be "in a great fright at the danger our Colonies are in from the French settlement at Mississippi." *Percival Diary,* Vol. II, p. 159.

[42] JC, Vol. V, pp. 68-69, 71 (April 8, 10, 1731).

[43] Extract of letter from Governor Burrington to Board of Trade, September 4, 1731, in William L. Saunders (ed.), *The Colonial Records of North Carolina* (10 vols., Raleigh: P. M. Hale, 1886-1890), Vol. III, p. 202.

[44] Board of Trade to Johnson, June 21, 1732, PR, Vol. XV, pp. 127-8.

notified. Johnson further explained that it was well known that the Catawbas of South Carolina had for a long time been at war with the Tuscaroras, but the Catawbas had made no expedition against their enemy. He said it was also true that the Five Nations were in collusion with the Tuscaroras, and that some of them had been with the party of Tuscaroras who carried slaves and horses away from South Carolina.

Johnson then described the Indian mode of operation, saying: "They seldom attack one another in such large bodys[.] Partys of 30 or 40 Men go out and if they can steal anything and kill 2 or 3 old Women or Men they soon return contented[.] 'Tis only such a War we hear of yet."

After Johnson's ultimatum to them, the Tuscaroras had done no damage in South Carolina. But Johnson declared that if they "had again insulted and robbed our Planters I believe we should have been obliged to have headed their Enemys the Catawbas against them."

Johnson distinguished carefully between Indian attacks upon other Indians and those directed against the white settlers, and he seemed startled that neither Governor Burrington nor the Board of Trade comprehended the distinction. The South Carolina Governor revealed his policy in concise terms when he wrote: "It is always the maxim of our Governm[en]t upon the Continent to promote war between Indians of different Nations with whom we Trade and are at peace with ourselves [,] for in that consists our safety, being at War with one another prevents their uniting against us."[45] The building of forts, his Indian policy, and the township plan, were operating together as Governor Johnson's overall defense of the Province.

---

[45] Johnson to Board of Trade, December 15, 1732, PR, Vol. XVI, pp. 3-4.

CHAPTER VIII

Enemies Within And Without

BEFORE leaving England to assume the royal governorship, Robert Johnson had memorialized the King concerning the defense of South Carolina, "the said Province being a Southern Frontier to the Continent." Johnson noted that four forts had been erected about 100 miles apart: one at Port Royal; another, Fort Moore, situated to the northeast, purposely "to awe the Northern Indians"; Pallachuccola fort, "to awe the Southern Indians"; and Johnson's Fort, which commanded Charleston harbor.

The Province had been put to the expense of hiring forces to man the fortifications, and since cost of employment of South Carolinians was three times that of soldiers sent from England, they had been weakly garrisoned. When Nicholson came over as governor, an Independent Company had accompanied him to America.[1] The soldiers were quartered in a fort on the Altamaha River which had deteriorated because the Province had been unable financially to maintain it. There was some indecision, too, in Carolina over whether the first line of defense would be made at the Savannah River or on the Altamaha, causing further worsening of the condition of the fort while the discussions went on.

The men at the Altamaha became thoroughly discontented with the deplorable state of their living conditions and because of their isolation. They were bothered also by the Spanish who objected to the fort's location, and complained to London where it was agreed that negotiations would be conducted on the local level about its future. The conference took place, coming to naught; and shortly afterward, in January 1725/6, the Altamaha fort was burned. When it was learned that twelve of the Englishmen stationed there had deserted to St. Augustine, the Carolinians charged the Spanish with the responsibility of its destruction. In the investigation that followed, Captain Edward Massey was named to conduct the inquiry. He found that the fort had not been burned by design, but on the other hand, the garrison stationed there had not attempted to put

[1] Memorial from Johnson to the King [n.d.], PR, Vol. XIV, pp. 306-7.

67568

it out, hoping to be quartered elsewhere if the fort were out of commission. The ending was a happy one for the soldiers; the Independent Company was moved to Port Royal. Departure of the garrison left the southern frontier unprotected, however, lowering still further South Carolina's defense against the enemy.[2]

Johnson's memorial to the King reported that only the Port Royal fort was manned, because the Province in its deplorable financial state could provide no funds for the other three. He also called attention to a discrepancy: New York had four Independent Companies, whereas far more soldiers were needed in the frontier Province of Carolina. Therefore, he begged the Crown to send an additional Independent Company of 100 men.[3]

Before he had sailed for America to become the South Carolina governor, Johnson had asked the Crown to furnish stores of war for the Province; and his first message to the Assembly expressed high hopes that the King would comply with his request.[4] A month later, in a message to the lower house, Johnson said a letter lately received from England led him to believe that the stores of war would soon be sent.[5] He also reminded the Assembly of the ruinous condition of Johnson's Fort [Fort Johnson], and of the Charleston fortifications, resulting from the hurricane, and strongly recommended immediate repairs.[6] Early in May, the Governor announced receipt of a copy of the King's order authorizing dispatch of the needed stores. The Commons expressed satisfaction at the King's consenting "to apply So large a Summ of money for the Defense of this his Province." Whereupon Johnson wrote his appreciation of the supplies and requested means be made available for repairing the fortifications which were in a "most ruinous condition."[7] He advised that the forts had been almost completely wrecked by storms and hurricanes, and were vital to defense.

---

[2] McCrady, *Royal Government,* pp. 74-77; Herbert E. Bolton and Mary Ross, *The Debatable Land* (Berkeley: University of California Press, 1925), pp. 69-71.

[3] Johnson to King, PR, Vol. XIV, p. 307.

[4] JC, Vol. V, p. 25 (January 21, 1730/31).

[5] JC, Vol. V, p. 48 (February 25, 1730/31).

[6] JC, Vol. V, p. 25 (January 21, 1730/31). After the hurricane the province was struck by a calamitous yellow fever epidemic. Robert Mills, *Statistics of South Carolina* (Charleston: Hurlbut and Lloyd, 1826), p. 144; City of Charleston, *Year Book, 1880,* pp. 253-4, 312.

[7] JC, Vol. V, pp. 72-73 (May 5-6, 1731); JCHA, pp. 669-670 (May 6, 1731).

Because the Crown had accepted Johnson's proposal to send stores of war to Carolina,[8] the Governor felt that this was not enough for full preparedness and that the Province should also be concerned about its defense. He had little success with the Assembly in his plea, and for more than a year after he had made his original request, he was still waiting orders to begin the repair work. Johnson was desirous that the King's purpose in furnishing the ordnance would not be defeated by local neglect.[9]

The decision was made to leave the Independent Company stationed at Port Royal, but to send a detachment to the Altamaha, where a new fort was to be constructed. In his Instructions, Johnson was given the alternative of either rebuilding the old fort or selecting a new site if he found some other place that was healthier or more convenient. His Instructions were specific in saying that the site selected should "secure the Embouchee and Navigation of the River Alatamahama," and the fort should be "always kept in sufficient repair capable to answer the aforementioned purpose."[10]

A Memorial from Captain Edward Massey, commander of the Independent Company at Port Royal, was received by Johnson soon after his arrival. Massey complained of the lack of necessary quarters and fuel which had resulted in much sickness and the loss of a number of men. The captain asked that the situation be rectified.[11]

The Governor forwarded Massey's memorial to the Commons House, and reminded the legislative body that it was "the Undoubted right of his Majesties Troops in all places to be provided with Quarters [,] Fireing and candles." He urged compliance with the King's order to send a detachment of the Independent Company to hold possession of the Altamaha River, an urgent necessity as the Spaniards laid claim to that area.[12]

Despite the urgency of his recommendation, several months later the same request had to be made again. He insisted that the Assembly make provision for the erection of a fort on the river.[13] Fortunately, this time the Assembly agreed and said that as soon as possible the fort would be constructed at a location considered

[8] Johnson to Board of Trade, November 14, 1731, PR, Vol. XV, p. 39.
[9] JC, Vol. V, p. 163 (February 3, 1731/2).
[10] PRO, CO 5: 192, p. 111 (Library of Congress transcript).
[11] JC, Vol. V, p. 46 (February 24, 1730/31).
[12] JC, Vol. V, p. 47 (February 25, 1730/31).
[13] JC, Vol. V, p. 127 (July 29, 1731).

suitable by the Governor.[14] Finally incorporated into the Appropriations Act was a provision for £5,600 (equivalent to £800 sterling) for the erection of the fort on the Altamaha and a new fort and barracks on a relocated site at Port Royal.[15]

In explaining this action to the Board of Trade, Johnson said he planned to visit the fort sites himself and give directions for the construction. The Assembly had called the £800 appropriation a loan to the King and said it hoped to be reimbursed in that amount because the action had been taken solely in compliance with his command. It was the opinion of the Assembly that soldiers with better accommodations would perform more effectively at Port Royal.[16]

After a few more months, Johnson reported that the barracks at Port Royal were ready, but that he had deferred building the forts. He thought they would be more durable if they were built with oyster shells and lime [tabby] instead of timber, and as this would incur more expense, he wished to consult the Assembly.[17]

The lower house adopted half of his recommendation, agreeing to using oyster shells and lime for the fort at Port Royal, but specified that the Altamaha fort must be constructed of timber to keep it from being excessively expensive.[18]

By December of 1732, the Governor was able to report that the Port Royal fort was well under way and that preparations had begun for the Altamaha fortification. At the same time, he was forced to ask for more money for construction.[19]

About three months later, he admitted that work on the Altamaha was at a standstill. His report to the Duke of Newcastle said that part of the timber had been sawed and squared for the Altamaha fort, but funds were insufficient to complete it, as all the money appropriated had been spent on the Port Royal fortification. Furthermore, he said the Assembly had refused to provide any more money for the Altamaha project because the founding of the Georgia colony had placed it outside the jurisdiction of the South Carolina

---

[14] JC, Vol. V, p. 131 (August 10, 1731).

[15] *Statutes,* Vol. III, p. 336.

[16] Johnson to Board of Trade, November 14, 1731, PR, Vol. XV, p. 38.

[17] JC, Vol. V, p. 170 (February 16, 1731/2).

[18] JC, Vol. V, p. 171 (February 17, 1731/2).

[19] *SCG,* December 9-16, 1732.

government.[20] Late in 1732, Johnson called attention to other needed defenses, particularly to the dismal condition of the Charleston fortifications.[21] The need for repairs became more urgent with the beginning of the Family Compact between France and Spain, and the outbreak of the War of Polish Succession. Despite the potential danger, in the spring of 1734 the Charleston fortifications were still described as in ruinous condition and the harbor open to sea attack. It was said that many thousands of pounds would be required to restore them and to build new accommodations for the ordnance sent over by His Majesty. The General Assembly complained that it had already agreed to tax the inhabitants more than £40,000 Carolina currency per annum, an amount equal to considerably more than one-third of all the currency in the Province. Also, by the King's order to the Governor, the duties placed on imported European goods had been discontinued, considerably lessening the colonial government's revenue. There was apprehension that any additional increase in taxes would cause many of the inhabitants to abandon the Province, and act as a hindrance to newcomers settling there.[22]

Governor Johnson was able to persuade the Assembly to provide £3,000 Carolina currency for mounting the ordnance, which he termed "a great point gained,"[23] and to consider other defense measures. Although Johnson had taken an extraordinary interest in defense, some accused him of neglecting to store the military supplies sent by the King, making derogatory remarks about him to the Board of Ordnance.

By the time Johnson heard of this attempt to discredit him, the Assembly had already provided the funds he had asked for mounting the ordnance, so the question was no longer valid. He did feel it necessary, though, to deny his enemies' charges and to inform the British authorities that the war materials in question had received the same care as was taken in His Majesty's Yards in England.[24] Johnson's statement was confirmed by Thomas Lloyd, gunner and

---

[20] Johnson to Duke of Newcastle, March 30, 1732/3, PR, Vol. XVI, p. 73.

[21] *SCG*, December 9-16, 1732.

[22] Governor, council, and Assembly of S. C., to the King, April 9, 1734, PR, Vol. XVI, pp. 397-8.

[23] Johnson to Duke of Newcastle, May 2, 1734, PR, Vol. XVI, p. 326.

[24] Johnson to Popple, May 24, 1734, PR, Vol. XVI, p. 336.

armorer of Charleston, who swore an affidavit that the supplies had been guarded in pursuance to the Governor's orders.[25]

It seems strange that Johnson should have been called upon to answer such trumped up charges. The supplies would not have been forthcoming had it not been for his continual pleading and insistence. Johnson's interest in the whole problem of defense went far beyond the implementing of existing plans and methods, leading him to pursue new avenues of protection. He had been particularly careful to secure the frontiers.

Soon after he began his administration, the Governor received a plea from the inhabitants of St. Helena Parish, requesting that more adequate measures be taken for their protection. They said:

> And as we have hitherto behaved with Strict Adherence and Submission to Government in the worst of times [,] So we are Still Resolved to Emulate the best of people in Loyalty and Obedience, hoping that the Warm Influence of your Excellencys Just and Wise Administration will dispell these Clouds & Discontents which have So long Unhappily attended us.

Governor Johnson replied that they could count on his "best Endeavors to Secure their Frontiers and those of the Province in General as farr as Lies in my power."[26]

Johnson had already formulated his plans for defending the southern area and for providing for the garrison at Port Royal, St. Helena's Parish. The Assembly had purchased 100 acres of land, and the fort and barracks were subsequently built. Other measures in that vicinity also improved defenses; and Johnson presented the British government a plan for establishing the town of Beaufort, to serve both for trade and defense. The Governor thought that the location was "convenient and of great importance," and felt that if the port and harbor were fortified and secured, it would be one of the best ports in America for use by the Royal Navy.

Because of this plan, Governor Johnson refused to grant any lots in the area, although many had requested permission to settle there; and a few lots had been granted prior to his administration. He said that he would issue no grants until he was informed which sections would be convenient for His Majesty's use for stores and docks, and for better fitting out of ships.[27]

---

[25] May 21, 1734, PR, Vol. XVI, pp. 338-9.

[26] JC, Vol. V, pp. 35-36 (February 12, 1730/31).

[27] Johnson to Newcastle, March 30, 1732/3, PR, Vol. XVI, p. 74.

Johnson not only took necessary precautions in the Province but also continually urged the British authorities to become awakened to the realities of the American scene. The English colonies on the American continent, especially the Province of South Carolina and the new colony of Georgia, he said needed encouragement, "because I am informed that the French increase very fast at New Orleans, and are Extending their Limits by building Forts, So that His Majesty's British Empire in America is more than one half Surrounded by the French from the Mouth of the Missisipi River to the Mouth of that of St. Lawrence."[28]

To meet possible attacks from French and Spanish, South Carolina and Georgia together were able to raise a militia numbering only 3,500 men.[29]

Another South Carolina danger was the continual importation of Negro slaves that raised the black population to an alarming level. On occasions, the slaves made attempts at revolt. In 1720—shortly after the change of government—a plot was discovered in which they intended to destroy all of the white people in the country, then to storm the town.[30]

Almost immediately after his return to South Carolina in December 1730, Johnson felt compelled to issue a proclamation to prevent any disturbances on the part of the Negroes during the holiday season.[31] Complaints were made against the misconduct of the slaves, enough to suggest that, except during and immediately after real or fancied insurrections, the slaves were often laxly controlled, especially around Charleston. More forcible measures were in effect at all times in the more southern reaches of the Province, because of the danger of slaves escaping to Spanish territory.

Of more danger to the Province, it should be emphasized, was the disproportion of settlers to slaves. In April 1734, the Assembly estimated that the number of Negroes in the Province was about 22,000, approximately three times the number of white inhabitants. A constant fear existed that the French would instigate insurrection

---

[28] Johnson to Board of Trade, November 9, 1734, PR, Vol. XVII, pp. 179-80.

[29] Memorial and Representation from Governor, Council, and Assembly of S. C., to the King, April 9, 1734, PR, Vol. XVI, pp. 388-92, 397.

[30] Letter to Joseph Boone, June 24, 1720, PR, Vol. VIII, p. 24.

[31] JC, Vol. V, p. 14 (December 18, 1730).

by promising the slaves their freedom,[32] a ruse also used by the Spaniards.

By the end of 1734, agents of South Carolina reported there were 24,000 Negroes in the Colony, who they said would probably join the Province's enemies in destroying the white settlers, if the slaves were assured they would be set free. In addition, the agents said they felt that the booty in slaves alone would be tempting to a foreign enemy, for if valued at only £20 sterling each, the total would approach £500,000.[33]

A satisfactory solution of the problem was not achieved, and about four years after Johnson's administration had ended, the Province suffered a major disaster in the Spanish-instigated Stono Revolt. Because of the pressure that traders exercised on the home government, it was impossible to stop the importation of Negroes, and the alternative was to induce more white people to settle in the Province for protection against internal and external enemies.

---

[32] Memorial and Representation from Governor, Council, and Assembly of S. C., to the King, April 9, 1734, PR, Vol. XVI, pp. 398-9; Edward McCrady, "Slavery in the Province of South Carolina, 1670-1770," in American Historical Association, *Annual Report,* 1895 (Washington: Government Printing Office, 1896), pp. 654-5.

[33] F. Yonge and P. Fury to the Board of Trade, March 8, 1735, PR, Vol. XVII, p. 300.

CHAPTER IX

Johnson's Plan Of Settlement

THE realization of the steadily mounting disproportion of slaves to white settlers led to several attempts to increase the white population. In 1716, as a result of the Yamassee War, an act was passed to encourage the importation of white servants, since "sad experience" had made it plain there were not enough white inhabitants for defense against the Indians, and the number of slaves was rapidly increasing. The act gave a bounty of £25 current money for each white male servant brought into the Province.[1]

In December 1725, another act was passed requiring landholders possessing 2,000 or more acres to furnish one indentured servant to serve in the militia for each 2,000 acres owned.[2] Some months afterward, another measure designed particularly toward the prevention of slave insurrections was enacted. It provided that every person in possession of a plantation or cowpen, owning any Negroes, should maintain a white man at the plantation or cowpen. Where there were twenty or more slaves, there should be at least one white man for every ten Negroes.[3]

The need for additional white inhabitants was imperative. Yet, prior to Johnson's appointment as royal Governor, there had been no large or rapid inflow of settlement, although the Province had gradually increased in size.[4] Thus it remained for Robert Johnson to suggest the first workable plan for enlarging the population to receive the approval and acceptance of the British authorities. This plan was the most significant part of Johnson's defense policy. In combination with other measures, the final means of protection was to make the Province so capable of counterattack as to dissuade any

---

[1] *Statutes,* Vol. II, pp. 646-9.

[2] *Statutes,* Vol. III, pp. 255-7.

[3] *Statutes,* Vol. III, p. 272.

[4] Ramsay, *History of S. C.,* Vol. I, pp. 5-6; Alexander Gregg, *History of the Old Cheraws* (New York: Richardson and Co., 1867), p. 42; Edson L. Whitney, *Government of the Colony of South Carolina,* in Johns Hopkins University *Studies in Historical and Political Science,* series 13, no. 1-2 (Baltimore: The Johns Hopkins Press, 1895), pp. 59-60.

potential enemy from warring against it. In Johnson's words: "Nothing is so much wanted in Carolina as white Inhabitants."[5]

Johnson's township plan formed the first section of his "Proposal for Improving and the better Settling of South Carolina" and he called on the Crown to grant 200,000 acres of land to be used by the Province for the development of townships on the frontiers. In area, each of the ten townships was to be 20,000 acres. As suggested by Johnson, there should be three townships on the Savannah River, one at the head of Pon Pon River, two on the Santee River; and one each on the Wateree, the Black, and the Peedee rivers. Where two or more townships were to be on the same river, they were not to be within twenty miles of each other. Only township residents were to secure grants, and no one was to be allowed more than one lot in the township. Each township would have the privilege of sending a member or two to represent its inhabitants in the Assembly.[6]

In another communication on the township plan, Johnson suggested that each township be laid out in a square tract. In the middle of the square, provision would be made for a small town of 200 lots, each lot consisting of no more than one-fourth acre. An additional fifty lots in the town would be reserved for tradesmen and for schoolhouses, churches, and other public functions. Altogether the town and commons would amount to about 250 acres, while the remaining 19,650 acres was to be divided into 200 parts and to belong to the inhabitants of the town. None was to have more than 100 or less than 75 acres. The parcels near the town were to consist of 75 acres, the remainder progressively increasing in size so that those farthest away from the town would contain 100 acres. The first settlers would get the parcels nearest the towns, the others farther away being granted as people came in to settle them.[7]

In an "Explanation of my Scheem given the Lords of Trade for Settling Townships," Johnson pointed out that his plan was designed "to Secure Convenient Settlements of good Land for the encouragement of poor People to come and Settle upon in Carolina." Also

---

[5] Letter from Johnson, December 19, 1729, PR, Vol. XIII, p. 425.

[6] "A Proposal for Improving and the better Settling of South Carolina," received by Board of Trade, March 7, 1729/30, PR, Vol. XIV, p. 58; David Duncan Wallace, *The History of South Carolina* (4 vols., New York: The American Historical Society, Inc., 1934), Vol. I, p. 334n.

[7] "Col. Johnsons Proposal for better improving & setling South Carolina," received by Board of Trade, March 18, 1729/30, PR, Vol. XIV, pp. 71-72.

he said it would "prevent those who have large Grants for Lands subsisting; from ingrossing the Lands in such Convenient Places." Therefore, by this "scheem," poor people would be encouraged to settle the townships and in turn would provide protection for the Province and themselves by constructing a fortification about their settlement.[8] By fortifying the town, they could defend themselves against any enemy, preventing a recurrence of the losses during the Yamassee War when many inhabitants were cut off for lack of places of protection.

Johnson believed that the Board of Trade's proposed quit rent of a penny per acre, which would apply to lands within or without the proposed townships, would greatly discourage new settlers from coming over. He felt it would deter people from taking up lands either within or outside the townships, especially since the Lords Proprietors had granted a good deal of land at only nominal quit rents; and also mentioned that such a high quit rent would discourage the pitch and tar industry. Further, he was afraid, he said, that the patentees with proprietary grants—once they saw their advantage—would take up all the good lands.

Johnson argued that it was questionable whether anyone would take up 1,000 acres of pine lands at the new quit rent rate because the lands could be used only three or four years out of every twenty. To him, it seemed more likely that such a grantee, after using all of the lightwood, would let the land escheat to the Crown, to prevent paying sixteen or seventeen years' rents on it when it could be put to no use.[9] He proposed allowing all persons, under proper regulations, to make use of the dead pine trees on the Crown lands, which would not harm them. A total of 640, or perhaps 1,000, acres would be sufficient for a family,[10] he thought.

Johnson's plan provided that no person be allowed to take up lands on the rivers selected as the sites of the townships until those townships had been laid out, a restriction applied at once. Lands laid out adjacent to rivers and other navigable streams were to have no more than one-fourth part of the linear measure of the grant located along the waterway. Exempted from this provision were the

[8] "Explanation of my Scheem given the Lords of Trade for Settling Townships," received by Board of Trade, April 30, 1730, PR, Vol. XIV, pp. 89-90.

[9] "Col. Johnsons Proposal," PR, Vol. XIV, pp. 71-74.

[10] "Explanation of my Scheem," PR, Vol. XIV, pp. 90-91.

townships, and it was provided that they should be set out for the best advantage of the inhabitants.

An unusual provision permitted all foreigners, as well as His Majesty's freeborn subjects, to take up reasonable amounts of land, and have the same voting privileges in the choice of assemblymen.

Since several persons held grants from the Proprietors for large tracts of land, Johnson suggested that no person be allowed to claim more than 640 acres under any grant within ten miles of any of the townships.

He had specified this limit originally for lands outside the townships, with the grantee agreeing to settle the land within two years, and if the person fail to comply with this provision, his grant would revert to the Crown. Persons already owning lands in the Province could not take up any more, unless they were able to settle the area within one year. In these cases, the Governor and Council would be left free to determine how much land the applicant should be granted, but the amount should not exceed 500 acres.[11]

Afterward, Johnson changed his mind about limiting the size of grants other than those of townships. He thought that he with the Council should have the power to allow a larger amount of land, which would be based on the number of slaves the grantee possessed and on how he intended to use it. Johnson thought that the larger grants would encourage pitch and tar production, as these industries required large land areas. Johnson thought that the amount should be 1,000 acres to every twenty Negroes to be employed, but presumably, the total amount to be granted would be left to the discretion of the Council after consultation with the Governor.

Johnson added a proviso that newcomers would not be required to settle in the proposed townships. It was reasonable to believe that people in good circumstances would not care to be restricted in such a fashion, and if compelled to live in the new townships, they might be discouraged from settling in South Carolina.[12]

Johnson received additional Instructions concerning his settlement and township proposals that had won the approval of the British authorities. The Instructions mentioned the inconveniencies that had arisen from persons claiming thousands of acres which they had

[11] "A Proposal for Improving and the better Settling of South Carolina," PR, Vol. XIV, pp. 58-60.

[12] "Explanation of my Scheem," PR, Vol. XIV, pp. 90-91.

failed to take up and cultivate, preventing others from settling and improving the land. To counteract this, the Governor was directed to urge the Assembly to pass a law requiring Proprietors' grantees either to take up and cultivate their lands within a certain time, or forfeit their claims to the Crown. To prevent similar happenings in the future, Johnson was instructed to include in grants *a vacating clause* on failure of cultivation. Also, grants were to be made only in proportion to the ability of the grantee to cultivate the land, based on the number of persons and slaves in his family. Thereby, no person was to be granted more than fifty acres of land for each white person or slave man, woman and child in his household at the time the grant was made.

In general, Johnson's proposals were followed. The Crown, however, specified that there would be eleven townships, one more than Johnson had suggested, and that they were to be located as follows: two on the Altamaha River, two on the Savannah River, one at the head of the Pon Pon River, two on the Santee River, and one each on the Wateree, Black, Peedee, and Waccamaw Rivers. This was considerably more than Johnson's original "scheem." The Instructions for two townships on the Altamaha, if carried out, would push the line of English settlement considerably farther southward.[13]

In contrast to Johnson's recommendation that the inhabitants be allowed to have tracts of 75 to 100 acres, the Instructions provided that there should be 50 acres granted for every man, woman, and child making up the grantee's family. Further, it was said that these grants could be augmented as the inhabitants grew capable of putting more land under cultivation. The lands within six miles of each township were to be reserved to the respective townships, so that only township inhabitants would be eligible to acquire them. This differed somewhat from Johnson's proposal of not allowing anyone who possessed a grant from the Lords Proprietors to take up more than 640 acres within ten miles of any of the townships.

Most of the other provisions followed Johnson's recommendations closely, specifically those in regard to the size of townships, of laying off town lots, and making provisions for a commons in each town.

He had specified that people in the townships be permitted to have representation in the Assembly. His plan provided that each

[13] PRO, CO 5:192, pp. 84-88 (Library of Congress transcript); A. S. Salley, *The History of Orangeburg County, South Carolina* (Orangeburg: R. Lewis Berry, 1898), pp. 1-2.

of the townships, with the contiguous six miles, be created into a distinct parish. When any of the parishes reached a population of 100 householders, it would have the right to send two members to the Assembly and enjoy simultaneously all of the rights and privileges of the existing Province parishes.

To increase white population, the Governor was instructed to recommend that the Assembly pass a law encouraging the importation of white servants, either men or women, to whom he would grant 50 acres of land after they had fulfilled their indentured agreements.

Lands granted by the Governor to people other than those within the township and to white servants were to be assessed rents to be determined by him and Council; but no land was to be granted at a lesser quit rent than four shillings per hundred acres. In any case, grants were to be free of quit rents for a period of ten years.[14]

Modified slightly by the Board of Trade, the township settlement plan was the final link in Johnson's overall plan of defense. In his long-range defensive strategy, the plan contained a strong element of offense, chiefly the township scheme. Johnson maintained that the best defense would be found in the expansion of settlements toward the frontier. He said these would present a phalanx of solidly settled and fortified communities, strong enough to withstand any enemy thrust, and having the potential to strike back.

When Johnson's township scheme had received the British government's approval, efforts were made to implement it quickly. Johnson sought and received the full support of the South Carolina Assembly, and made plans to recruit and receive new settlers from Europe, who would receive subsistence until they were able to provide for themselves. Because the new settlers were being placed in a frontier environment, they had to be supplied with housing, utensils, tools and food until they could clear the land and raise sufficient crops for their needs. This was doubly important for the newcomers, for many of them had come from manufacturing towns and had to become adjusted to an agrarian economy. By assisting these Europeans to find hope and home in the New World, South Carolina was also aiding itself by swelling its defense ranks.[15]

---

[14] PRO, CO 5:192, pp. 84-88 (Library of Congress transcript).

[15] Hewat, *Historical Account,* in Carroll, *Historical Collections,* Vol. I, p. 376; Gilbert P. Voight, "The Germans and the German-Swiss in South Carolina, 1732-1765: Their Contribution to the Province," in South Carolina Historical Association, *Proceedings,* 1935, pp. 17-18.

Even before Johnson had presented his township plan to the Board of Trade there had been an offer to transport settlers to Carolina. Jean Pierre Purry of Neuchatel, Switzerland, proposed to settle a group of his countrymen in the Province. Purry communicated with the English ambassador at Paris who sent his Memorial to the Duke of Newcastle. The letter was referred to the Board of Trade in 1724.[16] Purry described himself as "formerly Director General in the Service of the India Company in France," and said that he wanted to settle in Carolina with a group of about 600, consisting of workmen and soldiers, many of whom wanted to take their wives with them.

The conditions of Purry's offer were:

> That the King would grant him an area four leagues square, to be selected by him after his arrival in America, for which he was to enjoy the same rights and privileges as the other Carolina inhabitants;
>
> That from his group, he be allowed to form a Swiss regiment, all of whom would be from Switzerland and all of the Reformed religion, whose officers would have brevets from the King;
>
> That he (Purry) be given the rank of colonel and an appointment as judge, so that he would be able to settle differences among his people;
>
> That appeal from Purry's decisions could be made to the Chief Justice of the Province;
>
> That he (Purry) have the power to nominate and remove from office all officers in his settlement;
>
> That the King provide transportation for the group at Crown expense and that the expedition sail from some English port.

Because Carolina lands were still in the hands of the Lords Proprietors, Richard Shelton, secretary to the Proprietors, was requested to seek their advice on Purry's proposal.[17]

After consultations, Shelton reported that since the Proprietors were interested in encouraging settlement, they had agreed to donate

[16] Newcastle to Board of Trade, June 5, 1724, PR, Vol. XI, p. 127. Purry's Memorial is on pp. 128-31.

[17] A. Popple to R. Shelton, June 11, 1724, PR, Vol. XI, pp. 132-133; Board of Trade Journal, June 9, 1724, PR, Vol. XI, p. 13; Harriette D. K. Leiding, "Purrysburg, A Swiss-French Settlement of South Carolina, on the Savannah River," in Huguenot Society of South Carolina, *Transactions,* No. 39 (1934), pp. 27-28.

lands for this purpose, provided the grantees would pay a quit rent of twopence per acre after the first three years.[18]

Negotiations with Purry went on slowly. At one time, the Proprietors were reported to have made arrangements with Purry for transporting 1,200 Swiss natives to South Carolina.[19] This proposal came to nothing, as the Proprietors did not uphold their part of the agreement.[20]

While in England, Robert Johnson strongly championed the cause of Purry, whose last proposal was to transport 600 Swiss to South Carolina. He also learned that in addition to lands requested for new settlers, Purry wanted 12,000 acres free of quit rents for himself. Johnson recommended that the Board of Trade accept this proposal, provided Purry carried out his commitment within six years. Assimilating Purry's proposal into his own township defense scheme, Johnson recommended that the township should be laid out on the Savannah River, either near the Pallachuccola Fort or at some other convenient place to be chosen at the discretion of the Governor and Council.[21]

It was agreed that the Swiss newcomers would be treated in the same manner as were subjects from Great Britain, and were to be entitled to the same privileges. Upon their arrvial in Carolina, they were to take the oaths of allegiance, after which the Governor was to grant them their lands and settle them in the place and manner he supposed "most conducive to ye Interest & Security of the s[ai]d Province."

Purry, in view of his "Trouble, Labour & Expence," was to be granted the lands he wanted, free of quit rents, when proof was furnished by one of the customs officers in the Province that Purry had fulfilled his obligation.[22]

---

[18] Board of Trade Journal, July 23, 1724, PR, Vol. XI, p. 14.

[19] Board of Trade Journal, June 15, 1725, PR, Vol. XI, p. 252.

[20] PR, Vol. XV, p. 62; Crane, *Southern Frontier,* pp. 285-7; Meriwether, *Expansion of S. C.,* p. 34. It was during this period, as noted previously, that the tactics of the proprietary position on S. C. were changing from a claim of both government and lands to a proposed offer of surrendering the government in order to secure their land rights (plus quit rents). PR, Vol. XII, pp. 29, 66-71, and PR, Vol. XII, p. 253.

[21] Johnson to Board of Trade, July 20, 1730, PR, Vol. XIV, pp. 237-8.

[22] Board of Trade to Privy Council, November 30, 1731, PR, Vol. XV, pp. 61-64; Henry A. M. Smith, "Purrysburgh," in *South Carolina Historical Magazine,* Vol. X, No. 4 (October, 1909), pp. 188-91; South Carolina State Board of Agriculture, *South Carolina, Resources and Population, Institutions and Industries* (Charleston: Walker, Evans, and Cogswell, 1883), p. 383.

When Purry petitioned the Assembly for support, Johnson spoke of him as "a person that to my own knowledge has taken great pains [,] been at a Considerable Expence and is very Capable of Serving the Province in the manner he set forth." Johnson also sent the Assembly a copy of his Instructions relating to setting out the townships. The Assembly concurred, agreeing to make provision for the settlers, and granting Purry £400 for every 100 capable men brought over from Switzerland.[23] After his arrival in Carolina, Purry appeared before the Governor and Council to ask funds for defraying expense of a trip to the Savannah River to select a proper place for his intended settlement. The Governor, who said he was "very willing to give him all Due Encouragement," recommended that the Assembly provide Purry with £150 Carolina money,[24] and on the following day, the Assembly responded favorably. At the same time, a letter was sent to Captain Evans of the Pallachuccola Garrison, directing him to meet Purry at Port Royal, accompany him on his journey, and lend him all necessary aid. Colonel Deamour and Major Hassard at Port Royal were also asked to assist Purry.[25]

The Reverend F. Varnod of St. George's Parish, who preached in French to Purry's group at their request,[26] accompanied Purry on his trip up the Savannah River, where a site was selected. The best location was decided to be on the north side of the river, about thirty miles from its mouth where the land was known as the Great Yamassee Bluff.[27] Afterwards, Johnson made plans to have the township laid out for Purry, expressing the hope that the other townships could soon be settled.[28]

Purry, on making a return trip to Europe, petitioned the English government to increase his grant from 12,000 to 48,000 acres, and

---

[23] JC, Vol. V, pp. 50, 53, 58-59 (February 26, March 3, 18, 1730/31); Purry's suggestions, along with an exaggerated description of South Carolina, were drawn up in *Proposals by Mr. Peter Purry, of Newfchatel, for Encouragement of such Swiss Protestants as Should Agree to Accompany Him to Carolina,* and is reprinted in Carroll, *Historical Collections,* Vol. II, pp. 121-40.

[24] JC, Vol. V, p. 74 (May 6, 1731).

[25] JC, Vol. V, p. 76 (May 7, 1731).

[26] F. Varnod to Secretary of the SPG, February 13, 1730/31, SPG, Series A, Vol. XXIII.

[27] F. Varnod to Secretary of the SPG, August 9 and December 2, 1731, SPG, Series B, Vol. IV, Part 2.

[28] Johnson to Board of Trade, November 14, 1731, PR, Vol. XV, pp. 35-36.

the Board voted favorably on his request. It reported to the Privy Council, in words that reflected the ideas of Johnson, that "All ye British Colonies and especially the two Frontiers, should be peopled as amply & as soon as possible w[i]th white Inhabit[an]ts." The Board also thought that such matters were beneficial to the Crown and the public because "an accession of New Inhabitants in ye Plantations cannot fail to increase the Trade & Commerce of this Kingdom, whilst It creates an Augmentation of His Majesty's Revenues in his Quit Rents." In respect to the Province of South Carolina, the Board said, "As It is Our Frontier to ye Spanish and French Settlements, and is surrounded by a great number of Indian Nations, the well peopling of this Province Seems to be a very necessary Measure for the Defense and Security of all Our Plantations on the Contin[en]t of America."

The Board stated that it believed a chief reason for South Carolina's low rate of settlement was that "a Considerable number of People have never before made an Offer of Settling together in one place, & this Province is now so sensible of ye advantage and Security It would derive from such a settlement that they [the Board] have granted Monsr. Purry £400 Ster.," to bring over 100 men to Carolina.

The Board did not expect any adverse effects if Purry's request for 48,000 acres was allowed. It had learned that Purry did not intend to keep a large quantity of land for himself, but planned to sell it to various individuals who would be required to occupy and improve the lands. The Board qualified its permission by noting that the grant to Purry was not to be made until the Swiss settlers had arrived in Carolina.[29]

In the Privy Council, the Lords of the Committee for Plantation Affairs considered both Purry's proposal and the Board of Trade's favorable recommendation. They agreed to the proposition and said Purry could have the 48,000 acres contiguous to the township. The Board of Trade was advised to prepare an additional instruction for the Governor to that effect, with the proviso that all lands not cultivated within the period of ten years would revert to the Crown.[30]

---

[29] Board of Trade to Privy Council, May 26, 1732, PR, Vol. XV, pp. 113-20.

[30] June 6, 1732, PR, Vol. XV, pp. 121-2.

The Instructions to Johnson were drawn up,[31] and were subsequently approved by the Privy Council.[32]

In September 1732, the *South Carolina Gazette* printed a portion of a letter received in Charleston from Charles Purry, son of Jean Pierre Purry. The letter was written in May and stated that his father was in Switzerland, where he had bought up the time of a number of persons, and hoped besides to obtain a number of free men, and some women and children.[33] The same issue of the *Gazette* ran a June letter from a London merchant saying that Purry was due in England any day with about 200 people, and that two weeks following arrival, Purry and his party expected to sail for Carolina.[34] South Carolinians read this news eagerly, and began to make preparations to welcome the Swiss immigrants.

The Public Treasurer was ordered to provide the necessary tools, and provisions for three months; and to hire periaguas to go to Sullivan's Island to meet them and take them up the Savannah River. Only 150 of the expected 200 Swiss were due to arrive at this time, it had been learned,[35] and when later groups came over, it was planned to provide for them in the same way.[36]

In his report to the Board of Trade on December 15, 1732, Governor Johnson noted that Purry had arrived, bringing only 120 Swiss, including 50 men, and women and children. He reported that the new settlers had been furnished with provisions and "all sorts of necessarys," and that the first arrivals had already gone to Purrysburg — name of the new settlement — and that they had expressed great satisfaction at their reception."[37] Similarly, Purry's son told the Georgia Trustees that the settlers were "extremely well received," by the Governor and inhabitants of South Carolina.[38]

---

[31] PR, Vol. XV, pp. 124-6.

[32] July 21, 1732, PR, Vol. XV, p. 142.

[33] *SCG,* September 16-23, 1732.

[34] *SCG,* September 16-23, 1732. *Gentleman's Magazine* printed Purry's "A Description of the Province of South Carolina," Vol. II (August, September, October, 1732), pp. 893-70, 1017-8.

[35] JC, Vol. V, p. 212 (October 6, 1732).

[36] E.g., JCHA, p. 987 (March 17, 1732/3), which reports the arrival in the Province of about ten Swiss newcomers.

[37] Johnson to Board of Trade, December 15, 1732, PR, Vol. XVI, pp. 4-5.

[38] *The Colonial Records of the State of Georgia,* ed. by Allen D. Candler (26 vols., Atlanta: Franklin Printing and Publishing Co., 1904-1916), Vol. I, p. 100: *Percival Diary,* Vol. I, pp. 327-8.

CLXXXVI. *The Trials of Major* Stede Bonnet *and Thirty Three others, at the Court of Vice-Admiralty at* Charles-Town *in* South-Carolina, *for* Piracy, Octob. 30, *&c.* 1718. 5 Geo. I.

Tuesday, October the 28th, 1718. the Court met according to Appointment.

PRESENT

Nicholas Trott, Esq; Judge of the Vice-Admiralty, and Chief-Justice of the said Province of *South-Carolina*.

Assistant Judges,

George Logan, Esq;	*Samuel Dean*, Esq;
Alexander Parris, Esq;	*Edward Brailsford*, Gent.
Philip Dawes, Esq;	*John Croft*, Gent.
George Chicken, Esq;	Capt. *Arthur Loan*.
Benjamin de la Conseillere, Esq;	Capt. *John Watkinson*.

THE King's Commission to *Nicholas Trott*, Esq; Judge of the Court of *Vice-Admiralty*, and the Commission in the name of the Lord *Palatine*, and the rest of the Lords Proprietors, and Testified by the Honourable *Robert Johnson*, Esq; *Governor*, and the rest of the Lords *Deputies*, for holding the Court of *Admiralty Sessions*, was openly read.

Then the Grand-Jury was called, and twenty three of them were sworn; the Names of which are as followeth:

Michael Brewton, Foreman.	*John Breton*.
Robert Tradd.	*John Bee*.
Andrew Allen.	*Daniel Gale*.
Peter Manigault.	*Thomas Loyde*.
John Beauchamp.	*Laurence Dennis*.
John Bullock.	*Elias Foisin*.
Thomas Barton.	*John Shepherd*.
Anthony Matthews.	*John Simmons*.
Alexander Kinlock.	*George Peterson*.
Henry Perrineau.	*Solomon Legare*.
Paul Douxsaint.	*Abraham Lesuir*.
	John Caywood.

Sentence

That you the said Stede Bonnet *shall go from hence to the Place from whence you came, and from thence to the Place of Execution, where you shall be hanged by the Neck till you are Dead. And the God of infinite Mercy be merciful to your Soul.*

On *Wednesday December* the 10th, 1718. the said Major *Stede Bonnet* was *executed* at the *White-Point* near *Charles-Town*, according to the above *Sentence*.

Courtesy South Caroliniana Library

Venire of Jurors in the Trial; and the Sentence of Major Stede Bonnet, as Contained in Trott's *The Laws of the Province*.

CHAPTER X

Growth And Boundary Trouble

THE Johnson administration could be termed a period of expansion for South Carolina. During this time, the Province was extending its line of settlement on all of its landward sides, and there was much evidence of progress. On the western and southwestern frontiers, the township scheme of settlement was beginning its invaluable contribution, and, in the northern part, the Winyah area was growing and showing much promise of future development.

A Winyah representative of the Society for the Propagation of the Gospel as early as 1732 wrote that he looked forward to a very populous parish and thought the Society should begin to take steps to provide a sufficient supply of ministers. The missionary also said that he was awaiting hopefully the completion of the chapel that was under construction, for he was conducting services in a tavern and had "to officiate where so much discord and Confusion attends it that I cannot think of Administ[e]ring the Sacrament to them in such a place."[1]

Not quite three years afterwards, the minister wrote again concerning the parish, saying that "There is a considerable increase of People w[i]thin this few Years, insomuch yt [that] ye remotest parts are now become ye best settled."[2]

There was enough increase in population to cause a division of the Parish. One part retained the name Prince George's and the other received the designation, Prince Frederick Parish.[3]

The main town set out in this area was the port of Georgetown, which in early 1735 was reportedly more populous than Port Royal and had a larger church congregation than any other in the Province except Charleston.[4] A few months later, it was noticeable that

[1] T. Morritt to Secretary of the SPG, April 7, 1732, SPG, Series A, Vol. XXIV.

[2] T. Morritt to Bishop of London, February 3, 1734/5, SPG, Fulham Palace MSS, South Carolina, No. 69.

[3] Church Wardens and Vestry of Prince Frederick's Parish to Secretary of SPG, February 12, 1734/5, SPG, Series A, Vol. XXV.

[4] T. Morritt to Secretary of the SPG, February 3, 1734/5, SPG, Series A, Vol. XXV.

Georgetown was becoming a growing trade and business center, with about 200 inhabitants, and the number increased from day to day.[5]

Although Johnson's prime concern was settlement to protect the southern and western frontiers, he stoutly supported measures to attract newcomers throughout the Province. He had won the support of the Assembly to his cause, so that the importation of settlers took a prominent place in all the plans of the Province.

Commissary Alexander Garden felt that the Province could relieve the Society for the Propagation of the Gospel of the necessity of subsidizing missionaries in South Carolina, or at least in the richer parishes. In discussing this plan with Garden in the spring of 1735, Johnson said that the Assembly might be able to adopt the proposal in about two or three years. He pointed out that since the Province was engaged in importing poor Protestants at an annual expense of nearly £2,000 sterling, the Assembly might not readily adopt Garden's idea until financial obligations for new settlers were ended.[6]

Along the southern border, a new source of strength to the defense of South Carolina was the colony of Georgia. The people lent much encouragement and support to the establishment, although much of the settlement was carved from their own territory.

The secretary to the Georgia trustees was well aware of the reasons for the establishment of the colony, saying that they were: (1) "to provide a subsistence for those who were indigent at home and, consequently, a burden on the public"; and (2) "to make a barrier for South Carolina which had suffered, and lay still exposed to danger by the smallness of the number of her English inhabitants."[7]

---

[5] Vestry and Church Wardens of Prince George's Parish to T. Morritt, June 13, 1735, SPG, Series A, Vol. XXVI.

[6] A. Garden to Bishop of London, May 15, 1735, SPG, Fulham Palace MSS, South Carolina, Nos. 166 and 167.

[7] [Benjamin Martyn], *An Impartial Inquiry into the State and Utility of the Province of Georgia,* reprinted in Georgia Historical Society, *Collections,* Vol. I, p. 167. On motives behind the founding of the colony, see the Georgia charter, included in George White, *Historical Collections of Georgia* (New York: Pudney and Russell, 1854), pp. 1-13. Also see, Ettinger, *Oglethorpe,* pp. 110, 118; R. A. Roberts, "The Birth of an American State: Georgia: An Effort of Philanthropy and Protestant Propaganda," in *Transactions of the Royal Historical Society,* 4th series, Vol. VI, pp. 22-49. More recent accounts include Albert B. Saye, *New Viewpoints in Georgia History* (Athens: University of Georgia Press, 1943), pp. v, 8-42; Trevor Richard Reese, *Colonial Georgia* (Athens: University of Georgia Press, 1963), pp. 1-17; and Daniel J. Boorstin, *The Americans: The Colonial Experience* (New York: Vintage Books, 1964), pp. 71-96.

The provisions in the Georgia charter limiting land holding to 500 acres and prohibiting slave ownership—akin to Johnson's township plan—were inserted with concern for the colony's frontier and defensive aspects. The Trustee's secretary, Benjamin Martyn, stated: "The greater number of blacks, which a frontier has, and the greater disproportion is between them and her white people, the more danger she is liable to; for those are all secret enemies." Martyn also argued the point further by saying, "If a great number of negroes could have made South Carolina secure, she would not have wanted such a barrier."[8] A number of South Carolinians, Governor Johnson included, had been saying the same thing, except in different words, for some years.

The limit to 500 acres on Georgia-land ownership had been necessitated because Georgia "was designed to be a new frontier," and the perimeter had to be thickly populated by white settlers. Martyn stated that, as it turned out, ninety per cent of the inhabitants became 50-acre free-holders, an amount of land that would provide a comfortable subsistence but would not require maintenance by a large number of Negroes. The planters also felt they could rely better on white servants from Europe, who themselves would be eligible for land after they had completed their terms of indenture. In contrast to slaves, it was said that "The [white] servants will have no temptation to run away; from the hopes of a property they will be more industrious, and when they attain this, each man of them adds a strength to the colony."[9]

The South Carolina Governor notified British authorities that he stood ready to help in every way the establishment of the Georgia colony,[10] and had "subscribed very handsomely" from his own fortune to aid the settling of the new Province.[11] Benjamin Martyn wrote: "The governor is very hearty in promoting it, and has generously contributed towards it."[12]

---

[8] [Benjamin Martyn], *An Impartial Inquiry into the State and Utility of the Province of Georgia,* reprinted in Georgia Historical Society, *Collections,* Vol. I, p. 167.

[9] *Ibid.,* Vol. I, pp. 167-9.

[10] *Percival Diary,* Vol. I, p. 339; *Colonial Records of the State of Georgia,* Vol. I, pp. 68-69, 141-2; Leslie F. Church, Oglethorpe: *A Study of Philanthropy in England and Georgia* (London: Epworth Press, 1932), pp. 64-65.

[11] *SCG,* January 27-February 3, 1732/3; *Colonial Records of the State of Georgia,* Vol. I, pp. 92-93, Vol. III, pp. 65-67; *Percival Diary,* Vol. I, pp. 289, 304.

[12] [Benjamin Martyn], *Reasons for Establishing the Colony of Georgia,* reprinted in Georgia Historical Society, *Collections,* Vol. I, p. 224.

Oglethorpe arrived in Charleston on January 13, 1732/3 with the first group of people who had expressed a desire to settle in the new colony of Georgia.[13] Governor Johnson acquainted the Council of Oglethorpe's arrival, giving details of the voyage; and the Council, at his request, passed a resolution to offer all encouragement possible.[14]

The immigrants were reported to be in good health following the long sea voyage, and after a few days' rest, went to Port Royal, arriving there on the 19th. After a brief stay in Port Royal, Oglethorpe and his party then proceeded to the Savannah River, where he selected a site along the banks for the new settlement. This became eventually the city of Savannah.[15]

Several days after Oglethorpe had left Charleston for Port Royal, the Assembly responded favorably to a request from Johnson to supply him with 104 head of cattle, twenty-five hogs, twenty barrels of rice, and boats—including a scout boat—to transport the new settlers to Georgia. Captain McPherson and fifteen of the Rangers, a company of horse, were ordered to the new settlement, with instructions to take commands from Oglethorpe and to protect the colony if any danger were to arise. Johnson also sent notice to adjacent frontier garrisons to assist the new settlement in every way possible, and also informed friendly Indians of their arrival.[16]

Although the South Carolinians were generous, their aid to the Georgians was not altogether altruistic. Governor Johnson in effect admitted this when he said to the Commons House, "We should look upon the Effectual Settlement of this New Colony as the greatest

---

[13] *Percival Diary,* Vol. I, p. 339; *Colonial Records of the State of Georgia,* Vol. I, p. 102; *London Magazine,* Vol. II (May 1733), p. 266. Percival recorded on December 28, 1732, that the Trustees had read a letter from Governor Johnson to Oglethorpe, dated September 28, "advising the not making an embarkation this twelve months, because of the necessary preparations first to be made of houses, etc.," but Oglethorpe was eager to start the colony. *Percival Diary,* Vol. I, p. 304.

[14] JC, Vol. V, pp. 252-3 (January 12, 1732/3)

[15] Robert Johnson to Benjamin Martyn, February 12, 1732/3, in Georgia Historical Society, *Collections,* Vol. I, p. 237; Johnson to Board of Trade, January 8, 1732/3, PR, Vol. XVI, p. 31. When the new town of Savannah was run out, the public square was named Johnson Square, in appreciation for the governor's help. Charles C. Jones, Jr., *The History of Georgia* (2 vols., Boston: Houghton, Mifflin, and Co., 1883), Vol. I, p. 150; Coulter, *Georgia: A Short History,* p. 25.

[16] Johnson to Martyn, February 12, 1732/3, in Georgia Historical Society, *Collections,* Vol. I, p. 237; JC, Vol. V, pp. 264-5 (January 26, 1732/3); *SCG,* March 24-31, 1733; *Percival Diary,* Vol. I, pp. 364, 389, 398.

advantage to the welfare of this Province."[17] Oglethorpe was appreciative, however, and was quick to tell the Georgia trustees that "the governor and assembly have given us all possible encouragement."[18] It soon was discernible that Carolinian assistance benefitted both areas.

Colonel William Bull, a member of Council, who was familiar with methods of settlement, nature of the land, and habits of the Indians, was sent by Johnson to advise and assist Oglethorpe. "Had not our Assembly been sitting," wrote Johnson, "I would have gone myself."[19] He did provide a number of helpers besides Colonel Bull, a few sawyers and some friendly Indians to aid the newcomers in clearing the land.[20] Oglethorpe was kind to the Indians, and they were reported to be fond of him, and helpful as well.[21] When Oglethorpe arrived in this country, he had with him a copy of Sir Walter Raleigh's *Journal,* for he believed that his settlement was in the identical part of America as Raleigh's. He said:

> By the Latitude of the Place, the Marks and Tradition of the *Indians,* it's the very place where he [Raleigh] went a shore and talk'd with the *Indians,* and was the first *English Man* that ever they saw; and about half a Mile from *Savannah* is a high Mount of Earth, under which lies their chief King; and the *Indians* inform'd Mr. *Oglethorpe,* that the King desired before he died, that he might be buried on the Spot where he talked with that *great good Man.*[22]

When first in Savannah, Oglethorpe made a treaty with Tomochichi, the "mico" or chief of the Yamacraw Indians who were living near the new settlement.[23] In May 1733, on a visit to Charleston, Oglethorpe took Tomochichi and two of the chief's nephews with him.[24] On his return to Savannah, the general learned that while

---

[17] JC, Vol. V, pp. 346-7 (January 17, 1732/3).

[18] Oglethorpe to the Trustees for Establishing the Colony of Georgia in America, February 10, 1732/3, in Georgia Historical Society, *Collections,* Vol. I, p. 234.

[19] Johnson to Martyn, February 12, 1732/3, in Georgia Historical Society, *Collections,* Vol. I, p. 237; *The Journal of Peter Gordon, 1732-1735,* ed. by E. Merton Coulter (Athens: University of Georgia Press, 1963), p. 37.

[20] Martyn, *Reasons for Establishing,* in Georgia Historical Society, *Collections,* Vol. I, p. 224.

[21] SCG, March 17-24, 1732/3.

[22] SCG, March 17-24, 1732/3.

[23] SCG, March 24-31, 1733. Swanton identifies these Indians as a small band of Yamassee, *Indian Tribes of North America,* p. 116. In South Carolina, a chief was often referred to and commissioned as "king."

[24] SCG, May 5-12, 1733.

he was away, the headmen of all the tribes of the lower Creek Nation had come to negotiate a treaty. They had awaited his return, and receiving them in one of the newly constructed huts, the general made the usual formalities of address. The Indians told Oglethorpe that they claimed all of the land south of the Savannah River, but that they were willing to give up freely all the lands they did not use themselves. Negotiations and formalities went on for three days, after which the treaty was signed and presents were distributed to the Indians.[25] It was Oglethorpe's belief that it would pay to have some of the Indians visit England "both for authority and understanding," adding that by such a visit, the Indians "would be awed."

Oglethorpe, of course, had heard of the Cherokees' visit to England, which Sir Alexander Cuming had arranged, and spoke of the benefits that Carolina had derived which "probably will be felt with pleasure for an age to come."[26] His statement was very optimistic in view of the difficulties South Carolina was having with the Cherokees at that very moment.

Oglethorpe had not become familiar with the actualities of Indian affairs, and had not yet been forced to adopt as realistic an Indian policy as had Governor Johnson.[27] There were so many other difficult tasks to claim his attention, it is understandable that so inexperienced a person could not be expected to know the many, diverse ramifications of Indian affairs. In fact, few people ever visualized the needs and problems of Johnson's policy, and his handling of Indian affairs stands out as rare and distinctive.

Although Georgia's greatest importance to South Carolina was its defense contribution, the new colony assisted the Province in several other ways. It served as a deterrent to slaves running off to freedom

---

[25] *SCG,* May 26-June 2, 1733. This issue of the *Gazette* names the leading Indians from each tribe, and also gives the number attending from each.

[26] [James Oglethorpe], *A New and Accurate Account of the Provinces of South Carolina and Georgia,* reprinted in Georgia Historical Society, *Collections,* Vol. I, pp. 54-55.

[27] Johnson always exhibited the highest regard for Oglethorpe, characterizing him as "a hearty friend to this Province; he looking upon the Interest of Carolina and Georgia as inseparable." JC, Vol. VI, p. 2 (November 8, 1734); Henry Bruce, *Life of General Oglethorpe* (New York: Dodd, Mead and Co., 1890), p. 131. After Johnson's death a bitter dispute broke out between the two colonies over the Indian trade. *Report of the Committee to Examine into the Proceedings of the People of Georgia, with respect to the Province of South-Carolina, and the Disputes subsisting between the Two Colonies* (Charles-Town: Lewis Timothy, 1736); *Gentleman's Magazine,* Vol. VI (November 1736), p. 686; *Percival Diary,* Vol. II, pp. 212, 341; Church, *Oglethorpe,* pp. 106, 126-9; Ettinger, *Oglethorpe,* p. 180.

in St. Augustine, because the Negroes found in Georgia were known to be escapees. They were apprehended, and agreement was then made with Carolina for their return.[28] Also, the Province benefitted from the recapture of criminals. Shortly after his arrival, General Oglethorpe sent out a detachment to apprehend two escapees from the Charleston jail who had been hiding in Georgia, killing the horses and cattle of the settlers. These felons were returned to Charleston.[29]

While South Carolina's southern and western defenses were being bolstered by forts, townships, and the establishment of Georgia, its protection was still far from complete, and for many years, Charleston remained the most vulnerable point of attack, especially from the sea.

Soon, a different kind of problem arose along the Province's northern border, a dispute with North Carolina concerning the location of the boundary line dividing the two. In his earliest recommendations to the Board of Trade, Governor Johnson had emphasized the importance of determining this line. He had pointed out that one reason was to prevent South Carolinians from running away to Cape Fear and living there to escape their creditors.

Johnson was also mindful of the value of Cape Fear and thought that it should be declared to be within the bounds of South Carolina and that it should be made a port of entry, having a collector of customs in residence.[30]

The Board of Trade, in heeding Johnson's advice, worked to settle the dividing-line issue before Johnson's appointment as royal governor and before George Burrington became royal governor of North Carolina. Early in January 1729/30, before the departure from England of the two new governors, it was reported that the Board had agreed on a Boundary line.[31] Two weeks afterward, during a meeting, the Board after some discussion announced that the division decided upon was as follows:

"The Line to begin at 30 Miles South Westward of Cape Fear River and to be run at that paralel [sic] distance the whole course of the said River."[32]

---

[28] Martyn, *An Impartial Inquiry*, in Georgia Historical Society, *Collections*, Vol. I, p. 172.

[29] *SCG*, March 3-10, 1732/3.

[30] Johnson to Board of Trade, December 19, 1729, PR, Vol. XIII, p. 423.

[31] Board of Trade Journal, January 8, 1729/30, PR, Vol. XIV, p. 1.

[32] Board of Trade Journal, January 22, 1729/30, PR, Vol. XIV, p. 1.

Due to the unfamiliarity of the exact area under discussion, Instructions given the governors contained this qualifying statement:

> [Article 110]. And in order to prevent any Disputes that may arise about the Northern Boundaries of Our Province under your government, We are graciously pleased to signify Our Pleasure that a Line shall be run [by the Commissioners appointed by each Province] beginning at the Sea thirty Miles Distant from the Mouth of Cape Fear River on the Southwest thereof, keeping the same distance from the said River, as the Course thereof runs, to the Main Source or head thereof, and from thence the said Boundary Line shall be continued due West as far as the South Seas, But if Waggamaw River lyes within thirty Miles of Cape Fear River, then that River to be the Boundary from the Sea to the head thereof, and from thence to keep the Distance of thirty Miles Parralel from Cape Fear River to the head thereof, and from thence a due West Course to the South Sea.[33]

The addition of the Waggamaw [Waccamaw] provision, in time, created what was to become a long-standing dispute between the two colonies. The controversy arose over the interpretation of the last part "... But if Waggamaw River lyes within thirty Miles of Cape Fear River, then that River to be the Boundary from the sea to the head thereof, and from thence to keep the Distance of thirty Miles Parralel from Cape Fear River to the head thereof, and from thence a due West Course to the South Sea."

Johnson, in the fall of 1731, had written Governor Burrington, offering to send commissioners from South Carolina to meet with those from North Carolina, to settle the location of the boundary. Burrington, before Johnson's letter came, had sent a memorial on the boundary to British authorities, and did not reply to Johnson's letter until nearly a year later.[34] In his letter to Britain, Burrington asserted that to run the boundary line according to the Board of Trade's Instructions would cost £2,000 sterling; instead, he suggested that the Peedee River be made the boundary, with all lands

---

[33] PRO, CO 5:192, p. 112 (Library of Congress transcript). Cape Fear, like most other rivers of the Carolinas, flows in a southeasterly direction, but the Waccamaw flows southwesterly, almost paralleling the curve of the coastline. It is, therefore, nearly perpendicular to Cape Fear.

[34] Johnson to Board of Trade, September 28, 1732, PR, Vol. XV, pp. 233-4; JC, Vol. V, p. 348 (January 19, 1732/3).

north of the river included in the bounds of North Carolina.[35] The reply from the Board of Trade reminded Governor Burrington that the matter had been "thoroughly considered" before the Instructions for the boundary had been made up. The decision could not be altered, the Board said, because we "cant think of advising any alteration therein upon hearing one party only."[36]

After this rebuff, Burrington shifted his tactics, and centered the main controversy around the interpretation of the boundary Instructions, particularly the Waccamaw provision. Then he sent an announcement to the South Carolina *Gazette* in which he stated that he had received word that a number of people in South Carolina had obtained land warrants for survey of lands on the north side of Waccamaw River and he wanted to warn them that those lands were —by the King's Instructions—part of North Carolina. He further advised that anyone who desired to take up those lands must obtain grants from the government of North Carolina.[37]

Johnson countered by placing his own notice in the *Gazette* expressing disagreement with Governor Burrington's interpretation of the royal Instructions.[38] Further, he sent the Board of Trade a reminder that Burrington *before that body* had insisted that the Waccamaw River be the dividing line, but the Board had decided to place it thirty miles southward from Cape Fear. Burrington, he said, was now interpreting the Instructions to suit himself in claiming that because the Waccamaw River came within thirty miles of the Cape Fear River, the Waccamaw was to be the boundary from its mouth.

Johnson maintained that the Board's intention was to place the boundary thirty miles below the Cape Fear unless the *mouth* of the Waccamaw River was within thirty miles of Cape Fear, which was not so, its being about ninety miles away. He told the Board that the Waccamaw River flowed into Winyah Bay "as was made appear [apparent] to your Lordships by the Map then before You, for the

---

[35] Burrington to Duke of Newcastle, July 2, 1731, *Colonial Records of N. C.*, Vol. III, p. 154; Marvin L. Skaggs, *North Carolina Boundary Disputes Involving Her Southern Line,* in James Sprunt *Studies in History and Political Science,* Vol. XXV (Chapel Hill: University of North Carolina Press, 1941), pp. 34-35.

[36] A. Popple to Burrington, August 16, 1732, *Colonial Records of N. C.*, Vol. III, p. 355.

[37] *SCG,* October 21, 1732.

[38] *SCG,* November 4, 1732.

River keeps a course paralel to the Sea a great way, and makes a great neck of land, which would bring his Boundary into the Bowels of our present Settlements on that side of the province." Johnson expressed the hope that the Board of Trade would continue what he maintained had been their original intention in drawing up the Instruction.[39]

At this juncture, Burrington conveyed to the Board of Trade his alarming report that South Carolina Indians intended an attack upon North Carolina's Tuscaroras, with aid for the Tuscaroras expected from a large number of Iroquois warriors. The Board's attention was thus diverted, and it in turn reprimanded Johnson for his failure to inform members concerning the Indian matter. The South Carolina Governor discounted the seriousness of the crisis to the Board, but said nevertheless that this was the type of problem that may have contributed partly to the boundary dispute, intensifying and drawing out the matter and making agreement more difficult.

Later, Governor Johnson wrote again to the Board of Trade about the boundary line and asked for a re-interpretation of the Instructions. Simultaneously, he observed that should the Waccamaw River be declared the boundary, it would be extremely inconvenient to South Carolina. He pointed out that the river flowed into Winyah Bay where there was a considerable settlement, and that a collector of customs was located there. The latter, he said, would be powerless to prevent illegal trade, for a ship could travel a short distance into North Carolina and be out of the collector's jurisdiction.[40]

In March 1734/5, in what was possibly his last communication to England on this matter, Johnson noted that commissioners were to be sent from the Province to meet with those from North Carolina to stake out the line. He said that he held out little hope of success, for North Carolina held continually to its erroneous, stated position.

Johnson was not to live long enough to see the fruits of his arguments on the boundary issue. However, the King had been sufficiently impressed with his South Carolina plea to give the new North Carolina governor, Gabriel Johnston, specific orders on the problem. The appointment of commissioners from both provinces was the first Instruction, and after reaching agreement on the main point under dispute, the commissioners on May 1, 1735, began running

[39] Johnson to Board of Trade, September 28, 1732, PR, Vol. XV, pp. 233-4.
[40] Johnson to Board of Trade, December 15, 1732, PR, Vol. XVI, pp. 6-7.

the line at a point thirty miles southwest of the mouth of Cape Fear. By May 30, Lieutenant Governor Thomas Broughton reported on the commissioners' work saying that it was "an amicable Conclusion, so far as they have proceeded."[41] A large pie-shaped area from the mouth of the Waccamaw at Winyah Bay (Georgetown), running eastward of the Waccamaw and containing about eighty miles of seacoast, was retained for South Carolina; and officials of the northern province agreed to this disposition of the matter.[42] In 1763, the line that was begun during Johnson's administration as royal governor was approved by the Crown as the temporary line.[43] But the question over the boundary was not settled until the century following.

---

[41] Message of Thos. Broughton to Commons House of Assembly, JC, Vol. VI, Part 1, pp. 132-3. See also articles agreed to by commissioners of both provinces in Message of the Upper House, May 1, 1735, JC, Vol. VI, Pt. 1, pp. 123-4.

[42] The line was to proceed on a northwest course to the 35th parallel. Commissioners from the two Provinces, either separately or together, ran the line over 100 miles during 1735. See *The Colonial Records of North Carolina,* ed. William L. Saunders (Raleigh: Josephus Daniels, Printer to the State, 1887), Vol. V, p. xxxvii.

[43] Recommendation of the Board of Trade on Instruction to Governor Thomas Boone, March 29, 1763 (approved by the King in Council March 30, 1763), *The State Records of North Carolina,* ed. by Walter Clark (Winston: M. I. & J. C. Stewart, Printers to the State, 1895), Vol. XI, pp. 152-4.

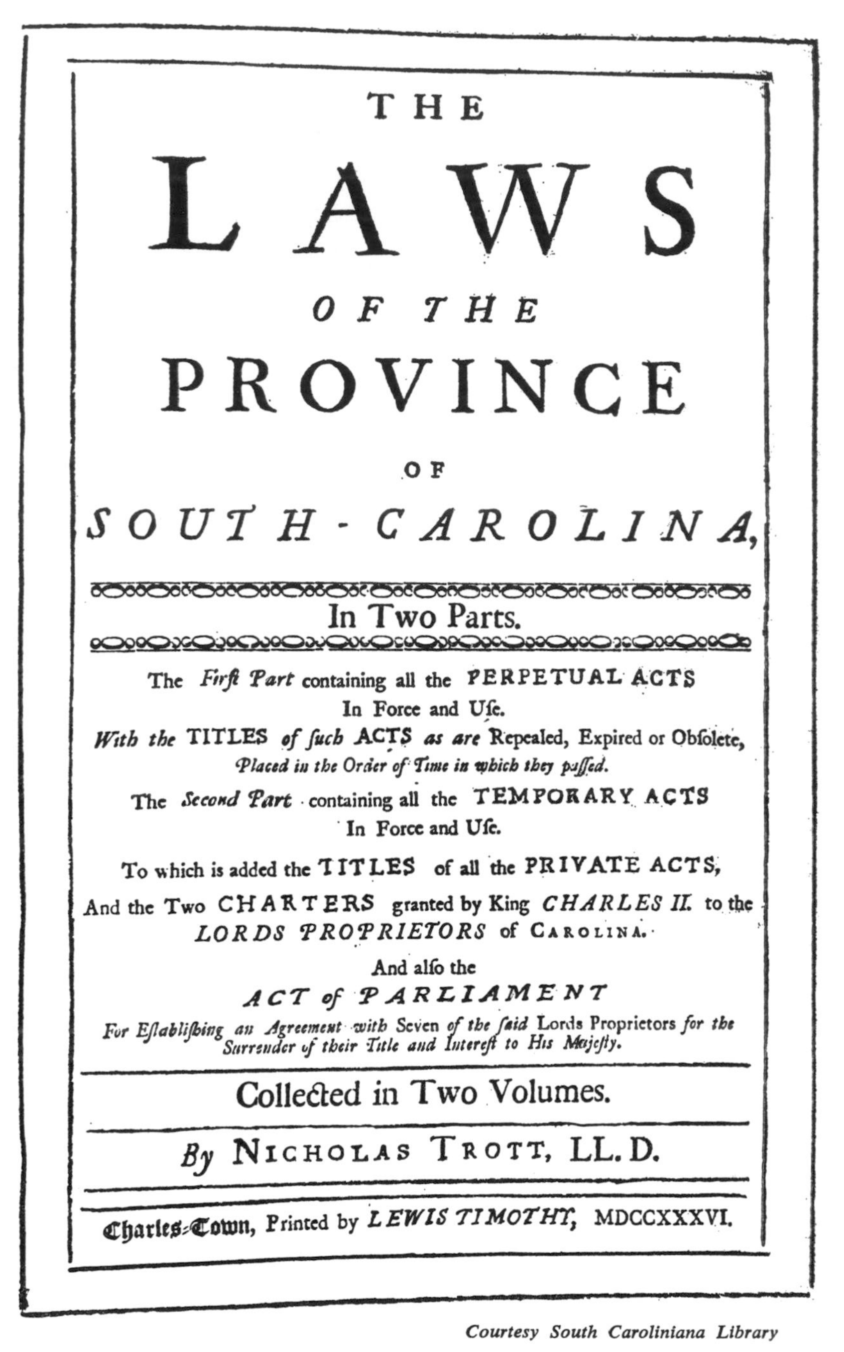

THE

LAWS

OF THE

PROVINCE

OF

SOUTH-CAROLINA,

In Two Parts.

The *First Part* containing all the PERPETUAL ACTS
In Force and Use.
With the TITLES *of such* ACTS *as are* Repealed, Expired or Obsolete,
Placed in the Order of Time in which they passed.
The *Second Part* containing all the TEMPORARY ACTS
In Force and Use.
To which is added the TITLES of all the PRIVATE ACTS,
And the Two CHARTERS granted by King *CHARLES II.* to the
LORDS PROPRIETORS of CAROLINA.
And also the
ACT of PARLIAMENT
For Establishing an Agreement with Seven *of the said* Lords Proprietors *for the Surrender of their Title and Interest to His Majesty.*

Collected in Two Volumes.

By NICHOLAS TROTT, LL.D.

Charles-Town, Printed by *LEWIS TIMOTHY*, MDCCXXXVI.

Courtesy South Caroliniana Library

Title Page of *The Laws of the Province of South Carolina,* compiled by Nicholas Trott and printed by Lewis Timothy. Trott's *Laws* was the first major work published in South Carolina.

CHAPTER XI

Paper Money And Quit Rents

THE insufficiency of a circulating medium for conducting trade and business had been a problem in the Province for some time. The need was most acute in the Indian War when bills of credit amounting to £30,000 were printed and were followed by subsequent issues. Merchants were inclined to object to the paper. Since they had the ear of the Crown, their influence forced the Province in the mid-1720's to make provision for sinking a considerable part of its paper money. The amount totaled £55,000.

The Assembly later changed its mind and wanted to re-issue all that was due for cancellation, but orders had been received from the Crown forbidding any change in the law. The Assembly sent pleas, emphasizing the need to defray the cost of defensive operations and expeditions against enemies of the Province. At the time that Johnson became royal governor, the request had not been acted upon, although the Assembly was insisting on its right. It wanted to re-issue the money and increase the amount in circulation to £140,000 (an amount equivalent to £20,000 sterling). This, it said, was the least amount that would be required to continue the trade of the Province, which the Assembly claimed amounted to £120,000 annually. But President Middleton and Council, bound by the royal command, stubbornly refused consent to such proposals. In return, the Assembly failed to provide tax money to be used for defense; or to engage in any other business. The deadlock had existed for nearly four years when Johnson arrived to take over the government.[1]

Before he left England, Johnson had taken a firm stand on the issue. He said that the number of bills in circulation in South Carolina amounted to £106,354, which he estimated was only a little more than £15,000 sterling. Johnson told the Board that a paper currency was an absolute necessity for the Province because the

---

[1] Johnson to Board of Trade, December 19, 1729, PR, Vol. XIII, pp. 421-2; JC, Vol. V, p. 24 (January 21, 1730/31); S. C. Council to the King, received by Board of Trade, July 7, 1729, PR, Vol. XIII, pp. 274-6; T. Morritt to Secretary of the SPG, September 1, 1729, SPG, Series B, Vol. IV, Part 2.

planters were heavily indebted to the merchants, and these debts were payable in the current paper bills. He emphasized that a decrease in the amount of paper in circulation would bring the remaining bills closer to the value of sterling and thereby ruin at least 19/20ths of the Province's inhabitants, while it would enrich only twenty or thirty persons.[2]

As a large planter himself, Johnson reflected the interests of that group in recommending paper money. Strangely, in view of the merchants' former opposition to paper currency, the Governor was able to secure the support of a group of "Merchants Trading to South Carolina" who memorialized the Board of Trade with a proposal favorable to paper money. These merchants pointed out that the annual exports from South Carolina were nearly £100,000 sterling, while the paper bills amounted to only £15,000 sterling. In addition, they declared that the Province was heavily in debt as a result of the Indian War, and it still had to maintain costly forces on the outskirts. These were matters the merchants had previously chosen to overlook, despite the many times they had been called to their attention by the government of the Province. The merchants then asked that the General Assembly be directed to call in all the old currency, and in its place issue £100,000 in new bills of credit. They proposed further that the law which provided for sinking the paper money be suspended for seven years, and that funds available for that purpose be used to buy tools and provisions for needy Protestant settlers.[3]

Johnson offered some explanation of the merchants' new attitude. He wrote that all the "considerable" merchants engaged in the Carolina trade had been consulted and thought that some paper currency was absolutely necessary because there was little gold or silver to use in its place. On the other hand, if perishable goods like rice, pitch, and tar were made a tender in payment, this would be "highly prejudicial to the Merchants & Trade of that Province." Johnson added that both merchants and planters now desired to retain a paper currency. The lone disagreement, he said, arose over the amount that should be kept in circulation, as in contrast to the

[2] "Col. Johnsons answers to Queries in relation to Paper Currency in South Carolina," received by Board of Trade, March 7, 1729/30, PR, Vol. XIV, pp. 54, 56.

[3] Merchants to Board of Trade, received February 4, 1720/30, PR, Vol. XIV, pp. 32-33.

merchants' suggested limit of £100,000, the planters wanted £140,000.[4]

Johnson, who had previously recommended the current amount of £106,354, proposed that either £105,000 of the existing bills be continued in circulation, or new bills for that amount be issued. He suggested that bills be allowed to circulate for seven years and that, after that time, the Act for sinking the bills be reapplied and £5,000 of the currency retired annually. He recommended further that if duties on Negroes, liquors and other imports—which were set aside for the retirement purpose—proved inadequate, the deficiency be made up from the general tax.

Johnson agreed with the merchants that during the suspension period the funds for sinking the paper money should go to the needy Protestant settlers. He also recommended that in his Instructions, the King should forbid the Governor to approve the suspension unless the proviso was included concerning the new settlers.[5] In effect, Johnson had made the fund another part of his settlement plan, believing it would help to promote new townships.

One article in Governor Johnson's Instructions from the King ordered him to veto an Act for setting up a new paper currency unless an emergency occurred. Even in such a case, he was warned that it must contain a clause suspending its execution until the royal pleasure concerning it had been discerned.[6]

A second article concerned "An Act for Calling in and sinking the Paper Bills." The Instruction read, in part:

> And it hath been represented to Us, that it would be a great Encouragement for the more speedy and effectual settling of Our said Province, if the Assembly were permitted for the Space of Seven Years to apply the Produce of such Revenue arising from that Act, as are now appropriated to the discharge of the old Bills of Credit to the Charge of Surveying and laying out Townships, and to the purchasing of Tools, Provisions, and other Necessaries for any Poor Protestants that shall be desirous to settle in Our said Province: We are graciously pleased to comply with the Request of the Planters and Merchants in this particular, and you are hereby impowered to give your

[4] Johnson, "A State of the Paper Currency in Carolina & a Proposal in Relation to the Same," received by Board of Trade, March 13, 1729/30, PR, Vol. XIV, pp. 63-66.

[5] Johnson, "A State of the Paper Currency," PR, Vol. XIV, pp. 63-67; "Col. Johnsons answers," PR, Vol. XIV, pp. 54-57.

[6] PRO, CO 5:192, pp. 74-75 (Library of Congress transcript).

> assent to a Clause in some Act for suspending the first design of the aforementioned Act, and for applying the said Sinking Fund for the Space of Seven Years to the purposes afores[ai]d.[7]

Then the Crown included a qualifying clause making the Act dependent upon the Assembly's passing a companion, effective law concerning the registering of land grants and the regulating of future quit-rent payments.[8] In this manner, the two issues became dependent upon each other.

Johnson made two recommendations regarding quit rents. He suggested that the Crown, which had paid the Proprietors £5,000 in consideration of their quit rents that were in arrears, might allow others to be put to such uses as the Assembly considered most advantageous for public affairs.

At this time, Province quit rents could be paid in produce, the value being determined by two members each of the Assembly and the Council, and therefore settled at scarcely more than one-fifth proclamation money. Johnson's second recommendation provided that future quit rents should be set at a certain, determined value, and for the future, therefore, should be paid in proclamation money,[9] or in paper money to the value of proclamation money. To "secure this Point effectually for the benefit of the Crown," Johnson proposed that he receive from the King His Majesty's "directive" not to consent to the use of the arrears of quit rents, or the seven-year suspension of the operation of the sinking fund, except on the condition that the future quit rents be secured in full value.[10]

In the Instructions that Johnson received, he was directed that the arrears be disposed of by allowing the Governor to assent to a law for remitting arrears. In this—as in other cases—the Crown was asking a price for its "Royal Bounty and Fatherly indulgence." By the same act, Johnson was instructed, the Assembly was to repeal a law entitled "An Act to ascertain the Prices of Land, the forms of Conveyances and the manner of recovering Rents for Lands, And the Prices of the several Commodities the same shall be paid in." Also, provision was to be made requiring all persons possessing land

---

[7] PRO, CO 5:192, pp. 73-74 (Library of Congress transcript).

[8] PRO, CO 5:192, p. 74 (Library of Congress transcript).

[9] The ratio of proclamation money to sterling was about four to three; that is, four pounds proclamation money equaled approximately three pounds sterling. Meriwether, *Expansion of S. C.*, p. 9n.

[10] Johnson, "A State of the Paper Currency," PR, Vol. XIV, pp. 67-68.

in the Province to register in the office of the Auditor General or his Deputy the grants by which the land was claimed. Two copies of this register, and of all grants made in the future, were to be sent to England. Finally, each person holding land in the Province by virtue of a grant from the Proprietors was in the future to pay the Crown in proclamation money the reserved annual quit rent.[11]

After Johnson's assumption of the royal government, he made these required recommendations to the Assembly, and added others of his own. He pointed out the importance of the measures and gave illustrations of the Crown's beneficence toward South Carolina. The Commons responded favorably by dividing itself into five committees for the examination and discussion of the various problems facing the Province and asked the Council to appoint members to consult with them, which was done.[12]

The Committee of Ways and Means made its report,[13] which was read and considered by the Council. The Council thought the report a "proper Foundation" on which to base bills concerning registering grants, paying quit rents in proclamation money, and "Suspending and Applying the Sinking Fund for payment of the Publick Debts."[14]

Prior to becoming Governor, Johnson had recommended to the Board of Trade that any money in the Sinking Fund be appropriated toward payment of the public debt, to March 25, 1730; and after that date that they be used for settlement purposes.[15]

Neither this nor his later recommendations were accepted, for the Crown did not heed his advice to apply the fund toward the payment of the debts. His Instructions suggested use of the fund for settlement purposes only. Overlooked was Johnson's advice that he be forbidden to approve suspension of the Act, unless the funds for seven years were used for settlement; and the only qualifying clause was concerned with registering grants and paying quit rents.[16]

The same report of the Ways and Means committee that dealt with land grant registration, quit rents, and the Sinking Fund, also

---

[11] PRO, CO 5:192, pp. 72-73 (Library of Congress transcript).

[12] JCHA, p. 619 (February 19, 1730/31); JC, Vol. V, pp. 43-44 (February 19, 20, 1730/31).

[13] JCHA, pp. 625-7 (February 28, 1730/31).

[14] JC, Vol. V, p. 51 (March 2, 1730/31).

[15] "Col. Johnsons answers," PR, Vol. XVI, p. 57. The Commitee on Ways and Means subsequently estimated the public debt at £80,000, and the balance in the Sinking Fund at £37,000. JCHA, p. 625 (February 28, 1730/31).

[16] PRO, CO 5:192, pp. 73-74 (Library of Congress transcript).

suggested the possibility of increasing the currency.[17] The Council opposed this temporarily, preferring to wait and see if local needs required additional currency.[18] Later, a bill was drawn calling in, reprinting, and exchanging paper bills of credit then in circulation.[19] When finally passed, the Act provided for the reprinting of £106,-500 of legal tender paper bills. The commissioners were empowered to exchange the new bills for the old, which were to be burned.[20]

The Assembly's bill for remission of quit rents in arrears was not entirely pleasing to the Council and a committee of both houses was appointed to work out differences. The Commons and Council added amendments to the bill.[21]

One item of disagreement arose when the lower house's version of the bill included a clause providing preferential grants for those "poor persons" who had settled lands without survey and made improvements upon them. Johnson told the Assembly he could not agree to the inclusion of such a clause because his Instructions called for making grants only in proportion to the grantee's ability to cultivate the lands. He said, in fact, that he was directed not to grant anyone more than fifty acres for each person, white or black, in his household. Governor Johnson did promise, however, that once he had proof of the number in a family and improvements made, he would allow them "what just preferrence of favour" he could.[22]

In mid-July, Johnson recommended that the Assembly handle all bills with dispatch, so that it could recess for two or three months until cooler weather, and escape the prevalent fever season. At the same time, Johnson reminded them of the Quit Rent Bill, saying, "And as you are very Senseable the Quit Rent Law is of very great Consequence to the Provinces[,] I must recommend to you to Employ an Agent [in England] to Sollicit that and the other Affairs of the Province." The Duke of Newcastle had already recommended Peregrine Fury as a proper person to serve as Agent for the Province, and Johnson urged the Assembly to select him. He said it

17 JCHA, p. 626 (February 28, 1730/31).

18 JC, Vol. V, pp. 51-52 (March 2, 1730/31).

19 JC, Vol. V, pp. 78-79 (May 12, 1731).

20 *Statutes,* Vol. III, pp. 305-7.

21 JC, Vol. V, pp. 62-64, 67-68, 74-75 (March 24, 1730/31, March 30-31, April 7-8, May 6, 1731).

22 JC, Vol. V, p. 68 (April 8, 1731).

was "highly necessary a person agreeable to his Grace Shall be Employed he having the Superintendency of the American parts in his province as Secretary of State." Johnson also advised setting up a joint committee to correspond with the Agent and send him proper arguments for supporting the Quit Rent Bill and other acts of the Assembly.[23]

On August 20, Johnson gave his assent to the bill for remitting the arrears of quit rents, and to ten other measures.[24] The Quit Rent Act, in general, followed the Crown's directives. It provided for the registering of proprietary patents and grants and for future quit rents, with payments to be made in proclamation money. It also set forth that from the time of the King's approval of the new legislation, the "Act for Ascertaining the Prices of Lands," would be repealed.[25] The withdrawn Act, or "Archdale's Law" of 1696, permitted payment of quit rents in produce, a law of which the people were very fond. In the past, it had been the foundation of disputes between the former Lords Proprietors and the people and had occasioned non-payment of Quit Rents for twenty or more years.

Johnson wrote the Board of Trade that the new Quit Rent Act had taken up much time and had caused much discussion and debate between Council and Assembly. He said he hoped the Crown would approve it and thereby confirm all Proprietary titles despite those titles' deficiency.

The Governor had already experienced personally some difficulty over imperfect land grants, and a patent that Johnson had inherited from his father had been submitted to the Attorney and Solicitor Generals for their opinions. They ruled that the grant was not valid because the location of the lands was not specified and there was nothing in the grant upon which this could be determined.[26] Johnson brought the South Carolina Assembly's attention[27] to this incident, and mentioned it again some months later.[28]

---

[23] JC, Vol. V, p. 112 (July 15, 1731). In representing the Province, the Agent would appear before the Board of Trade and perhaps the Privy Council, but not before Parliament.

[24] JC, Vol. V, p. 148 (August 20, 1731).

[25] *Statutes,* Vol. III, pp. 289-304.

[26] July 28, 1730, PR, Vol. XIV, pp. 246-7. A copy of Sir Nathaniel Johnson's patent (April 1, 1686) for two baronies and the dignity of a cacique is found in PR, Vol. XIV, pp. 80-82.

[27] JC, Vol. V, pp. 53-54 (March 3, 1730/31).

[28] JC, Vol. V, p. 113 (July 15, 1731).

The Governor was unable to win support for excluding large-sized grants of landgraveships, caciqueships and baronies from the Act[29] because many people, following the closing of the land office, had purchased land under patent laws. Therefore, he saw no hope of getting any measures passed until patent titles were confirmed, no matter how deficient the instruments appeared under the law. Under the many sales and conveyances made by patent title, purchasers pleaded equity, as they had paid sizeable amounts and made many improvements. The Assembly pointed out that the law it had agreed to repeal confirmed deficient titles, and Johnson observed to the Board of Trade that since quit rents on patent lands were payable to the King, he and the Council approved the law. He described the law as "what was absolutely necessary for the peace and Tranquillity of the Province," and said that he hoped it would win the Crown's approval.[30]

Further, Johnson gave the Board of Trade notice of the passage of a clause suspending the sinking of the paper bills for seven years. The revenues in this sinking fund, accumulated from the duties on Negroes, liquors, and other imports, had reached a total of £40,-000, which was to be applied toward the payment of the debts and charges of government amounting to £104,775-1s-3d. New bills of credit to this latter amount were to be printed, he said.

Duties were averaging £13,000 per year, Johnson reported, of which £5,000 was to be appropriated annually for aiding and subsisting new settlers and for the expense of laying out townships.

---

[29] Johnson to Board of Trade, November 14, 1731, PR, Vol. XV, pp. 33-35.

[30] Johnson to Board of Trade, November 14, 1731, PR, Vol. XV, pp. 33-35. It should be noted that the Proprietors *sold* land, whereas the Crown *gave* land subject to annual rent; thus a "land office" was not needed in a royal colony. Johnson, later, in his defense of the Quit Rent Act, observed that there were other patent grants that were not so deficient as his own, since his grant did "not so much as name the province it is whether South or North Carolina, nor indeed any Carolina at all." In such a situation, Johnson thought it permissible to "infer that perhaps if fuller grants had been shown to the Attorney Gen. his opinion might have varied." Johnson to Board of Trade, September 28, 1732, PR, Vol. XV, p. 231.

It should also be mentioned here that while the determination of Johnson's grant had been by law officers' opinion, some years earlier a chancery court decision in the Province had confirmed purchases made under an inherited patent grant. Plats of these purchases, as well as of future sales under the grant, were to be returned to the office of the Surveyor General, who was ordered to certify them. Obviously, although by implication, this decision necessarily assumed the validity of inherited patent grants. Ruscoe *v.* Trench (1726), in Gregorie, *Records of the Court of Chancery of S. C.*, pp. 323-5.

The remainder was to be applied toward the payment of the public debts during the seven-year suspension period.[31]

Opposition to this arrangement was forthcoming from the merchants trading with Carolina. They chose to center their attack on the Appropriation Act, but the motives behind their antagonism antedated the passage of the act. Even before Johnson had left England, London and Bristol merchants had petitioned the Board of Trade to eliminate the South Carolina import duty on Negroes.[32]

It was recommended that Johnson try to change the duty law, so that it would be paid by the purchaser rather than the importer. Payment of duties by importers, it was declared, discouraged the importation of Negroes,[33] and that, of course, was a prime purpose of the law; it had not been designed as a revenue-producing measure. If it were changed to facilitate importation of Negroes, the full effect of Johnson's defense scheme (which was directed against internal as well as external foes), might well be nullified. Consequently, the South Carolina Assembly chose to apply Negro and other import duties to discourage more slaves being brought in.

Immediately, the issue became more complicated. After passage of the Appropriation Act—but before it had gained the attention of the Crown—Governor Johnson received Instructions from Newcastle not to consent to any law imposing duties on Negroes imported from Africa or felons from England. Johnson replied that he would take care to obey the order in the future, but advised that such a law was already in force in the Province. Because £5,000 of the duties were to be used annually for the encouragement of settlement, Johnson said he hoped the merchants would not go so far as to ask for the disallowance of the Appropriation Act.[34]

The matter was not settled easily or quickly. The English merchants continued to push the issue, and two years afterwards the Governor, Council, and Assembly sent two communications to the

---

[31] Johnson to Board of Trade, November 14, 1731, PR, Vol. XV, pp. 35-36; *Statutes,* Vol. III, pp. 289-304, 334-41. There is a £500 discrepancy concerning the use of the £13,000, between the Quit Rent Act and the Appropriation Act.

[32] Petition from several merchants of London and Bristol trading to South Carolina, to the Board of Trade [no date], PR, Vol. XIV, pp. 75-76.

[33] PRO, CO 5:192, p. 114 (Library of Congress transcript).

[34] Johnson to [Newcastle], June 25, 1732, PR, Vol. XV, p. 133; Johnson to Board of Trade, June 26, 1732, PR, Vol. XV, pp. 135-6. *See also* Robert K. Ackerman, "Colonial Land Policies and the Slave Problem," *Proceedings,* South Carolina Historical Association (1965), p. 32.

Crown on the matter. They maintained that even ordinary expenses of government could not be met unless the King allowed the Appropriation Act to stand,[35] and said if the act were repealed, "the poor protestant families must go back disappointed who had expected the bounty." Concerning the slave problem, they stated significantly:

> The Importation of Negroes . . . is a Species of Trade that has exceedingly increased of late in this Province where many Negroes are now trained up to be Handicraft Tradesmen, to the great discouragement of Your Majestys white Subjects, who came here to settle with a View of Employment in their several Occupations, but must often give way to a People in Slavery which we daily discover to be a great Obstruction to the Settlement of this Frontier with white People.[36]

One month later, Johnson emphasized the whole matter to the King, saying he feared it would be extremely difficult to obtain the necessary sum of £104,775 by any means but the Appropriation Act. He said he did not feel that the money could be raised by a tax on land and slaves, and that import duties were essential if provision were to be made for subsisting newcomers.[37]

In England, meanwhile, the merchants had become alarmed when they heard a report that the South Carolina Assembly might pass a law to prohibit importation of Negro slaves if the Appropriation Act were voided. They asked the Crown to instruct the Governor specifically not to permit such action, declaring that slave importation was necessary to preserve "part of a Branch of Trade, which has been always Judged highly valuable to Great Britain, by the Extending and Better Settling of his Majestys Plantations in America."[38]

The issue finally reached the Privy Council which rendered a decision in October 1735 to let the Appropriation Act stand, but on a probationary basis. In effect, this was a victory for South Carolina. At the same time that it ruled on the Appropriation Act, the Privy

---

[35] Memorial and Representation from Governor, Council, and Assembly of South Carolina, to the King, April 9, 1734, PR, Vol. XVI, p. 399.

[36] Remonstrance from Governor, Council, and Assembly of South Carolina, to the King, April 9, 1734, PR, Vol. XVI, pp. 382-3.

[37] Johnson to A. Popple, May 24, 1734, PR, Vol. XVI, pp. 336-7.

[38] Wm. Wood (on behalf of Bristol traders) to [Popple], September 10, 1734, PR, Vol. XVII, pp. 32-33. Obviously there was quite a difference of opinion between the English traders and Governor Johnson on what type of settlers the Province wanted.

Council approved the recommendation made by the Board of Trade that duties should be applied first to settlement.[39]

Several months before, the South Carolina Assembly had passed an act to that effect as the £5,000 appropriation per annum had proved insufficient for settlement purposes. The Assembly accepted the recommendation of Johnson to apply the funds during the entire period set by the original law, but confirmation was delayed because the Governor "was so extremely ill, in fact so bad, that his life was despaired of." The bill was signed in June 1735, however, by Lieutenant Governor Thomas Broughton.[40]

---

[39] October 13, 1735, PR, Vol. XVII, pp. 392-4.

[40] *Statutes,* Vol. III, pp. 409-11; Extract of Letter from Samuel Eveleigh to George Morley, May 1, 1735, PR, Vol. XVII, p. 340.

THE PREFACE.

W*HEN first I made a Collection of the* LAWS of the Province of SOUTH-CAROLINA, *it was designed only for my own Use, and I had then no Thoughts of publishing the same. But afterwards being desired, and encouraged by his present Excellency* ROBERT JOHNSON Esq; *Governor, and the Honourable the Council and Assembly of the Province, I undertook to make this Collection of the* LAWS *to be published for general Use, and accordingly I have now made the following Edition of them.*

As to the Method and Design of the Work, tho' the same may be understood by the Title Page, and is so plain and easy, that I suppose it needs little Explication; however I think it will be necessary, by way of Preface, to say something of it.

Immediately after this Preface, *I have added an* Historical Introduction, *wherein, after having mentioned the two* Charters *granted from the Crown to the* Lords Proprietors, *which are afterwards exemplified at large, I have given an Account of the several* Fundamental Constitutions *agreed upon by the then* Lords Proprietors, *as a Scheme or Model of Government, and designed to be passed into a fundamental unalterable* Law, *but was never done.*

Then follows the Succession of the Governours *from* Coll. WIL-

b LIAM

Courtesy South Caroliniana Library

Preface to Trott's *Laws*

CHAPTER XII

St. John And The Quit Rent Law

PAPER bills had received such acceptance in the Province that their value had remained constant for nine or ten years.[1] In 1731 the Commons House Ways and Means Committee proposed doubling the amount in circulation, but action was postponed until the next meeting of the Assembly to allow for full discussion.[2]

The subject was sidetracked, however, after the question of quit rents came violently to the fore in the form of an Assembly dispute with James St. John, surveyor general of the Province. The Quit Rent Act had not met with universal approval, and St. John had emerged as chief spokesman for the dissidents.

He not only voiced his objections in the Province, but bypassed the Governor, Council, and Commons House and sent his opinions directly to British authorities. His actions showed that he failed to understand the prevailing state of mind in South Carolina. A Province which had just effected a successful revolution against a group of Lords Proprictors had no intention of bowing down before a mediocrity the size of St. John. His actions aroused the full fury of the Commons House.

At about the same time that the Commons House received from the Council the Surveyor General's communications on laying out eleven townships, it noted that some persons were writing, or planning to write, to England to voice objections to the Quit Rent law.

A committee of both houses was appointed to consider St. John's Memorials, and he was ordered to attend the Governor and Council to hear the report, which dealt with two matters. First, on his recommendations concerning surveying the townships, the Assembly decided that the Governor should appoint officers to select sites for the townships along the various rivers, and name the towns. The body thought this method expedient in view of the uncertainties attending the arrival of settlers. The Governor's appointees were to draw up a plan of each respective town, which, if approved by

[1] Their ratio to sterling was seven to one.

[2] Johnson to Board of Trade, November 14, 1731, PR, Vol. XV, pp. 35-36; JCHA, p. 626 (February 28, 1730/31).

the Governor, was to be a rule for the Surveyor General in running out the lots when the settlers arrived. The fees for the Surveyor General were to be provided through the Appropriation Act. The Act also suspended temporarily the sinking of paper bills so that bounties could be offered new township settlers who could have their lots free of charge.

To do this surveying, St. John was demanding one penny in proclamation money per acre for the six-mile reserve contiguous to the township, in addition to the 20,000 acres of the township itself. The committee calculated that on this basis, surveying about 138,-000 acres for each township and environs would cost more than the Province could bear immediately—about £25,000 Carolina money. Such expense would, in fact, frustrate the plan of encouraging newcomers to enter those lands free of cost. The committee said it was not trying to deny the Surveyor General his fees; it proposed paying him the full sum when the townships were peopled.[3]

The Governor and Assembly hoped to stagger surveying costs by meeting initial expenses for general township outlines and paying for individual surveys as settlers arrived. St. John, on the other hand, wanted detailed surveys on each township as soon as possible, and expected to be paid on a per-acre basis for marking off the six-mile-reserve contiguous to each township. The Assembly pointed out that survey marks were perishable. If individual surveys were made immediately, the work would have to be done again for settlers arriving three years later, and, the Province would have to pay twice for the surveying—a notion which St. John did not appear to oppose.

The second part of the report dealt with St. John's opposition to the Quit Rent bill. He made public statements that he intended to write to "Some persons of his Majesty's Ministry"[4] to secure disallowance of the measure. Since the act was considered of such importance, the committee said it desired the Governor to interrogate St. John before the Council to learn what his objections were. Its reason, the committee said, was "that we [the Assembly] may have an Opportunity of either amending the Said Law or otherwise be Enabled to Instruct our Agent to Support the Same." If St. John refused, the committee felt that the Crown would "look upon Such a procedure as Acting ex parte."

---

[3] JC, Vol. V, pp. 154-156 (November 19, 1731); JCHA, pp. 811-813 (November 19, 1731).

[4] JC, Vol. V, pp. 151-152 (November 18, 1731).

Although the Commons House was sensitive to criticism, it was not trying to stifle voices raised in opposition to the Quit Rent law. There were other, very good reasons, a chief one being that it objected to anyone writing to England concerning laws without its knowledge. Due to the slowness of communication, the house was concerned that British authorities might be unduly influenced on hearing only one side of a case, and did not want important legislation acted on without its knowledge. Unless the agent could be instructed in advance, he would be helpless to do more than stall proceedings until the Assembly was heard from. But St. John duly appeared before the Governor and Council, and was requested at his convenience to present a copy of the objections he planned to send to England.[5]

It was customary when controversy arose for the Governor to transmit the varying opinions to the Crown, after both sides had read and commented upon the other's case. This method eliminated secret reports and discouraged the submission of additional reports by either side.

As to the case in question, the Assembly viewed it as especially serious since St. John held his commission from the Crown. It construed it as a part of the continuing struggle between royal prerogative and its privilege as a governing body. St. John either did not understand this struggle or chose to ignore it, thinking that his supporters in England were powerful enough to raise him above the whole issue.

After this first meeting, Johnson wrote to the Board of Trade but did not mention the Surveyor General or the disagreement with him, hoping to settle the matter within the Province. Johnson spoke of the Quit Rent Act, referring to it "in a Manner almost suspended" until he had received the King's directions. Until the King's pleasure could be learned, the Governor advised that he was refusing to grant warrants for surveying or laying out lands claimed by patents from the Proprietors, because he feared it might strengthen their titles. At the same time, he said he found that people were slow in regis-

---

[5] JC, Vol. V, pp. 156-7 (November 19, 1731); JCHA, pp. 811-3 (November 19, 1731). The Assembly, naturally enough, was unfavorably disposed toward any individual or group trying to bypass the established chain of command.

tering their titles until they found out whether the Quit Rent law was to stand. Johnson asked an early decision from the Crown.[6]

Governor Johnson knew how to control the Assembly, but he never underestimated its potential. He did underestimate, or misjudge, St. John. In his first message to the Board of Trade, Johnson should have stated the case against St. John, or at least, recounted the Surveyor General's actions, such as his obdurate refusal to survey the townships in the manner specified by the Governor, Council and Assembly. Later, in his own defense, Johnson was forced to make complaint because St. John, besides attacking the Assembly, made personal accusations against the chief executive. Unfortunately, St. John's charges reached British authorities before they had any complaint about his misconduct from either Johnson or the legislative body of the Province.

Because Johnson failed to take the offensive, he unwittingly put himself and his government on the defensive, taking the edge off the charges when he did make them finally against St. John. The Governor's mistake not only hurt him with English officialdom at the time, but later compromised his reputation with historians. Johnson, at first, delayed action because St. John held a royal commission. His failure to act until too late was predicated on the Governor's optimism that the matter could be settled within the Province.

St. John's refusal to survey the townships as ordered had brought forth a reaction from the Commons House. It appointed a joint committee to look into the fees allowed by law to the Surveyor General.[7] The committee reported that as the law failed to provide

---

[6] Johnson to Board of Trade, December 16, 1731, PR, Vol. XV, pp. 67-68. For accounts extremely critical of the Quit Rent Act, and which also are exceedingly hostile toward Johnson, but most favorable to St. John, *see* W. Roy Smith, *South Carolina as a Royal Province, 1719-1776* (New York: The Macmillan Co., pp. 34-48, and Beverley W. Bond, Jr., *The Quit-Rent System in the American Colonies* (New Haven: Yale University Press, 1919), pp. 318-49. Both of these writers tend to look upon the Governor, Council and Assembly as land speculators, who had their schemes opposed by St. John and Whitaker, two public-spirited citizens, eager to protect the interest of the Crown and the welfare of the inhabitants.

[7] JC, Vol. V, p. 161 (January 28, 1731/2). Johnson, at first, made no report to the Board of Trade against St. John because the latter held a royal Commission. His later failure to act, predicated on Johnson's optimism that the matter could be settled within the Province, was evidence that the Governor had misjudged the character of his antagonist, St. John. St. John had apparently taken the Surveyor General's office because he believed it was a lucrative position. His determination to profit from the office did not remove him far from other royal officials in America with similar designs; but he was more insistent than most in achieving his own ends.

fees for the deputy surveyors, those for the Surveyor General were "given in full Satisfaction of the Fees and perquisites, and all other Demands whatsoever that may happen, or arise to The Surveyor Genll., or his Deputys on running out any Lands within This Province." St. John had taken for himself the full fee for lands run out by the deputies, the deputies receiving their fees from the persons for whom the lands were surveyed, at a rate of two pence per acre in Carolina money, or three pounds per day.[8]

After he finally decided to complain about St. John, Governor Johnson called attention to the Surveyor General's practice of keeping for himself the entire survey payment fee from the Province. In order to have their lands run out, the people had agreed to pay the deputies, although it was contrary to the law's intention and the practice of former surveyors. Their policy had been to give half their fee to the deputy surveyor. During St. John's tenure as surveyor general, every person who received lands from the King had to pay at least six pence—and some paid eight pence—per acre for the survey, which Johnson observed made the Assembly and the people "very uneasy."[9]

The joint committee discovered that after a settler had been granted a warrant for lands, and before he could have the use of them, he was required by the Surveyor General to take out a precept to the deputy surveyor through payment of a fee, although no such fee was permitted by law. Besides, the grantee was forced by the Surveyor General to take out a separate precept for each parcel of land located in a different county.

The committee recommended that a bill be drawn up to prevent similar abuses in the future, eliminating irregularities in the Surveyor General's office, and to insure that no undue preference be given in certain cases. The committee proposed that the bill require the deputy surveyors to write down "in words" at length, and record in their office the course and distances of all plats.[10] A bill incorporat-

---

[8] JC, Vol. V, p. 161 (January 28, 1731/2). By an act passed in 1721, the Surveyor General was allowed one penny per acre in proclamation money for running out land. The fee was changed to four pence Carolina money in April, 1733, when it was specifically stated that the Surveyor General would pay half the four pence per acre to his deputies, who actually did the survey work. Numerous other fees were also collected by the Surveyor General. *Statutes,* Vol. III, pp. 343-7.

[9] Johnson to Board of Trade, June 26, 1732, PR, Vol. XV, p. 136.

[10] JC, Vol. V, p. 161 (January 28, 1731/2).

ing the committee recommendations was drawn up and passed by the Commons House. The Commons also read and passed a bill extending the time for land claimants to register their titles with the Auditor General and to confirm grants, a measure designed "for the ease and quiet of His Majties Subjects, against all pretended Concealm[en]ts of Titles."[11]

On receiving word of these bills, St. John requested that he receive copies and that he be heard. Both requests were granted.[12] At this date, the Governor and Council were still treating St. John with the utmost regard and respect. The Commons House requested that the Surveyor General be questioned by Johnson, who said afterward that he and the Council thought the result "so very reasonable that we make no doubt but you will Look upon it as Satisfactory."[13]

The lower house, however, was not mollified. Its appointed committee found St. John guilty of extreme partiality in executing warrants for surveying land, as he gave undue preference to some and postponed others without cause. The House committee also complained of St. John's order restricting his deputies to specified districts and refusing to let them work in other areas.[14]

Notwithstanding these and similar charges, the Council once more defended St. John, saying that the Assembly's charges were both unilateral and too general. Since its own members had not helped to conduct the inquiry, the Council demurred saying "to Stigmatize an Officer of His Majesty in so considerable an Employment without being our Selves well Satisfyed the Facts charg'd are true, and giving him (if he desires) an opportunity to acquit himself."[15]

Despite this, St. John's case was to take a downward turn from about that time forward, and very soon he lost the support of the Governor and Council.

Once again St. John was asked to lay out the eleven townships, his remuneration to be at the rate of £500 Carolina money for each. Once again St. John refused, demanding instead the rate of four pence Carolina money, per acre. The sum required, on St.

---

[11] JC, Vol. V, p. 169 (February 12, 1731/2).

[12] JC, Vol. V, p. 170 (February 16, 1731/2).

[13] JC, Vol. V, p. 172 (February 17, 1731/2).

[14] JC, Vol. V, p. 177 (March 2, 1731/2).

[15] JC, Vol. V, pp. 179-180 (March 3, 1731/2); JCHA, pp. 870-71 (March 3, 1731/2).

John's terms, would have amounted to £25,344 exclusive of other costly expenses and charges specified by the Surveyor General.

Laying out the townships was of prime interest to the Governor, and had been ordered by the King; furthermore, it was imperative to prevent private persons from running out lands in the township areas. Since the Province at that time could not pay the large amount the Surveyor General demanded, it had to find a way to have the work done at lower cost. To resolve the crisis, the Council members turned surveyors. Chief Justice Robert Wright and Alexander Skene were directed to mark out three townships on the Black, Peedee and Waccamaw Rivers. Francis Yonge was designated to lay out one at Savannah Town and another at the Congarees. Colonel William Bull was instructed to mark out Purrysburg township on the Savannah River, at a site selected by Jean Pierre Purry, and Thomas Waring was to run out a township at the head of the Pon Pon River. These Councilmen-Surveyors were ordered to return plats of their work to the Council, and £500 Carolina currency would be allowed for each township marked off.[16]

Later, after Francis Yonge had made plans to go to England as the Province's Agent, Henry Yonge was substituted in his place to lay out the Congarees' township; and it was ordered that additional townships be marked out by John Baily and George Hunter. One was to adjoin the Congarees and to extend on the south side of the Santee in the direction of Mill Creek. The other was to be located at the mouth of the Wateree River.[17]

At the time the Councilmen began their surveys, St. John probably still could have had the job of running out the townships if he had offered to do the work at the government's price. Instead, he remained obdurate, although by then it was evident that he could not set his own terms. As a result of his stubbornness, St. John lost a considerable sum of money that normally would have been his, but was promised future survey work for the individual settlers entering new townships. Disgruntled, the Surveyor General used his leisure time in April 1732 to write the Board of Trade about practices in granting lands and remitting and collecting quit rents which were, in his opinion, of "a very peculiar and extraordinary nature."[18]

[16] JC, Vol. V, pp. 192-3 (March 10, 1731/2).

[17] JC, Vol. V, pp. 322-3 (June 7, 1733).

[18] St. John to Board of Trade, April 6, 1732, PR, Vol. XV, p. 111.

It was not long before Council members began to return their plans of the surveys of the townships, for which they were paid.[19] In his report to the Board of Trade late in June 1732, the first time Johnson mentioned St. John's conduct to the Board, the Governor noted that six townships had already been laid out by Council members. He also observed that these surveys done for the £500 consideration included the limits of the six miles around the townships, whereas St. John had insisted on being paid on a per acre basis.[20]

St. John continued to complain at home and in messages sent abroad that all of the townships had not been laid out. Councilman Alexander Skene, who visited St. John at the request of the Governor and Council, made affidavit that he had received the impression that St. John would consider undertaking the work at Council's figure; but later St. John refused to do so. Called to appear before the Governor and Council, he was reminded of his refusal to do the work except on his own terms. At St. John's charge that delayed township surveys were holding up individual grant surveys, the Council countered that his exorbitant fees were more likely the cause of the hindering. Councilman Thomas Waring told St. John that he had heard numerous people cite high fees as the chief reason for not having run out their lands.[21]

Nevertheless, the Council appointed a committee to consider St. John's complaints. Its subsequent report, reciting events leading up to the Governor's appointment of Council members as township surveyors, pointed out that it was the Governor's prerogative to appoint anyone he thought capable to do the surveying. The report also denied any encroachment on the Surveyor General's office because his fees were derived through parceling and distributing lands to the inhabitants.[22]

St. John made further complaints. He charged that persons holding patent grants from the Proprietors were daily running out lands, but were filing no returns of the surveys in his office. In reply, the Governor and Council tried to embarrass him for his opposition to the Quit Rent Law. They observed that patentees registering their plots [plats] in the office of the Surveyor General did not show what

---

[19] JC, Vol. V, p. 202 (June 2, 1732).

[20] Johnson to Board of Trade, June 26, 1732, PR, Vol. XV, pp. 137-8.

[21] JC, Vol. V, pp. 210-11 (October 6, 1732).

[22] JC, Vol. V, pp. 234-7 (November 24, 1732).

rents were due the Crown. Under the provisions of the Quit Rent Act, they said, all persons, including patentees, were required to register their lands and the tenure by which the lands were held. This law served thereby the vital purpose of enabling a rent roll to be drawn up for the King, the officials reminded.[23]

During this time, dissatisfaction grew throughout the Province over St. John's conduct of his office. The Governor and Council, disturbed over "the General Clamour and uneasiness of the Inhabitants" caused by the Surveyor General and his deputies' excessive fees, again called St. John before them for questioning.[24]

When St. John was asked why he retained for himself the whole four pence per-acre fee allowed by law for running out lands and allowed his deputies to take further fees from the people, he acknowledged the amount of his fee but said he was not aware of what his deputies took. St. John was then asked why, without authorization, he claimed fees for precepts, and on a number of occasions, on the same warrant. To this he replied that he took no precept fees, but did not know about his clerks. Further, St. John denied the accusation that he detained plats, even though they were demanded and on which fees were paid. When he was asked why he and his deputies received more than twice the fifty shilling fee for each plat and certificate allowed by law, St. John denied that this was true. The Governor and Council thereupon responded that St. John's deputies were taking such fees and that the Surveyor General was responsible for the actions of his deputy surveyors. At this stricture, St. John replied, "If they did what they could not answer [for] they ought to Suffer for it."[25]

If, as St. John pretended, he knew little about what his subordinates were doing, the reason may have been his preoccupation with other matters. Besides his extensive letter-writing to England, he had assumed a new title for himself and had become active in another phase of Provincial affairs, one involving patents and grants.

---

[23] JC, Vol. V, p. 217 (November 10, 1732).

[24] JC, Vol. V, p. 199 (June 1, 1732).

[25] JC, Vol. V, pp. 201-2 (June 2, 1732).

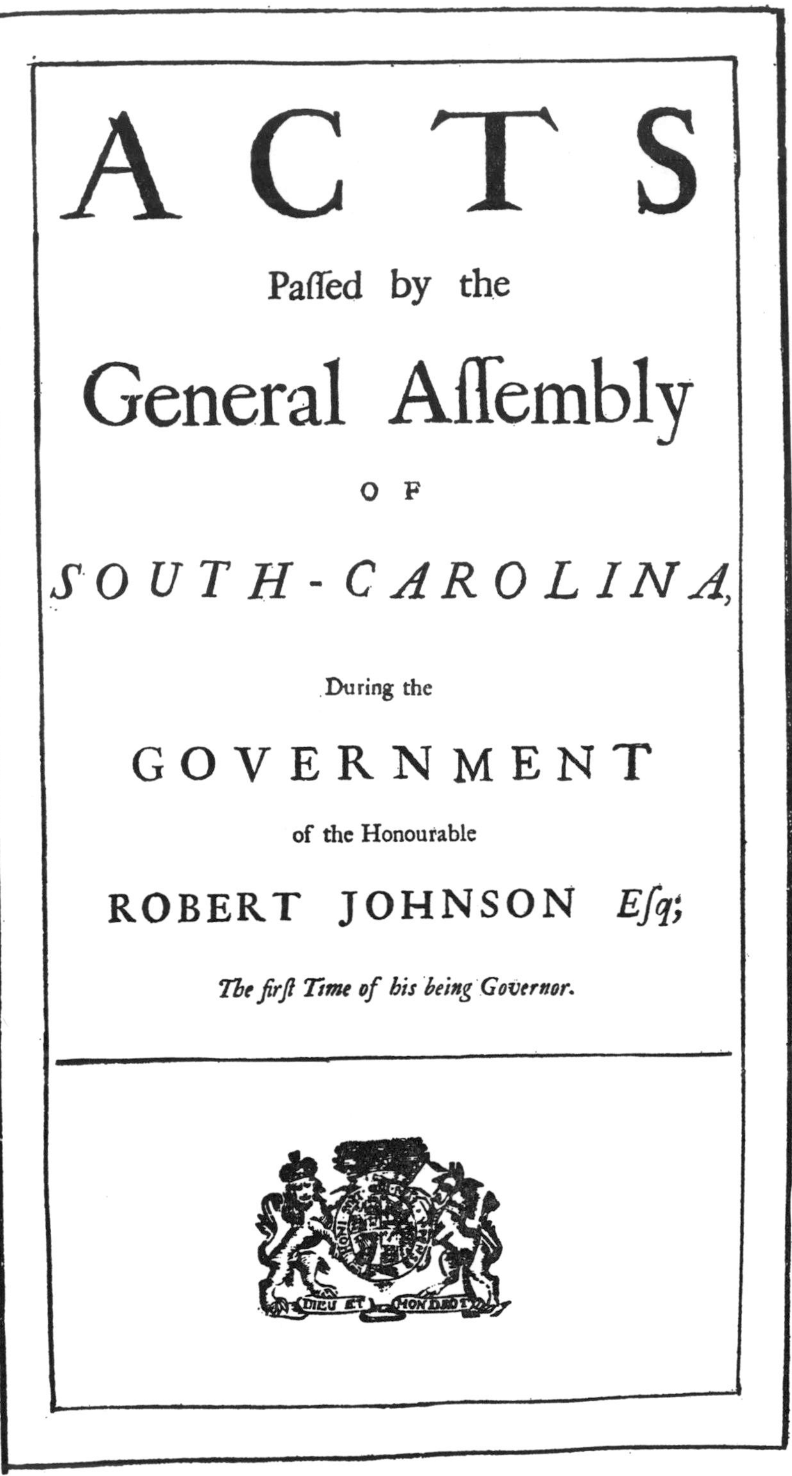

ACTS

Paſſed by the

General Aſſembly

OF

SOUTH-CAROLINA,

During the

GOVERNMENT

of the Honourable

ROBERT JOHNSON *Eſq;*

The firſt Time of his being Governor.

Courtesy South Caroliniana Library

Acts Passed by the General Assembly during the Government of Robert Johnson, a Leaf from Trott's *Laws*.

CHAPTER XIII

Another Clash With St. John

A NEW dispute soon erupted over an additional office that St. John assumed separately from his commission as Surveyor General. Under the Quit Rent Law, passed in August 1731, all persons were required to register within eighteen months their deeds and titles in the office of the King's auditor or his deputy. As a follow up to this, in November a notice was published that James St. John was the Auditor General of the Province and that people were required to register their grants and patents at his office. The notice was signed by George Rolfe, who styled himself "Deputy Auditor." When asked if Rolfe were the deputy of Horatio Walpole, Auditor General of America, St. John replied that Walpole held no claim as Auditor of South Carolina because his patent had been given prior to the Crown's purchase of the Province. His statement was immediately challenged by John Hammerton, Secretary of the Province, who claimed that he alone had the right of registering such official documents.[1]

This dispute led to a St. John memorial, and on the last day of May 1732, he appeared by invitation before the Governor and Council. In support of his claim to registering titles, St. John produced a writ from Walpole appointing him as his deputy. St. John was asked why he had acted as auditor general for more than six months without establishing his authority to do so, and why he had not taken the oaths required by Parliamentary statute. St. John answered that he had informed the Governor of Walpole's deputation and that the notice had been published in all the parish churches. Johnson, facing St. John, flatly denied the statement, saying that he knew nothing of the deputation until he read St. John's memorial of May 29. The notice signed by Rolfe was then held up and St. John was asked if that was what he meant when he said he had published his deputation. He replied that it was.

St. John was next asked why he had assumed the title of Auditor General, claiming an appointment from the King, when his appoint-

[1] Johnson to Board of Trade, January 8, 1732/3, PR, Vol. XVI, pp. 29-30.

ment as deputy was by Walpole. St. John replied peculiarly that the notice was published without his order. In answer to why he had not taken the oaths qualifying himself as deputy auditor, he said he had already taken them as surveyor general, and thought there was no need to do so again. He was prepared to subscribe at any time, since they were required, he said, and at that point the oaths were administered.

The interrogation, however, was not over. St. John was asked why he had assumed the authority to appoint a deputy auditor when he was but Walpole's deputy. St. John did not answer as he had grown tired of being questioned. He told Council to put any questions it might have in writing and he would answer in the same fashion.

He was informed that such was not the usual proceeding of Council, and reminded sharply that the Governor was given the power "to inspect into the conduct, behaviour, and capacity of the officers, to call them to an account, and to suspend them in case of misbehaviour." Council demanded that he then and there answer the question. St. John still refused to answer.

Regarding his failure to provide Council with copies of his letters to England complaining of mistreatment at its hands and that of the Governor, St. John answered that he did not think he had kept any. It was recalled to him that he had been offered the job of marking out of townships at £500 each, but St. John refused to admit that this was true. He maintained instead that an offer had been made to him by Johnson in which he would share the fees with the Council. Alexander Skene interrupted St. John to ask how he could make such a statement when, at the Governor's request, he had spent more than an hour with him trying to persuade him to lay out the eleven townships for £5,500. The Governor and Council forthwith denied that any such proposal had been made in which Council would share surveying fees; and then reprimanded the Surveyor General for his extravagant demand of more than £25,000 to lay out the townships.

Immediately, St. John was told that he was guilty of misconduct, because he had neither produced the deputation nor qualified for the position of deputy auditor, thus being liable to forfeiture of the post and a large fine. St. John replied, "What you please."

An effort was made to resume the questioning, but St. John refused to be queried *viva voce,* saying he would not permit the clerk to record his statements. After St. John had left the chamber, George Rolfe was brought before Council. Rolfe stated that he had received orders from St. John to sign the notice as Deputy Auditor, since he [St. John] claimed the post of Auditor General of the Province, but acknowledged that he had no written deputation from St. John.[2] Two days later, Council reviewed St. John's having acted as Auditor General without having announced his deputation and being sworn into office. It then passed a resolution charging that St. John was guilty of a misdemeanor.[3]

The same afternoon, Council examined some of St. John's activities as Surveyor General, and passed another resolution forbidding him to certify irregular plats in the future. Council also served notice that it was on guard to St. John's halting some plats that he said were not properly surveyed, whereas he had certified others with identical deficiencies.[4]

If St. John was in any way affected by this strong criticism, he showed only vexation, not regret, and made little, if any, basic changes in the conduct of his offices. About nine months later, Council requested him for the third, (and it emphasized, the last time), to remit a copy of his "Powers & Instructions" from Walpole, adding that noncompliance would be his responsibility. St. John at last complied, sending copies of his Commission and Instructions.[5]

During this activity, St. John made complaint of patentees running out lands without returning them in his office. The Governor and Council replied that following St. John's arrival to assume his post, and His Excellency's Proclamation forbidding patents,[6] they knew of none on the Governor's orders. The only exception was Lord Carteret, they said, whose right was protected when the Province was surrendered to the King. The Surveyor General was advised that if he knew of any other baronies run out by unqualified

[2] JC, Vol. V, pp. 195-8 (May 31, 1732).

[3] JC, Vol. V, p. 200 (June 2, 1732).

[4] JC, Vol. V, p. 201 (June 2, 1732).

[5] JC, Vol. V, p. 287 (March 14, 1732/3).

[6] A copy of the proclamation may be found in Douglas C. McMurtrie, *A Bibliography of South Carolina Imprints, 1731-1740* (Charleston: Privately printed, 1933), p. 5, and in Douglas C. McMurtrie, *Four South Carolina Imprints of MDCCXXXI, Together with Complete Facsimiles of These Imprints from the Presses of George Webb and Thomas Whitmarsh* (Chicago: John Calhoun Club, 1933), No. 1.

persons, he should inform the Attorney General of the Province whose instructions were to prosecute such offenders.[7]

Later, St. John requested the establishment of a Court of Exchequer, and Council complied, appointing Chief Justice Robert Wright as chief baron of the court. It also named several assistant judges who were appointed puisne barons. Orders were given that messages be sent to the Duke of Newcastle and to the Board of Trade informing them of this action and of the Province's need for a regular court of that type.[8]

St. John's troubles were not over. He was again placed on the firing line when the Governor put before Council a letter he had sent St. John, instructing him to furnish an account of the lands marked out in compliance with the Governor's warrants. St. John had replied that he would not place his office records before the Council, or allow them out of his possession, although he would supply information concerning a particular record at the Council's request.[9] Council protested to St. John that his refusal to open his records left the Governor and Council uninformed on how the lands were set out. This action, the house told him, was contrary to the King's Instruction empowering the Governor to inquire into the behavior of all officers and to suspend any of them if need be.

The Council thereupon resolved that St. John was guilty of contempt of the King's orders and of the Governor's authority in the Province. Again Governor Johnson sent a letter to St. John, calling upon him to report what lands were run out under the Chief Executive's order and to enumerate those set out on the Surveyor General's order without warrants from the Governor.[10]

By then the Council's patience with St. John was exhausted. It made a representation to the Governor reciting St. John's actions in pretending to be auditor general, and his mishandling of his position as Surveyor General. Council said that he had been treated with favor and indulgence, but there had been so many complaints made against him that it believed he was guilty of "partiality and unfairness" in the execution of his office. Council complained further that

---

[7] JC, Vol. V, pp. 217-8 (November 10, 1732); [Newcastle] to Johnson, April 1731, PRO, SP, Dom. Geo. II, Bundle 151, No. 10 (Library of Congress transcript).

[8] JC, Vol. V, pp. 217-8 (November 10, 1732).

[9] St. John to Johnson, November 7, 1732, PR, Vol. XV, pp. 249-52.

[10] JC, Vol. V, pp. 220-21 (November 10, 1732).

not only had he expedited some surveys while delaying others, but he had also given "an undue preference of good Land and Soil to some, to the great disappointment of many others who expected a fair Mixture and distribution pursuant to His Majesty's instruction for the purpose." St. John, Council said, had denied the Governor's authority to examine the proceedings of his office, and continued to take fees unwarranted by law despite orders to the contrary from Governor and Council. St. John's retort to these accusations was that he "did not value a Fig the Governor and Council here nor what they could do." The Council concluding that St. John should be suspended from office and another put in his place, requested the Governor to write to England to ask for St. John's permanent removal."[11]

In reviewing the St. John episode to the Board of Trade, Governor Johnson accused Benjamin Whitaker of being the real culprit in the case, or at least the directing genius behind St. John. Johnson referred to Whitaker as "the Carolina Craftsman," saying that it was upon Whitaker's advice that St. John continued to disregard authority of Governor and Council. These two men, along with their associates, Johnson asserted, tried to discredit the government in the eyes of the public "by all the Vile ways imaginable." Johnson said that under Whitaker's influence, the Surveyor General had spoken his maledictions against the Governor and Council in an effort to justify his own misconduct, and to make it appear that only St. John and his friends had regard for the King's concern. Johnson remarked, "and by St. John's great Interest which he Brags he has [,] Whitaker hopes to profit himself in England as well as here."[12] Whitaker, one time Attorney General of the Province, had been appointed Deputy Surveyor by St. John.[13] In the controversy, Whitaker lost nothing, for a few years later, following Johnson's administration, he was appointed Chief Justice of the Province.

As to St. John, Governor Johnson expressed to the Board his hope that once his conduct had been revealed fully, all of his offices would be taken from him. Johnson had finally been brought around to this opinion, and although he was urged by Council to suspend St. John, he chose to refer the entire matter to the authorities in

---

[11] Representation of Council to Governor Johnson, December 15, 1732, PR, Vol. XVI, pp. 43-48.

[12] Johnson to Board of Trade, December 15, 1732, PR, Vol. XVI, p. 5.

[13] JC, Vol. V, p. 202 (June 26, 1732).

England. He hoped that relief would be forthcoming, and that official action would be taken against St. John.[14]

The St. John clique, meanwhile, was busy defending itself in vigorous letters to England, many of which expressed opposition to the Quit Rent Act. Whitaker even charged that St. John, from the time of his arrival in the Province, had been treated distantly by the Governor, which left St. John no opportunity for free conversation with the chief executive. Whitaker also made certain to put himself and other St. John supporters in the most favorable light, reporting: "It was his [St. John's] fortune after he had been here a few months to meet some persons who had no interest or concerns in the public affairs other than as wellwishers to the Society they lived in but who from a long residence in the country and having been engaged in former administrations were pretty intimately acquainted with the present as well as former transactions."[15]

Johnson had said the Quit Rent Law effectively secured His Majesty's quit rents in proclamation money, that the inhabitants of the Province had approved the act as making them secure in their property, and they considered it the "Magna Carta of Carolina."[16] James St. John and Benjamin Whitaker took a completely opposite view to Johnson.[17]

The Surveyor General in his letter asserted that if the Quit Rent Act should receive Crown approval it would "be very prejudicial to His Matys [Majesty's] Interest, will be a great hindrance to the settling and strengthening the province of South Carolina and will tend very much to the disquet of the Inhabitants of the said Province."[18]

Both St. John and Whitaker were adamant in their condemnation of the Quit Rent Act's affirmation of land titles based on proprietary

---

[14] Extract of letter from Johnson to Hutcheson, December 21, 1732, PR, Vol. XV, p. 267.

[15] Letter from Whitaker, September 21, 1732, PR, Vol. XV, pp. 206-8.

[16] Johnson to Board of Trade, June 26, 1732, PR, Vol. XV, p. 136.

[17] St. John, "The Case of the Patents granted to the Landgraves an[d] Cassiques in South Carolina," received by Board of Trade, September 6, 1732, PR, Vol. XV, pp. 149-58; "Observations on ye proceedings of ye Governor Council and Assembly of So. Carolina concerning the granting his Majtys Lands and the payment of Quit Rents—The copy of the Report of Mr. Whitaker late Attorney General of that province. With copies of several Memorials of Mr. St. John and other papers on the same subject," received by Board of Trade from St. John, September 6, 1732, PR, Vol. XV, pp. 159-205.

[18] St. John, "The Case of the Patents," PR, Vol. XV, pp. 155-6.

patents. Their objections were many, and included the following: (1) That lands taken up under the patents had not been recorded in any public office, so what quantity of land was held by each patentee was unknown; (2) that the lands had been run out in large tracts, fronting rivers, and had included the most select lands; and (3) that under the Act, the King's quit rents would be lessened by £1,000 per year.[19]

St. John's first objection was contradictory to terms of the Quit Rent Act. It stated that all patents and grants be registered in the Auditor General's office, with information on tenure, location, and the rent reserved on them, and that lands not so registered within eighteen months were to be regarded as vacant lands.[20]

As to his second objection, this was contrary to St. John's own actions in which the Governor had accused him of engaging in the identical practices, and which Johnson had tried to prevent. However, proprietary grants had specified only the size of the grant, allowing the grantee to select a location in unoccupied lands. Because of this provision, grantees naturally selected those lands considered to be the choicest. This situation antedated Johnson's arrival in Carolina, and there was no ready solution, for the choice had to be made from two possibilities: either the titles could be confirmed or else be invalidated. By the Quit Rent law, the General Assembly had decided titles should be confirmed.

St. John and Whitaker so beclouded the issue that the purpose behind this provision of the Quit Rent Act became obscured. Since the land office had been closed for many years, anyone desiring to purchase lands had to buy them from holders of patents or from those with grants made prior to that time. The Quit Rent Act confirmed these purchases and made the buyers secure in their lands. The fact that the Act also worked to the advantage of large landholders who had not parceled out and sold their grants was probably an unavoidable consequence. The alternative would have been invalidation of all such titles and this could have wrought chaos.

Johnson, prior to his service in Carolina, had tried to take steps to prevent similar, future problems. Following his recommendation to the Crown, he received Instructions carrying directives on the size of future grants, the amount of the land that could front on a river,

[19] St. John, "The Case of the Patents," PR, Vol. XV, pp. 156-7.
[20] *Statutes,* Vol. III, pp. 290-92.

and other restrictions. His Instructions further ordered that the Governor and Council must require all land applicants to take the oath that the land for which they were applying was for their own use, and that there was no present view or design of selling the grant.[21]

The third objection voiced by the St. John group in letters to England was a weak one, because they overlooked the fact that no quit rents had been paid for a great many years. The Quit Rent Act required however that all landholders indicate under what yearly rent they possessed their land, and what payment was to be paid to the Crown. Under the law, reasonable distress could be made on goods and chattels of the owner if rents had gone unpaid for three months; and if they remained unpaid for five years, the land forfeited to the Crown.[22] This meant that holders of large, uncultivated and unimproved tracts either had to settle them or sell them to prospective settlers, to avoid payment of annual quit rents on unproductive lands.

Johnson, who had not been at all pleased with the Quit Rent Act at its passage,[23] had finally approved it as the best legislation obtainable. Having accepted the Act, he gave it his full support, and made numerous appeals to the British ministry, carefully and cogently pointing out the reasons why the Act should receive royal endorsement. He continued his efforts on behalf of the Act, even as his antagonists gained support for their position, and it appeared that the Act would be disallowed. The English treasury, after hearing from Benjamin Whitaker, informed the Board of Trade that it viewed the Act as "not proper for his Majestys Royal Approbation." The reasons cited were those of Whitaker and St. John.[24] After taking the matter under consideration, the Board of Trade likewise reported unfavorably on the Act, preparing a draft of a representation to repeal it.[25] When the Board made its recommendations to the King, it followed the St. John-Whitaker line of reasoning.[26]

---

[21] JC, Vol. V, p. 272 (February 9, 1732/3).

[22] *Statutes,* Vol. III, p. 294.

[23] Smith, *S. C., as Royal Province,* pp. 34-48, and Bond, *Quit-Rent,* pp. 318-49.

[24] J. Scrope to A. Popple, October 6, 1732, PR, Vol. XV, p. 239.

[25] Board of Trade Journal, October 25, November 1, 1732, PR, Vol. XV, p. 85.

[26] Board of Trade to the King, November 1, 1732, PR, Vol. XV, pp. 240-46.

Meanwhile, Johnson had reported to the Board of Trade that if the King allowed the Act, he thought additions or changes could be made in it. If it were repealed, he said, "Our dutys are lost, provisions for newcomers defeated, Our debts unpaid, and All Taxes left to be raised upon real and personal Estates only which no Colony does and what I am afraid they will never come into, tis my duty to give my sentiments but submit all to your Lord[shi]ps better judgement."[27]

Despite reverses at the hands of the Board of Trade, Johnson continued his efforts. He urged the Crown to delay its disallowance, at least until the rent roll could be completed. The Governor pointed out that the registering of deeds had been greatly delayed by St. John's actions in the Auditor General fiasco, and by some "Cavilling Lawyers" who tried to defeat the law, and cause trouble. Because of the uncertainties thereby created, people had been hesitant in having their titles recorded in the Auditor General's office, he said.

The Assembly had wanted to lengthen the time given for registering, but Johnson had refused to assent. The Governor felt that the eighteen-month time limit should be calculated from June 10, 1732, the day on which St. John subscribed to the oath as Walpole's deputy.

In this way, Johnson felt that no question could arise concerning the legality of the eighteen-month period and he requested the Crown to use this oath date in determining it, and asked the Crown not to repeal the law until the period for registering the deeds had elapsed.[28]

Governor Johnson revealed a particular type of opposition to the Quit Rent Act when he recited the case of Thomas Lowndes, who held a grant of five baronies of 12,000 acres each. Lowndes was reported to have sold almost all of this land, giving no warrant for same, but being paid for it between £2,500 and £3,000 sterling. He was now opposing the Act, the repeal of which would leave his buyers without land or money.[29] Similar hardship cases were coming to light, Johnson said.

[27] Johnson to Board of Trade, September 28, 1732, PR, Vol. XV, pp. 230-31.

[28] Johnson to Board of Trade, January 8, 1732/3, PR, Vol. XVI, pp. 29-30.

[29] Johnson to Board of Trade, September 28, 1732, PR, Vol. XV, p. 231.

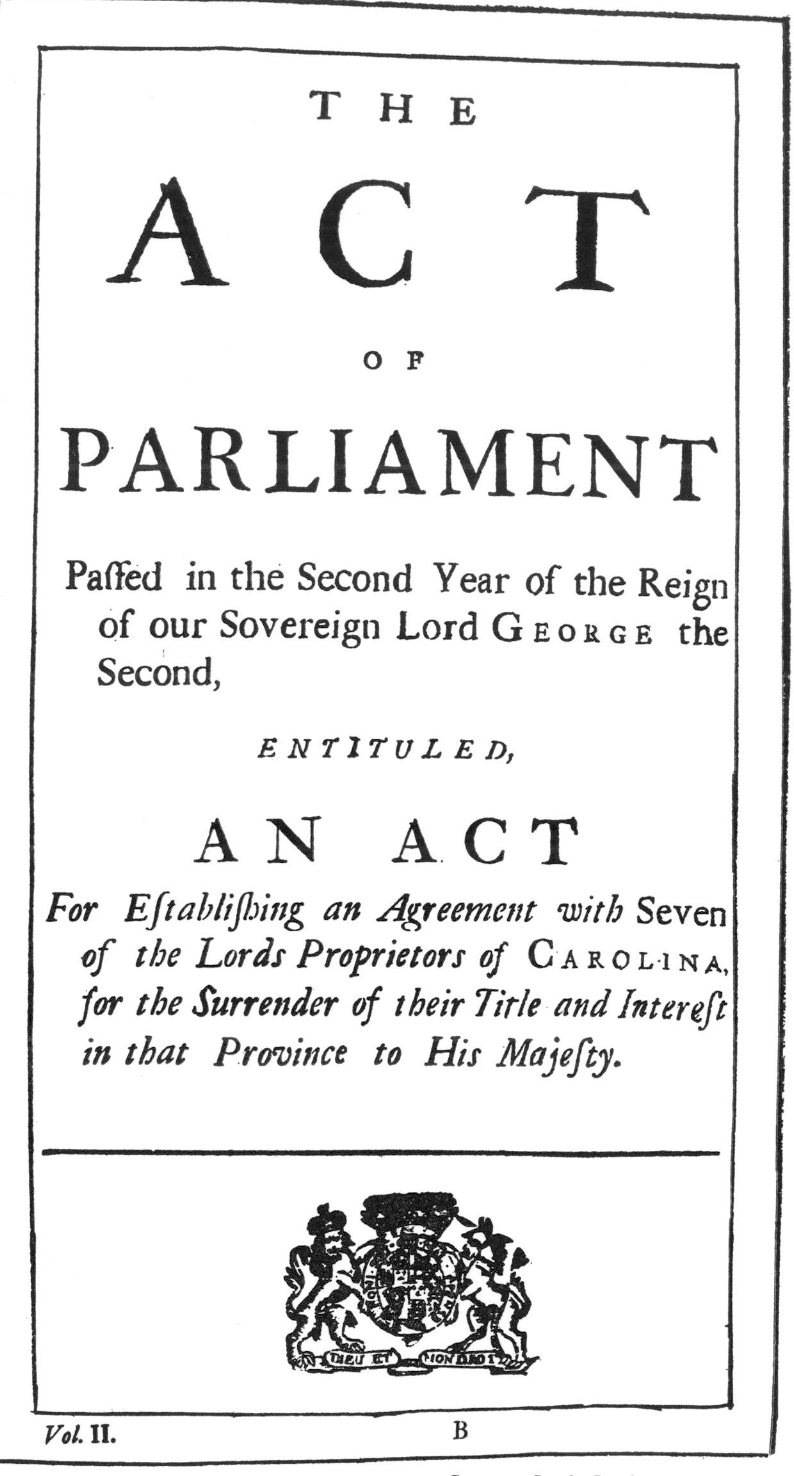

THE

ACT

OF

PARLIAMENT

Paſſed in the Second Year of the Reign of our Sovereign Lord GEORGE the Second,

ENTITULED,

AN ACT

For Eſtabliſhing an Agreement with Seven *of the Lords Proprietors of* CAROLINA, *for the Surrender of their Title and Intereſt in that Province to His Majeſty.*

Vol. II. B

Courtesy South Caroliniana Library

Leaf from Trott's *Laws,* an Agreement with the Lords Proprietors.

CHAPTER XIV

The Legislative-Judiciary Fight

WHEN news of the Board of Trade's unfavorable report on the Quit Rent Act reached Carolina, the friends of St. John, without waiting to see what the King would decide, made their move. By their actions they revealed the motives back of their opposition to the measure.

On February 1, 1732/3, the Commons House addressed the Governor, complaining that several persons were running out lands that had been surveyed previously by virtue of patents. Such a practice, the House said, if permitted to continue, might "tend greatly to the disquiet of the Inhabitants of this Province." Members asked the Governor to take measures to prevent those "pernicious Proceedings."[1]

At the same time, Council observed that some people had made agreements to dispose of lands before they received grants, making it obvious that they had no intention of settling and improving the lands. A resolution passed to require all potential grantees to take an oath that the lands applied for were for their own use.[2]

Governor Johnson, already the chief target of those opposing the Quit Rent Act, soon found himself in the midst of a land scandal which had a strange beginning. Robert Hume, at that time Speaker of the Commons House, took out five *caveats* against the Governor's granting himself land in Granville County, claiming that the lands had been granted to other people. Johnson informed the Commons of Hume's action and said that the lands had long since been surveyed for him by Colonel Bull, a sworn surveyor. Johnson demanded to know by what authority Hume was swearing out *caveats* in other people's names,[3] and presented evidence to show that in some cases the *caveats* had been entered without the knowledge or consent of the persons whose names were used.[4]

---

[1] JC, Vol. V, p. 362 (February 1, 1732/3).

[2] JC, Vol. V, pp. 366-7 (February 2, 1732/3).

[3] JC, Vol. V, p. 370 (February 9, 1732/3), JCHA, pp. 921-2 (February 9, 1732/3).

[4] JC, Vol. V, p. 370 (February 10, 1732/3); JCHA, pp. 926-7 (February 10, 1732/3).

Summoned to appear before Council about this time in regard to quit rents was an attorney named Thomas Ellery. Ellery admitted that he had visited a Mrs. Catherine Bettison in an effort to have her sign a false paper stating that she had sold a warrant for 400 acres of land to a fictitious person. Mrs. Bettison had refused to sign, she told Council, because she had not sold her land or precept to anyone. When the Council asked Ellery by whom he was employed, he replied, "Robert Hume."[5]

Hume was deeply involved in the land scandal. Attorney General Charles Pinckney refused to have drafts made of land grants when Hume applied for them. In that respect, the Attorney General received support from the Council which declared:

> The said Lands are not duly surveyed and are most of them, if not all lay'd out on Patent Lands contrary to His Excy's Warrant, and the Survey[o]rs usual precept, and an Act of Assembly of this Province, and are purchased by the said Hume and others, and not design'd for the use of the Persons in whose names the said Platts are return'd.

Meanwhile a report was made by a committee appointed to inquire into the duplication of patent and previously surveyed lands. The report seriously implicated St. John, stating that he had been active "to promote and Carry on the Pernicious designs of a Set of men (with whom your Comm[itt]ee believes the said Surveyor Gen[era]l [is] deeply interested) who have agreed, and Confederated for their own Private advantage to run out and Survey Patent Lands, and Lands formerly Surveyed."[6]

Boldly striking at the St. John clique, the Commons House recommended that the Governor suspend St. John from the office of Surveyor General "until his partial arbitrary and unprecedented Proceedings" could be related to the imperial authorities. Curiously enough, that message to the Governor was signed by the Speaker of the Commons who was none other than Robert Hume.[7] Shortly afterward, Hume found it judiciously convenient to resign as speaker, and soon sailed with Benjamin Whitaker for England.[8]

---

[5] JC, Vol. V, pp. 274-5 (February 10, 1732/3).

[6] JC, Vol. V, p. 374 (February 10, 1732/3).

[7] JCHA, p. 926 (February 10, 1732/3).

[8] JC, Vol. V, p. 379 (February 23, 1732). Hume said he intended to represent interests of himself and his associates before the proper authorities.

The Governor and Council called attention to the case in a letter to Lord Carteret, who quite naturally had a great interest in patent lands. In part, they said:

> But here are a sett of men who on a rumor only that the Quit Rent Law will be repealed have taken upon them to run out all Lands heretofore admeasured by patents and are sending home two Solicitors Mr. Hume & Whitaker to solicit for Grants for them having been refused them here and those persons are the same who complained of engrossing vast Quantities of Lands in a few hands in prejudice of the Country But appear now to have complained only, that the Lands might be taken up by themselves Whether they will shew any more respect to your Lordship is very doubtful they having yet shewn none to anyone.[9]

Despite commands to the contrary, warnings and scoldings, the St. John associates continued to survey lands as it suited their pleasure, in direct defiance of constituted authority. But the long-suffering South Carolina Commons House in 1733 served notice that it would no longer tolerate such effrontery.

The first move in the Commons' counterattack was an order to its messenger to take into custody four of St. John's deputies: James Ferguson, Robert Godfrey, William Staples, and William McPherson. Although these men were only carrying out directions, they were aware that they were involved in illegal proceedings.[10]

A week later, the Commons touched persons nearer the inner circle when it ordered the commitment of Job Rothmahler and Thomas Cooper[11] "for aiding [,] assisting & superintending the Deputy Surveyors in running out Patent Lands and Lands already survey'd."[12]

---

[9] Governor and Council to Carteret, February 28, 1732/3, PR, Vol. XVI, pp. 54-55.

[10] JCHA, pp. 916-7 (February 3, 1732/3). Certainly the St. John group must have been aware of possible consequences if it continued in open defiance of the authority of the Governor, Council and lower house. Presumably, the "land jobbers," as Johnson called them, were willing to lose an early round, feeling confident that they would win the final decision which would be handed down in England.

[11] January 9, 1733/4, PR, Vol. XVI, p. 204. Whitaker also appeared before the Georgia trustees and told that body that Rothmahler "had been very serviceable to the new colony in Georgia." *Colonial Records of Georgia,* Vol. I, p. 113. Whitaker and Hume later charged in England that commitments against Rothmahler and Cooper had been brought about at the "Instigation & incitement" of Governor Johnson.

[12] JCHA, p. 921 (February 9, 1732/3); Hewat, *An Historical Account,* in Carroll, *Historical Collections of S. C.,* Vol. I, pp. 297-8.

In petitioning to be discharged from the custody of the Commons House, Cooper asserted that he had not been engaged purposely in any act designed to trespass on the lower house's privileges or had any intention to scorn that body's authority.[13] Hume and Whitaker, testifying in England, declared that the lands Cooper was charged with running out were vacant lands which had not been surveyed for anybody, due to a lack of "any lawfull Authority derived either from Yo[u]r Majesty or the late Lords Proprietors."[14]

The case became more involved when a serious clash between the Assembly and the Chief Justice developed. The newest dispute made the issue something more than land grabbing and evolved during adjournment of the Assembly. James Graeme took out a writ of habeas corpus for Cooper, but the messenger of the Commons House, John Brown, refused to obey it. Graeme then brought suit in the Court of Common Pleas against Brown for refusing to make return of the writ of habeas corpus. When the Commons reconvened, it committed Graeme and Rowland Vaughan, who delivered the writ to the messenger. Graeme tried to escape from the custody of the House by asking Chief Justice Wright to issue writs of habeas corpus.[15]

The action of the Chief Justice in issuing the writs evoked the especial ire of the Commons House. The body thereupon passed a set of resolutions clearly indicating the wide scope of the powers it claimed for itself:

> Resolved, That it is the undeniable Privilege of the *Commons House of Assembly* to commit into Custody of their Messenger, such Persons as they judge deserve to be committed.
>
> Resolved, That the Freedom of Speech and Debates, or Proceedings of this House, ought not to be impeached or questioned in any Court or Place out of this House.
>
> Resolved, That it is a great Contempt and Violation of the Privileges of this House, for any Person whatever, to impeach or call in Question any Commitments of the *Commons House of Assembly:* And that no Writ of *Habeas Corpus* lies, or

---

[13] PR, Vol. XIV, pp. 190-91.

[14] January 9, 1733/4, PR, Vol. XVI, p. 205. With this statement, Hume and Whitaker ignored the fact that the work had been done in manifest violation of the authority of the Governor, Council, and Assembly, who, separately and together, constituted the highest executive, legislative and judicial power within the Province of Carolina.

[15] PR, Vol. XVI, pp. 207-9; JCHA, pp. 992, 1002 (April 5, 7, 1733).

> ought to be granted in Favour of any Person committed by this *House* during the sitting of the same. And that any Proceedings by Writ of *Habeas Corpus,* or in any other Manner, but in *Assembly,* is an express Contradiction of the *Declaration of Right,* 1 *Will. & Mar. cap.* 2. which says, *That the Freedom of Speech and Debates, or Proceedings in Parliament, ought not to be impeached or questioned in any Court or Place out of Parliament.*
>
> Resolved, That no Person committed by this *House,* for Breach of Privilege or Contempt of this House, ought to be by any Writ of *Habeas Corpus* made to appear in any other Place, or before any other Judicature, during that Session of Assembly, wherein such Person was so committed. That the Messenger attending this House, do make no Return, or yield any Obedience to the said Writs of *Habeas Corpus,* and for such his refusal that he hath the protection of this House. . . .[16]

The Chief Justice opposed the actions and statements of the Commons House. He said:

> These unwarrantable *Resolutions* are of the utmost ill Consequence to this Province, as they strike at his Majesty's Prerogative, the Liberty's of the Subject, and the fundamental Laws of the Land; and should I condescend to, or countenance them, so far as to act in concert with those who made and published them, I should break my Oath, betray my Trust, give up his Majesty's Prerogative, and the Liberties of the People, in a most shameful and dishonourable manner. . . .[17]

In South Carolina, the two opposing forces of legislative omnipotence and judicial supremacy came to the fore. Wright stood alone in resisting legislative power in such cases.[18] The Carolina Commons not only viewed itself as holding the ultimate legislative authority but strongly indicated its claims to judicial supremacy (i.e., short of appeal to England).

One member of the Council, Francis Yonge, defended the actions of the Commons and expounded upon the extent of its powers. As the St. John group had used the Governor abusively, Yonge chose to open his speech with a defense of the chief executive. He said:

---

16 *SCG,* April 7-14, 1733; JCHA, pp. 1000-1002 (April 7, 1733).

17 *SCG,* April 21-28, 1733; JC, Vol. V, pp. 306-8 (April 13, 1733).

18 McCrady, *Royal Govt.,* p. 161. Because Johnson's administration will be judged largely by his success or failure in dealing with the Assembly, one comment is in order: the development of the South Carolina Commons House was in a great many ways paralleling or following the development of Parliament in England.

> It is with the utmost Concern, that I see our Feuds and Dissentions carry'd to such a Hight, as in all Probability will retard the public Business, and consequently be detrimental to the whole Province; and all this not under the Government of a Tyrant, or One that has deserved ill of any Body, but (I hope, it will not be thought Flattery in me to say) under the *mild* and *just Government* of One that has always made it his Study, to do all the Good he can to every individual Person; and yet (such is the Frailty, or rather Corruption, of human Nature) that all the Good he has, or can do, shall not be able to preserve him from the *Envy* and *Malice* of some People; but, I hope, they are not many.[19]

Yonge took to task those who were speaking of the Commons' action as arbitrary and unwarranted, by his declaration that:

> Liberty is now become the grand Theme! And who shall speak against so great a Blessing? But therefore let such as want it consider well whether they have not done anything to forfeit it; for if they have, themselves are the Authors of their own unhappiness.[20]

Yonge examined the history of commitments as practiced by Parliament and then turned his discussion to Cooper, Graeme, and Vaughan. His stand against Cooper is especially telling:

> And is not Dr. *Cooper's* Case as well questionable before them, as any of these: Has he not been dividing, and disposing of other People's Properties, contrary to Law? And if this Step of the Commons House had not been taken, I mean the taking him into Custody, together with the Surveyors that assisted him, where might it have ended? They might have enquired who's Titles were deficient, or whose they thought so, then have surveyed their Lands, and protested against the Governor for not granting them, as they have others. And (if the Quit-Rent Law should be repeal'd, which their Endeavours have not been wanting to get effected) I fear, there will be but few legal Titles in this Province, and then there may be fine Fishing; but what Distractions must this produce? and how general the Calamity? And does not a general Calamity require a Parliamentary Enquiry?[21]

The Council supported Yonge's stand rather than that of the Chief Justice. In a series of resolutions, the Council declared that Yonge's speech was agreeable to the opinion of that body, and that

---

[19] *SCG,* April 14-21, 1733.

[20] *SCG,* April 14-21, 1733; JC, Vol. V, pp. 421-4 (April 19, 1733).

[21] *SCG,* April 14-21, 1733.

it gave full support to the lower house, asserting that the privileges of the Commons House were the same as those enjoyed by the House of Commons in England.[22]

In the interim, the trio of committed persons was still under confinement, and obviously they were not going to be released by habeas corpus writs. Yonge had pointed out that this was not the correct procedure, the usual manner of release being by submission. The Chief Justice had suggested the Governor dissolve the Assembly which presumably would have automatically released the prisoners, but the Council opposed that suggestion. Finally, Vaughan, Graeme, and Cooper made their submission, petitioned the Commons House, and were released from custody.[23]

The Commons House, having won that victory, turned its displeasure upon the Chief Justice and requested that he be disciplined by the Governor. Shortly afterward, it requested Johnson to suspend him immediately from the occupation and execution of his office.[24] Johnson wisely ignored the Commons' requests. He realized the real struggle was against the land speculators and not the Chief Justice. The two separate quarrels, he felt, involved different points of contention: one with St. John and the land group and the illegal surveying of patent or occupied lands; the other, a result of the first, basically with the privileges of the lower house. As viewed by the Chief Justice, the latter was a struggle between royal prerogative and assembly privilege. Significantly, the St. John group used its endeavors to confuse the two issues and clothe itself with an aura of respectability, if not altruism.[25] In a similar manner, the situation was later presented in England by agents for St. John's group.

An observer of the political situation who had come from Savannah to Charleston, commented: "These people give me a Strong idea of the Committees in our Times of Confusion, for their

[22] *SCG,* April 21-28, 1733.

[23] *SCG,* April 14-21, 1733.

[24] *SCG,* April 28-May 5, May 5-12, 1733.

[25] It is wrong to consider Wright a supporter of the St. John group. Both Wright and St. John were at odds with the Commons House at the same time, but, as pointed out, over different issues. Wright, it will be remembered, was one of the Council members undertaking the surveying of the townships, following St. John's refusal to do the work on the government's terms. Bond, however, erroneously speaks of the Assembly as reducing Wright's salary because of his opposing the "land frauds" (i.e., in the point of view of Bond and Smith, those supposedly committed by the Governor, Council and Assembly), *Quit-Rent System,* p. 331.

Heads seem to be Turn'd by a Notion they have got that they Themselves are the whole Legislature, regarding neither his Majesty nor the British Parliament."[26]

The Assembly, extremely provoked, had passed "An Act for the Prevention of Suits and Disturbances of His Majesty's Judges and Magistrates in this Province, on account of the Habeas Corpus Act," the piece of legislation to which the Savannah writer referred. At the time that he reached Charleston, opponents of the Act had magnified it all out of proportion to its purpose or intent, so that he became misinformed on the merits of the issue.

The Act was designed to protect those officers who had carried out, or acted in accordance with, the will of both houses of Assembly. It excused from prosecution those magistrates who had refused to grant writs of habeas corpus and those officers who had refused to obey such writs when granted.[27] In reporting the Act to the Board of Trade, Johnson said he had assented to it because "there was the greatest Necessity to put a Stop to such litigious Proceedings as was threatened by some Lawyers, who had been comitted by the Lower House of Assembly for Contempts and breach of Privilege and who had industriously procured those Comittments in order to raise Contributions from the Magistrates."[28]

The Act was criticized when word of its passing reached England. Hume and Whitaker opposed it, and the Board of Trade reported against it. Less than a year after its passage the Act was disallowed by the King in Council.[29]

In South Carolina, Governor Johnson was able to calm the Commons House, and gradually secured the needed harmony within his government, although trouble was still brewing over the land problem. Even so, the Commons could not forgive Chief Justice Wright, and made no provision for paying his salary, despite Johnson's

---

[26] H. Herbert to Bishop of London, April 20, 1733, SPG, Fulham Palace MSS, South Carolina, No. 81. Undoubtedly that observer overpainted the existing situation, especially when he with seriousness mentioned in the same letter that the Assembly was talking of making itself "septennial."

[27] *Statutes,* Vol. III, pp. 347-8. This provision was restricted to cases involving persons committed by either house, and was limited in time to the session of the Assembly which ran from February to May.

[28] Johnson to Board of Trade, May 4, 1733, PR, Vol. XVI, p. 105.

[29] Whitaker and Hume to Board of Trade, PR, Vol. XVI, p. 211; Board of Trade Journal, January 25, February 15, 1733/4, PR, Vol. XVI, pp. 226, 228; *Statutes,* Vol. III, pp. 348-9.

efforts to secure it.[30] By this unfriendly gesture, the Chief Justice learned the disadvantage of not having a Province civil list, which the Governor by the narrowest of margin had failed to get established. The Commons, on the other hand, was convinced of the wisdom of its refusal to establish offices by law, and declared that when it came to salary, it was in the body's discretion "to give or not to give."[31]

---

[30] *SCG,* May 26—June 2, 1733.
[31] *Ibid.*

Johnson's Return.

Courtesy of Bettmann Archives

When Robert Johnson returned to South Carolina as the Royal Governor, he was the escort of a group of Cherokee Indians who had been in England. The Indians (shown in back ground), had gone to England with Sir Alexander Cuming, as a move of friendship to win them to the British side. The Cherokees were presented at court and received with grandeur everywhere they went.

CHAPTER XV

Land Scandal Hits Carolina

THE land crisis continued; and some men seemed willing to go to any extreme to gain their ends. An incident well illustrating the seriousness of the St. John group's intentions involved Thomas Cooper and his advertisement placed in a public place at Port Royal in the name of Cooper, Rothmahler, and Company. The announcement stated that the King's lands would be disposed of to those desiring them, who applied to the company. When this news reached the Governor, he advised the Collector of Customs at Port Royal to send the advertisement to him and Council. The Collector complied, by placing it in a sealed letter addressed to the Clerk of the Council. The letter never reached its destination and sworn statements were given that it had been forcibly taken from the lodgings of the bearer by Cooper.[1] This interception of official government mail showed that the land problem was becoming even more involved. It had again come to the forefront after being sidetracked in the Assembly-Chief Justice conflict. During that interim, Surveyor General James St. John had virtually disappeared from sight.

When the Council and the Commons House requested the Governor to suspend St. John as Surveyor General, Johnson agreed it should be done, declaring, "It will be impossible to support the Authority of the Government and to do the King's business, if St. John and Whitacre meet with encouragement."[2]

Since this statement represented Johnson's true opinion of St. John, it is difficult to determine why the Governor did not suspend St. John temporarily from office, pending presentation of the case to the British ministry. Instead, Johnson recommended to England that St. John be removed. Johnson used restraint in the matter to prevent censure by the Board of Trade, an act that would have been regarded as a victory by the land speculators.

---

[1] Francis Yonge to Board of Trade, received May 7, 1734, enclosing affidavits of Louis Patereau, May 11, 1733, Joseph Raper, May 25, 1733, and Elizabeth Patereau, May 25, 1733, PR, Vol. XVI, pp. 328-35.

[2] Extract of letter from Johnson to Hutcheson, December 21, 1732, PR, Vol. XV, p. 267.

The Assembly, however, was not in a comparable position, and was provoked by the excess of St. John's impertinencies. When St. John had received a prohibitory order preventing his survey of lands for anyone without a specific warrant from the Governor, he replied by verbally attacking the Governor and Council as enemies of the country. Then he turned his venom on the Assembly, ridiculing their speeches and making himself highly offensive to the legislative body.[3] The day after the Commons had ordered its messenger to commit Rothmahler and Cooper, St. John was taken into the custody of the body "for a gross affront, and high Indignity, offered to the Honour of that House."[4]

After St. John's case had been presented in England with the backing of Hume and Whitaker, the Board of Trade, writing to Johnson, said it had reason to believe "that had there been no Resentment ag[ains]t him, on Account of ye Information and Observations, which according to his Duty he gave here upon ye passing ye Quit-Rent Law, the Assembly would not have been so exasperated ag[ains]t him." The Board asked Johnson to try to secure St. John's release, adding "nothing being more disagreeable to Us, than that any Persons especially those Employ'd in His Ma[jes]tys Service should suffer for having discharged their Duty, by giving any Information whatever to this Board, which they shall judge may contribute to the publick service."[5] The message created no problem for Johnson or the Assembly because St. John had been discharged from custody almost a month before the Board sent its letter.[6] The

[3] Hewat, *An Historical Account,* in Carroll, *Historical Collections of S. C.,* Vol. I, p. 298.

[4] *SCG,* February 10-17, 1732/3; *Gentleman's Magazine,* Vol. III (June 1733), p. 329, (July 1733) pp. 383-4.

[5] Board of Trade Journal, June 5, 7, 1733, PR, Vol. XVI, pp. 24-25; Board of Trade to Johnson, June 7, 1733, PR, Vol. XVI, pp. 145-6. Whitaker and Hume had gained a quasi-official status in England, appearing as the "late Attorney General in South Carolina" and the "late Speaker of the Assembly," respectively. Hume's title was particularly misleading. Although he had been the speaker, his connection with the land group had placed him completely without the tenor of the Commons House.

[6] *SCG,* May 5-12, 1733. It is of no little interest to observe how various authors have written of St. John's subsequent behavior. Smith writes: "Seeing that he was not properly supported by the authorities at home, Mr. St. John relaxed his efforts," *S. C. as a Royal Province,* p. 48. According to Bond, "St. John had learned his lesson, and was not inclined thereafter to expose the designs of the official coterie of land speculators in South Carolina," *Quit-Rent System,* p. 326. These two accounts should be compared with Meriwether's unimpassioned observation: "He held his office for ten years more, but appears to have offered the strong-willed Commons neither indignity nor opposition," *Expansion of S. C.,* pp. 23-24.

message emphasized the prime need—already undertaken by the South Carolina government—for more agents, for better representation and presentations in England of its needs and concerns, especially in matters before the Board of Trade. The Agent employed by South Carolina, Peregrine Fury, had not been remiss in his duties, but the position was so involved that he could not handle all of the details alone. The Assembly had decided that what was needed was official representation by a South Carolinian who was intimately associated with affairs of the Province and could give first-hand accounts. Therefore, it had already acted.

But before the letter arrived, in which wishes of the Board of Trade would be made known, the government of the Province (including the Governor, the Council and the Commons House), had unanimously approved the selection of Francis Yonge, a member of Council, to present its case in England. Yonge gave evidence of being a most fortunate choice for the difficult task, as he enjoyed the full confidence of the Governor, Council and members of the Commons House of Assembly. His chief assignment in London was to emphasize the Quit Rent Act and answer the objections that had been raised to it.[7]

When the new Agent departed for England, he took a letter to the Bishop of London from Commissary Alexander Garden, D.D., a member of the Privy Council. Doctor Alexander wrote at the request of the Clergy of the Province, always strong in its support of Governor Johnson. The letter referred to Governor Johnson as one "who has always shown all favorable Countenance & Regard, to the Interests of Religion, the Church of England, and the Clergy in this Province & that we have every Motive to engage our dutiful Affection to his Person & Government."[8]

The letter was a timely one, for Johnson was losing favor in some official circles. He was being denounced in some places because of the effectiveness of the approach of Whitaker and Hume in influencing the Board of Trade in favor of St. John. Too, the insecurity of his position was becoming even more noticeable when application was made—with strong support—to replace him as Governor of South Carolina.

---

[7] Johnson to Board of Trade, April 6, 1732, PR, Vol. XVI, pp. 79-80.

[8] A. Garden to Bishop of London, April 7, 1733, SPG, Fulham Palace MSS, South Carolina, no. 37.

Due to the influence of the Duke of Newcastle, such actions were quashed. The Duke called a halt to such notions, saying in one instance that "there is no Resolution taken, to remove Mr. Johnson, nor are as I know of, any of the Complaints against him yet heard, so that at present there is no vacancy and indeed I am not sure there will be any."[9] Again, the Duke said, "Tho' there are Complaints against Governor Johnson, there has yet, as I apprehend, been no Determination upon them; nor is there any Resolution taken to remove him from his Government: so that there is at present no Vacancy."[10]

Some time later, Viscount Percival heard that the British government had pressed Oglethorpe to accept the South Carolina governorship, but said he learned that he "absolutely refused, because 'it would be turning out Governor Johnson, who has been a favourer of our Colony . . .'."[11]

From Carolina, St. John's land group renewed its attacks upon Governor Johnson, sending further appeals to the Board of Trade. The group, claiming that Johnson and a few others were defeating the King's plans for peopling the Province by taking large tracts of land, completely overlooked the fact that Johnson had drawn up the settlement plans and had been their chief advocate. The land group, in its memorials, further charged that poor people who had settled the southern frontier in the vicinity of Port Royal had lost their lands to those who had run out patent grants before the land office was opened. By this devious reasoning, Johnson's enemies connected him with the "conspiracy," and belittled him before the Board of Trade. On the one hand the group claimed that the "poor" people had been forced to abandon their lands upon the outbreak of the Indian war in 1715, and on the other said that "these people" had come to the Province because of a manifesto Johnson published in Ireland in 1718 when he was Proprietary Governor.

None of the petitioners had obtained legal titles to the lands they claimed. They had arrived in the Province at different times, and whether they had occupied the lands was questionable, but irrelevant. The people held no titles and the petitions stated that they had left the lands they were now reclaiming, some having been vacated fifteen

---

[9] Newcastle to the Solicitor General, June 22, 1733, PR, Vol. XVI, p. 162.

[10] Newcastle to Lord Craven, June 22, 1733, PR, Vol. XVI, p. 164.

[11] *Percival Diary,* Vol. II, p. 159; see also, *ibid.,* Vol. II, pp. 183 and 187.

years previously. It was evident that the petitioners had no intentions of claiming the lands but were spurred to do so when they began to increase in value as a result of Johnson's plan to settle and defend the frontiers, and aid in the establishment of the Colony of Georgia.

The Board of Trade, strangely enough, thought that the petitioners' claims, although they were equitable, and not legal, should be given a hearing, with as little expense as possible to the claimants. This recommendation was contrary to the Board's action in reporting against the Quit Rent Act to which it had objected, saying that the Act confirmed titles not strictly good in law.

The petitions of the "poor" settlers, included the names of Robert Hume, Thomas Cooper, Job Rothmahler, and William Frewin, among the chief objectors to the Quit Rent Act. Its provisions would have offered them the opportunity to confirm any valid claims although they might be legally incomplete or press them if they had been residents and made improvements on the claimed land.[12]

Johnson pointed out that those who complained most loudly had done so at the prospect of personal gain. No sooner had they heard of the unfavorable report of the Board of Trade on the Quit Rent Act, than the discontents formed a company to run out lands, "purchasing poor peoples Warrants for a trifle." At the same time, Johnson said, they were soliciting grants in England while "their Notarys and Lawyers threatened me very hard for refusing to give them Grants here." Johnson made it clear that he had not put into execution that part of the Quit Rent law which validated patents, and that he would not do so until he had learned the King's pleasure concerning the law.[13]

This brought the whole affair of the commitments into review again, for the land group managed to weave skilfully into the argument the Chief Justice's objections. The Board of Trade was kept apprized of these events in Carolina by inveterate letter writers, one of whom, Will Frewin, said:

[12] Will Frewin to Board of Trade, May 12, 1733, PR, Vol. XVI, pp. 113-9; Petition of Robert Hume, Thomas Cooper, Job Rothmahler, *et al.*, and Petition from Port Royal and other parts of Granville County, PR, Vol. XVII, pp. 110-116, 116-21; Board of Trade to the King, December 19, 1734, PR, Vol. XVII, pp. 241-8.

[13] Johnson to Board of Trade, April 6, 1733, PR, Vol. XVI, pp. 79-80. The Governor by his announcement wanted to make sure that the Crown's interest and/or revenue would not suffer from the Act.

> The Gentlemen in power here, both by their speeches and Actions, seem to have entirely forgot that they are Subjects or dependents, the Commons House of Assembly look upon themselves as the Supreme Court of Judicature, and nobody here that has the power offered to dissent to their Jurisdicion, their Interests are one and the same, which is the occasion of the perfect harmony and good understanding between them.[14]

Frewin, in his communication to the Board of Trade, said that on his arrival in the Province, he had presented letters of recommendation to the Governor which "never influenced Mr. Johnson to do me the least good office." He added that he had been much befriended by Benjamin Whitaker before that gentleman left the Province on his mission to England.[15] Such attacks and accusations lowered Johnson in the estimation of the Board of Trade, and unfortunately, he was to be further discredited in the Board's eyes by St. John over certain developments within Purrysburg, a new Province township.

When the land was surveyed originally for Purrysburg by Colonel William Bull, he discovered that several people had run out tracts of land in the area, despite the Governor's Proclamation that no one could take up land within six miles of the township. In mentioning this to the Governor and the Council, Colonel Bull injected the fact that there was enough vacant land along the Savannah River to make up the deficiency, and that it would be just as convenient for the Purrysburg inhabitants. Governor Johnson took Colonel Bull's suggestion and issued another Proclamation that the people of Purrysburg could make use of the contiguous, vacant lands on the Savannah River that were most convenient to them.[16] Then, to prevent a like situation from occurring where other townships would be laid out, Johnson drew up a Proclamation forbidding anyone to run out lines within six miles of any township, and ordered that this clause be inserted in all land grants.[17]

Purry, who led the settlers in the township that bore his name, was in Charleston when the question of the land deficiency arose,

---

[14] Will Frewin to Board of Trade, May 12, 1733, PR, Vol. XVI, pp. 113-9. The lower house claimed the same powers as the House of Commons in England. Ample illustrations of divergent ideas and notions within the governing bodies served to belie the charges of identical interests or complete accord. That the legislative and executive branches of the South Carolina government were able to work in harmony must redound to Johnson's credit. This cooperation rarely existed, either before or following the time of his administration.

[15] PR, Vol. XVI, p. 112.

[16] JC, Vol. V, p. 206.

[17] JC, Vol. V, p. 214.

and posed no objection to the substitution arrangement, according to Colonel Bull. Later, Purry changed his mind and petitioned Council for the original six-mile reserve. Governor Johnson advised Purry that the Council would consider his petition and "do the Township Justice." The matter was not taken up immediately and because Purry did not pursue further, Council presumed that it was concluded.[18]

Instead, Purry had petitioned the Crown, stating that the Governor at the time had doubted that he had the authority to remove those persons who had settled within the six-mile limit previous to the survey. Purry maintained that they had not taken up the lands before the survey, but following the selection of the township site, and after Governor Johnson had issued his proclamation forbidding settlement there. He begged the King to order the Governor to designate the six-mile reserve for the use only of Purrysburg, and again asked for the 48,000-acre grant that was due him for fulfilling his part of the settlement agreement.[19]

Meanwhile, Surveyor General St. John had sent the Board of Trade a list of tracts that had been taken up within the limits of the Purrysburg reserve. It included the name of Robert Johnson, the Governor, who reportedly had 8,000 acres there.[20]

The first that Governor Johnson heard of Purry's discontent and of the St. John list containing his own name, was in a message from the Board of Trade. The Board advised that those pretending to hold lands in the area could have no right or title, if—as the Board assumed—they had claimed the lands subsequent to the Governor's proclamation.[21] The Board of Trade's order was followed by one from the King to the same effect. The Crown's letter to Johnson instructed him to set aside the original six-mile reserve exclusively for the use of Purrysburg.[22]

In its letter, the Board of Trade added sarcastically that it could not "help observing that 8,000 acres of those very Lands have been

---

[18] Johnson to Board of Trade, November 9, 1734, PR, Vol. XVII, pp. 185-7.

[19] Purry to the King, received May 11, 1734, PR, Vol. XVI, pp. 318-23; *Percival Diary,* Vol. I, p. 451.

[20] From St. John, September 15, 1733, PR, Vol. XVI, pp. 343-4.

[21] The Board said that after consultation with the proper legal authorities it had concluded that the Governor's proclamation in conjunction with the King's instructions could be considered equal to a grant of land for the King's use. A. Popple to Johnson, August 22, 1734, PR, Vol. XVII, pp. 8-9.

[22] February 13, 1734/5. PRO, CO 5:196, pp. 105-107 (Library of Congress transcript).

Surveyed in your Name." It then concluded its Instructions by asking the Governor to issue another proclamation reiterating that settlement was forbidden within six miles of the other townships.[23]

Johnson replied to the Board's letter, stating that he had issued the Proclamation as requested; and then related the Council's dealings with Purry, and explained his ownership of the 8,000 acres. He stated that he had acquired the land before the area was surveyed for Purrysburg, as had other people whose lands lay within the area of the township. He said that the settlers had made honest errors in staking out their lands because it was impossible to judge distances in the forests, not because they were prone to disregard the Governor's Proclamation. To prevent such future mistakes, he said that the South Carolina government had surveyed and marked both the 20,000 acres and the six-mile reserves of other townships, and he was having a new survey made of Purrysburg. He did not add—but might well have done so—that this work was being delayed considerably while the Council tried unsuccessfully to induce St. John to do the surveying.

Johnson further informed the Board that he believed the people of the Province would be willing to part with their lands that fell within the township because of the current law prohibiting settlement within township reserves.[24] He also made the point that Thorpe's Barony — run out on Lowndes' patent — that was reputed to be within the Purrysburg township, had been surveyed by St. John without a warrant from the Governor. Johnson then lamented to the Board that he was "misrepresented in every thing I do, while they [St. John's group] by deceipt and Fraud endeavor to rob me and others of their rights, and the Legislature of the Worthy C[h]aracter they deserve."

Regarding his land in Purrysburg in his letter to the Board, Johnson said that when Colonel Bull surveyed the land for him, he was assured that it was thirty miles from Purrysburg. Then, however, he said he was convinced that 300 to 400 acres of the 8,000 lay within

---

[23] Popple to Johnson, August 22, 1734, PR, Vol. XVII, p. 9.

[24] Johnson to Board of Trade, November 9, 1734, PR, Vol. XVII, pp. 185-7, 189, 191. Johnson's ownership of the 8,000 acres came about in an entirely innocent way. About the time that Purry had been selecting the location for his town—which he accomplished by marking a tree—Colonel Bull mentioned to Governor Johnson that he knew of some fine land that he might like to own and that he would survey it for him, if he wished.

the six-mile line, and he had told the Purrysburgers that if this were true, he would relinquish it.

He said further that the 8,000 acres originally had been a 12,000-acre tract that was run out on his patent, and inasmuch as its quit rent was higher than the rent at which the Governor was empowered to grant land, it had not affected the King's revenue adversely. Johnson said that when he heard of the Board's opposition to the section of the Quit Rent Act confirming patents, he set a good example by relinquishing his patent right and issuing a warrant to resurvey 8,000 acres of the tract for himself. He had qualified for same, he said, under his family right (i.e., fifty acres for each man, woman and child, white and slave). Then Johnson recounted some strange and unjust things that happened, saying that St. John, his deputy and the "Land Jobbers" contrived to be on the land a day before the other deputy arrived with Johnson's warrant, and surveyed the best land for themselves "without regard to the Justness of the Survey or the Kings Instructions for Surveying." When the plats were brought to St. John's office, Johnson said, the Surveyor General certified theirs but refused his.

Johnson had appealed the matter to Council, placing that body in a dilemma. Its decision was favorable to the Governor, and although it was accused of being less than impartial, Council ordered St. John to certify Johnson's plat. St. John refused to do so; and his land group appealed Council's decision to England, making Johnson feel that he had been "put upon Tryal" over whether he was to have any land, either by patent or family right. The Governor added significantly to the Board of Trade, "and those are the People who at the same time represent I have run it upon the 6 Miles of Purrisburgh, but dont think that [is] an Objection to having it themselves, being striving for it at this time."[25]

Johnson at first was not in accord with the omnibus Quit Rent bill, in its confirmation of patent grants and titles derived from them. However, after considerable consultation with the Assembly, and following concessions on both sides, he accepted the bill as the best that could be obtained. By his support of it, he came under the ire of St. John's group.

The Quit Rent Act as passed, even aside from its merits, was vital to the stability and quietude of the Province, a fact grasped by Gov-

[25] Johnson to Board of Trade, November 9, 1734, PR, Vol. XVII, pp. 187-9.

ernor Johnson. Although he was a large landowner and a wealthy planter,[26] there was little that he could gain personally from the Act; he was only complying with a request from the Assembly to help the poorer people in land matters.

The reason the land clique chose Johnson as its antagonist in the Purrysbury matter is not difficult to discern. It was obvious that if the Governor were embarrassed at home and discredited abroad, his reports revealing the schemes of St. John and his associates would carry little weight with the British Government. By intimidating him, and blackening the reputation of the Governor within the Province, they believed they could bolster their power to achieve success.

Governor Johnson, the soldier who had fought courageously and defeated pirates, the strategist who had dealt effectively with war-like Indian tribes, the statesman who had coped successfully with French or Spanish threats, was frail in the defense of his own reputation against the land speculators.[27] Whatever he said had little effect on the Board of Trade which had, apparently, lost confidence in him for no other reason than the charges of his enemies.

---

[26] Johnson's will revealed that he was the owner of more than 25,000 acres of land. Lothrop Withington, "South Carolina Gleanings in England," in *South Carolina Historical Magazine,* Vol. V, No. 2 (April, 1904), pp. 105-7; Henry A. M. Smith, "The Baronies of South Carolina: The Seewee Barony," in *S. C. Hist. Mag.,* Vol. XII, No. 3 (July, 1911), p. 115; Mabel L. Webber, "Sir Nathaniel Johnson and His Son Robert, Governors of South Carolina," in *S. C. Hist. Mag.,* Vol. XXXVIII, No. 4 (October, 1937), pp. 113-4; Vere L. Oliver, "Carolina Wills," in *S. C. Hist. Mag.,* Vol. XII, No. 4 (October, 1911), p. 215.

[27] St. John continued to hold his post, but made no further trouble in the Province. Whitaker later became chief justice, receiving his appointment from the Crown. The Privy Council decided to permit the Quit Rent Act to stand provisionally, a decision that did not eliminate large landholdings, as these had been in existence since the proprietary period. Since the Act was never disallowed, this meant a victory for its supporters, and precluded any future, violent struggle over land titles that could wreak havoc in the Province. The implementation of the township plan, and its further extension, resulted in an area of small landholdings in the backcountry, with resulting antagonism between Up Country and Low Country. This hostility was manifested in the Regulator Movement in South Carolina and continued at least to the period of the Civil War, despite some signs of unity. To illustrate this contention, John Henry Logan dedicated his book "To the People of Upper Carolina, and the Citizens of Charleston, Intimately Associated, and Closely United by Ties of Trade, and of Common Struggles, and Sufferings, from the Earliest Periods of their Contemporaneous History; and now Constituting, after the Lapse of More than One Hundred Years, the North and South Poles of Our Political Magnet." Logan, *A History of the Upper Country of South Carolina: from the Earliest Periods to the Close of the War of Independence,* Vol. I (Charleston: S. G. Courtenay, and Columbia: P. B. Glass, 1859; Spartanburg: Reprint Company, 1960).

CHAPTER XVI

Prelude To Prosperity

ROBERT Johnson's administration as Royal Governor of South Carolina opened lands for peaceful settlement, providing an outstanding method of colonization. Once the people had secured their lands and felt safe from their enemies, they were then able to turn their thoughts to the economic aspects of the Province that had been obscured and long neglected.

It was Johnson's hardship and South Carolina's misfortune that so much of his administration was taken up with the land struggle. The Robert Johnson who left England in 1730 to assume the governorship of South Carolina was a person full of confidence in the future of the Province. His plans for its defense against the internal slave threat and against the Indian and European enemies, especially as expressed in his township scheme, gave renewed hope for security. He felt that once these things had been solved, he could put into force his plans to move the Province forward along the economic front.

Johnson's preliminary planning involved studies of the greater advantages to be derived from the main staples of the Province: rice, pitch, tar, deerskins and pelts; and what new industries might be introduced.

In an appearance before the Board of Trade, he made significant recommendations concerning naval stores, and methods for increasing the production of rice. He also suggested the possibility of other crops, including hemp, flax, the culture of silk and potash mining.

In regard to naval stores, Johnson told the Board that he believed that pitch and tar production could be greatly increased without harming the King's timber, by making use of dead lightwood trees on lands both patented and not patented, and by tapping others. He emphasized that dead trees would steadily diminish as the people burned their lands to clear them for spring planting, and as other lands were put into use for making naval stores. He mentioned that the Parliamentary bounty on green tar had not been successfully exploited, and requested the Board to send over some informed person to teach the inhabitants how to render it. Johnson thought this would be a great encouragement to the Carolinians and would help at the same time to conserve the forests and make "Perpetual the Supplys which this and the Neighboring Provinces might afford to Great Britain."[1]

Following Johnson's first year in office, he expressed concern over the diminishing returns on rice. Although its production had increased, 50,000 barrels of the cereal had brought in less in sterling money in 1731 than 22,000 barrels had in 1721; and he feared comparable losses in the future. In the doubling of the harvest, he noted, twice as much land had been put into cultivation, twice as many Negroes had been used to work it, and twice the amount of shipping had been needed, which, in the latter case, plus the sale of English-made clothing to Carolinians, was "no small advantage to the British nation."

But the Assembly felt that either the acreage had to be cut to insure better prices or additional markets for sale of rice would have to be found. It said that if production were restricted by allowing planters to cultivate limited acreage, it might "prevent their being ruined by their own industry," but Johnson looked on this as a measure that would affect adversely the King's revenues and British shipping.

Once in South Carolina, Johnson had been able to pursue the subject of rice economy further. The Acts of 1706/7 placing rice on the "enumerated" articles that could be exported only to England had been a severe blow to the Carolina planters who had been selling the product to Spanish and Portugese markets also. Finally, in 1730, Parliament modified this arrangement and permission was granted Carolinians to ship rice to points south of Cape Finisterre.[2]

Johnson was not convinced that this would return prosperity to the rice industry, and strongly urged that planters be allowed to ship the product anywhere south of Ushant, which would open up a direct French market. He also requested that they be permitted to ship to all parts of the North American continent and the West

---

[1] Johnson to Board of Trade, January 2, 1729/30, PR, Vol. XIV, pp. 29-31; Johnson to Board of Trade, November 9, 1734, PR, Vol. XVII, p. 181. The French likewise were expressing an interest in pitch production. Diron d'Artaguette to Maurepas, March 25, 1734, in *Miss. Prov. Archives,* Vol. I, p. 248.

[2] Wallace, *South Carolina: A Short History,* p. 189.

Indies.[3] Three years later, conceding that great advantages had been derived from the trading south of Finisterre,[4] Johnson again asked the Crown for a widened sphere.

Besides concentrating his attention on rice, Governor Johnson began experimenting with new products for economic improvement of the Province. Some plants were grown on trial to see if the Carolina soil was suitable, especially hemp and flax. He sought also to encourage the mining of potash, the enlargement of the silk industry that had been tried on a small scale for a number of years,[5] the manufacture of drugs, and greater production of timber.

Johnson recommended to the Board of Trade that some such incentive as a large bonus be given to the first person who could make a tun of good wine, with smaller prizes for other top producers. He also asked that a bounty be provided silk growers and removal of the English import duty on the product. He pointed out that wine production and silk culture required much labor and heavy expenditures before there could be any return, and present experiments with both were discouraging. Johnson added that because the Province was not financially able to meet such expenses, bounties would have to come from the Crown.

Three years later, writing to the Board of Trade, Johnson again expressed interest in the possibilities of raising hemp and flax. He stated that neither had been grown in quantity enough to prove feasible, and mentioned a man, Richard Hall, who, possessed of considerable knowledge and skill as a planter, believed that hemp and flax could be cultivated in several parts of the Province. The Assembly, he said, had induced Hall to remain in the Province an additional three years, to experiment with planting. Again, Johnson asked the Crown to supply premiums, stating that hemp and flax harvests were so bulky that freight charges for shipping them to England was very costly.[6]

Concerning ship's timber, the Governor spoke of huge supplies of excellent live oak, thought to be better than English oak; yellow

---

[3] Johnson to Board of Trade, December 16, 1731, PR, Vol. XV, pp. 66-67; *Percival Diary,* Vol. II, p. 154; O. M. Dickerson, *American Colonial Government, 1695-1765* (Cleveland: Arthur H. Clark Co., 1912), p. 310.

[4] Johnson to Board of Trade, November 9, 1734, PR, Vol. XVII, p. 179.

[5] Johnson to Board of Trade, received January 26, 1731/2, PR, Vol. XV, pp. 87-88.

[6] Johnson to Board of Trade, November 9, 1734, PR, Vol. XVII, pp. 178-83.

pine, superior to New England white pine, for masts; and cypress, which could be used for docking and other purposes.[7] The only difficulty, he said, was logging the trees which grew so great a distance from the water across the marshy countryside.

He expressed the difficulties in a report to the Board of Trade:

> The Country has not yet had Inhabitants who were Inclined or Capable of making many Trails for New Products, which leaves the more room to Hope for Improvements; as they found Rice, Tarr and Pitch gainful Commoditys, very little prospect appeared of employing their time and Labours to more advantage than in those Articles, and indeed considering Our Situation, and the several Staple Products of the Brittish Colonies, there seem few Articles left to fall to our Share, Our great hope has been Silk, Wines and Pot Ash, neither of these being yet made to Perfection, I mean any Quantity, and how far we may in time advance in them or other new Products cant yet be determined. The Granting a Premium on these or any other Articles and procuring proper Persons to be sent over to Instruct, will no doubt in a few years discover what this Province is Capable of.[8]

Unfortunately, Hall's experiment with hemp and flax planting was delayed. The seeds he was importing arrived too late for the first season, and planting had to be put off for a year. Governor Johnson apprized the Board of the circumstances, and forwarded Hall's suggestions and comments on the prospects.[9]

In the meantime, Johnson continued trying to broaden the base of the economy. At times he worked almost single-handedly, and where others were satisfied with the usual staple crops, he wanted to expand both types and varieties.

During his administration, times were good. Crops were flourishing,[10] business improved, and there was general optimism through-

[7] Johnson to Board of Trade, November 9, 1734, PR, Vol. XVII, pp. 183-4, 192-3.

[8] Johnson to Board of Trade, November 9, 1734, PR, Vol. XVII, pp. 183-4.

[9] Received by Board of Trade, December 31, 1734, Pr, Vol. XVII, pp. 160-173. Coincidentally, hemp and flax seeds also arrived tardily at New Orleans where several Frenchmen planted seeds that failed to sprout. Bienville and Salmon to Maurepas, April 3, 1734, in *Miss. Prov. Archives,* Vol. III, p. 644. In addition, the French were experimenting with cotton; e.g., "The mill that had been made to gin the cotton is not yet in a state of perfection. Father de Beaubois is working to make it so and flatters himself that he will succeed at it." *Ibid.,* p. 644.

[10] Will Dry to Secretary of the SPG, September 30, 1734, SPG, Series A, Vol. XXV.

out the land.[11] How responsible the Governor was for this prosperity cannot be assessed except in terms of the distraught condition of the Province before Johnson came into office, and the great improvement during his administration. When he had returned to South Carolina in 1730 with plans for almost every phase of colonial life, he was able to transform many of his ideas into action. While he was not always able to find the correct solution to a pressing problem of the Province, he did recognize and understand what it was, and possessed enough courage and wisdom to meet it. Johnson used the experience he had gained from his first administration to make a success of the second, one that was termed "the most popular and most successful of the royal administrations."[12]

Johnson had the unique distinction of being the last Proprietary Governor of South Carolina and the first Royal Governor. Governor Nicholson was appointed governor provisionally but served before South Carolina was, in the strictest sense, a royal province. Johnson presided at the demise of one government, and saw the birth of another.

When the Assembly was convened in November 1734, Johnson was present but was not well enough to address the body. His short speech, read by Secretary John Hammerton, made brief recommendations concerning defense, fortifications, current expenses, subsistence for new arrivals in Purry's settlement.

The address was closed in these words:

> I am persuaded You will continue to make His Majesty's pleasure and Interest the Measure of Your Proceedings, which is the only Means of being Prosperous in all Our Undertakings, his Views tending always to the good and Welfare of his people. I flatter myself the same good Harmony will Subsist between the two Houses of Assembly, as has done ever Since my having the Hon[o]r to Govern, which I shall promote to the utmost of my Power, with a just regard to His Majestys Rights and Prerogative, In which Gentlemen of the Council I am satisfied of your Assistance.[13]

---

[11] A. Garden and W. Guy to Secretary of the SPG, April 16, 1735, SPG, Series A, Vol. XXVI.

[12] Meriwether, *Expansion of S. C.*, p. 24.

[13] JC, Vol. VI, pp. 1-2 (November 8, 1734).

Governor Johnson's physical condition steadily declined, and when the Assembly met in April 1735, he was unable to be present.[14] On May 3, Johnson succumbed to his long illness.[15]

The South Carolina Gazette paid its heartfelt, final tribute:

> On Saturday last, between twelve and one o'clock, died after a long and lingering Sickness, His Excellency Robert Johnson, Esq; Captain General, Governor and Commander in Chief in and over this his Majesty's Province, and was decently interred on Monday last in a Vault near the Altar in Charles-Town Church [St. Phillips]. His Pall was supported by the Gentlemen of the Council, and his Corps[e] was attended to the Grave by the Lower House of Assembly, headed by their Speaker, and a numerous Body of Gentlemen and Ladies who came from all parts of the Province, where timely Notice could be had of his death, to pay their last Respects to one whom they might justly look upon as their common father. The Troop and the two Compagnies of Charles-Town Foot appeared on this melancholy Occasion, to add to the Solemnity of the Procession. The principal Mourners were his Excellency's two Sons and two Daughters, his Brother in Law Thomas Broughton Esq; our present Governor, and his Family.
>
> His Excellency died in the 59th Year of his Age, and in the 5th of his Government. He had on his Advancement disposed of all his Patrimony in England, so that his Interest might concur with his Inclinations in promoting the Welfare of that Country His Majesty had done him the Honour to intrust him with the Care of, and accordingly always kept up a good Correspondence with the Assembly, as they were all fully convinced by the whole Tenor of his Conduct, that the Interest of the Province lay principally at his Heart. But it will be needless to enlarge upon a Life & Character so well known, and which have render'd his Death so universally and deservedly lamented over the whole Province.[16]

---

[14] *SCG,* April 12-19, 1735; JC, Vol. VI, p. 90 (April 16, 1735).

[15] Thomas Broughton to Board of Trade, May 6, 1735, PR, Vol. XVII, p. 308; Board of Trade Journal, June 24, 1735, PR, Vol. XVII, p. 262. Governor Johnson was survived by three sons, Robert, Nathaniel, Thomas and two daughters, Margaret and Mary. A fourth son, William, had died of yellow fever in 1732. The Governor's daughter Mary married Benjamin Stead. Margaret married Henry Izard, and their son Ralph [pronounced Rafe] became a United States Senator. Mabel L. Webber, "Sir Nathaniel Johnson and his Son Robert, Governors of South Carolina," in South Carolina Historical Magazine, Vol. XXXVIII, No. 4 (October 1937), pp. 114-5; A. S. Salley (ed.), *Marriage Notices in the South Carolina Gazette* (Albany, N. Y.: Joel Munsell's Sons, 1902), p. 13.

[16] *SCG,* May 3-10, 1735. The death of Governor Johnson "universally lamented in that Province," was reported in *Gentlemen's Magazine,* Vol. V (June, 1735), p. 332, and *London Magazine,* Vol. IV, (June, 1735), p. 335.

The Assembly, remindful of Johnson's friendship and leadership, placed a tablet to his memory in St. Philip's Church.[17]

The inscription read:

> Near this place lyes the body of His Excellency Robert Johnson, Esquire, His Majesty's First Captain-General, Governor and Commander-in-Chief, and Vice Admiral of this Province, after the purchase thereof from the Lords Proprietors, who dyed the 3d day of May, Annoque Domini, 1735, aged 58 years. To whose memory the General Assembly gave this marble to be erected as a mark of peculiar esteem and gratitude for his mild, just and generous administration. And beside him lyes his beloved consort, Mrs. Margaret Johnson, an amiable, sensible lady, of exemplary piety, charity, and oeconomy, who dyed the 5th day of July, Annoque Domini 1732, aged 45 years."

Upon the Governor's death, Richard Hall, the hemp and flax expert, wrote:

> I am now apprehensive of meeting with Greater difficulties than expected in carrying on this undertaking, being my only pillar His Excellency Governor Johnson departed this life the third Instant and as your Honor hath had a personal acquaintance of that worthy Gentleman the late Governor it would be needless for me in giving his character.[18]

In addressing Council and the Commons House after taking over the reins of government, Lieutenant Governor Thomas Broughton asked the two houses to continue the good understanding and harmonious relations that had existed within the government during Johnson's administration. Broughton referred to the late chief executive, his brother-in-law, as "that good man," and said that he had served as a "Beneficient, Humane, and Prudent Governor."[19]

There is little wonder that the chief executive was remembered by the people as "good Governor Robert Johnson,"[20] for the prosperity—for a time—ended at his death.

---

[17] City of Charleston, *Year Book, 1880,* p. 270; Frederick Dalcho, *An Historical Account of the Protestant Episcopal Church in South Carolina* (Charleston: E. Thayer, 1820), p. 122n.

[18] Letter from Hall, May 8, 1735, PR, Vol. XVII, p. 314.

[19] JC, Vol. VI, pp. 125-6 (May 29, 1735).

[20] McCrady, *South Carolina under the Royal Government,* p. 167.

At the time of Johnson's death, there had been disagreement—but tempered with respect—between him and the Commons House over defense requirements.[21]

The amiable relationship that he had worked so diligently to achieve between the two houses of Assembly broke down, and major clashes flared up between them. A year after his death, paper bills were exchanged at great discount and the Province, it was said, seemed "to grow poorer dayly,"[22] while "Georgia & this colony are all to pieces 'bout the Indian trade."[23]

During his lifetime, Johnson, with skill, understanding and forcefulness of character, had taken a distressed Province which had only recently practiced the art of revolution, and shaped it dramatically through word and deed to show the great advantage of royal rule. His art of ruling was the major step in developing South Carolina into a firm and loyal Province of the British Crown.

There was a lesson for the British government in Johnson's administration. The lesson was not learned, and the resulting loss, to Britain's regret, was South Carolina and twelve other of its American colonies.

---

[21] The House considered Pallachucola Garrison useless because of settlements in Georgia and Purrysburg and wanted to reduce the number of men at Fort Moore because the area was no longer vulnerable. Johnson, while pleased at the good results of his settlement plan, recommended that the Province not yet relax its guard, exerting himself to the last as a defender of the Province. JC, Vol. VI, p. 95 (April 18, 1735).

[22] F. Varnod, to Secretary of the SPG, June 29, 1736, SPG, Series B, Vol. IV, Part 2.

[23] A. Garden to Samuel Quincy, July 20, 1736, SPG, Series B, Vol. IV, Part 2.

End

Bibliographical Essay

In the recounting of its history, South Carolina has been fortunate in having its story told by many dedicated and competent authors throughout the years. While sometimes writers find it almost too easy to praise or condemn, South Carolina has been doubly fortunate in that a number of its better known historians, naturally close admirers, have exercised a judicious critical faculty, thereby easing the burden of those who follow in the historical train.

The purpose here is to mention some of the materials that have been helpful in completing this study. Among the usual bibliographical aids, first attention is directed to J. H. Easterby, *Guide to the Study and Reading of South Carolina History, South Carolina Bibliographies,* No. 1 (Columbia, 1949) and No. 2 (Columbia, 1950). At the same time, anyone pursuing a topic in the colonial period might well survey the standard accounts that have weathered the test of time, including Edward Channing, *A History of the United States,* 6 vols. (New York, 1910-1925); Herbert L. Osgood, *The American Colonies in the Eighteenth Century,* 4 vols. (New York, 1924); the landmark work of Charles M. Andrews, *The Colonial Period of Amercian History,* 4 vols. (New Haven, 1934-1938); J. A. Doyle, *English Colonies in America,* 5 vols. (New York, 1882-1907); and such specialized studies as G. L. Beer, *British Colonial Policy, 1754-1765* (Gloucester, Mass., 1958); O. M. Dickerson, *American Colonial Government, 1696-1765* (Cleveland, 1912); and Evarts B. Greene, *The Provincial Governor in the English Colonies of North America* (Cambridge, 1898). Special mention must be given to the major reinterpretation presented by Lawrence Henry Gipson, *The British Empire before the American Revolution,* 10 vols. (New York, 1939-1961); and the influence of Sir Lewis Namier, *The Structure of Politics at the Accession of George III,* 2nd ed. (London, 1957).

Further insights into English personalities and politics are provided in Stebelton H. Nulle, *Thomas Pelham-Holles, Duke of Newcastle: His Early Political Career, 1693-1724* (Philadelphia, 1931); W. Baring Pemberton, *Carteret: The Brilliant Failure of the Eighteenth Century* (London, 1936); two important books by Basil Williams, *Carteret & Newcastle: A Contrast in Contemporaries*

(Cambridge, 1943) and *The Whig Supremacy* (Oxford, 1939); Mark A. Thomson, *The Secretaries of State, 1681-1782* (Oxford, 1932); and Trevor Richard Reese, *Colonial Georgia: A Study in British Imperial Policy in the Eighteenth Century* (Athens, 1963).

In South Carolina, Charleston was the center of politics and society. Frederick P. Bowes furnishes an excellent account of *The Culture of Early Charleston* (Chapel Hill, 1942). An older but still fascinating book is Harriott H. Ravenel, *Charleston, The Place and the People* (New York, 1906). Added color is provided in John B. Irving, *A Day on Cooper River,* enlarged and edited by Louisa Cheves Stoney (Columbia, 1932); and Samuel Gaillard Stoney, *Plantations of the Carolina Low Country,* 3rd ed., edited by Albert Simons and Samuel Lapham, Jr. (Charleston, 1945).

David Ramsay, *History of South Carolina,* 2 vols. in one (Newberry, S. C., 1858) is usually considered a milestone in American historical writing for its improvement in source selection and critical evaluation over the author's earlier account of the American Revolution. Of much value are William J. Rivers, *A Sketch of the History of South Carolina to the Close of the Proprietary Government by the Revolution of 1719* (Charleston, 1856) and *A Chapter in the Early History of South Carolina* (Charleston, 1874). Absolutely fundamental to any study of the period are two volumes by Edward McCrady, *The History of South Carolina under the Proprietary Government, 1670-1719* (New York, 1897) and *The History of South Carolina under the Royal Government, 1719-1776* (New York, 1899). Also noteworthy are Edson L. Whitney, *Government of the Colony of South Carolina,* Johns Hopkins University *Studies in Historical and Political Science,* Series 13, No. 1-2 (Baltimore, 1895); A. S. Salley, *The History of Orangeburg County, South Carolina* (Orangeburg, 1898); and Yates Snowden, *History of South Carolina,* 5 vols. (Chicago, 1920). More recent, and outstanding for its scholarship, is David Duncan Wallace, *The History of South Carolina,* 4 vols. (New York, 1934). The same material is used in the excellent one-volume work, *South Carolina, A Short History,* reprinted by The University of South Carolina Press, Columbia, 1966.

For the Johnson background, it is essential to consult Robert Surtees, *The History and Antiquities of the County Palatine of Durham,* 4 vols. (London and Durham, 1816-1840); William Wardell

Bean, *The Parliamentary Representation of the Six Northern Counties of England* (Hull, 1890); and *The Register of Freemen of Newcastle upon Tyne,* ed. by Madeline Hope Dodds, Newcastle upon Tyne Records Committee *Publications,* Vol. III (1923); John Guillim, *A Display of Heraldry,* 6th ed. (London, 1724); Wm. A. Shaw, *The Knights of England,* 2 vols. (London, 1906); and *Alumni Oxonienses: The Members of the University of Oxford, 1500-1714 . . . being the Matriculation Register of the University,* by John Foster, Vol. II (Oxford, 1891). Brief but thoughtful accounts are found in Hayes Baker-Crothers, "Sir Nathaniel Johnson," *Dictionary of American Biography,* Vol. X, p. 111, and Mabel L. Webber, "Sir Nathaniel Johnson and His Son Robert, Governors of South Carolina," *South Carolina Historical Magazine,* Vol. XXXVIII, No. 4 (October, 1937), pp. 109-115. Also helpful are Sir Alan Burns, *History of the British West Indies* (London, 1954) and J. W. Fortescue, *A History of the British Army,* 13 vols. in 14 (London, 1899-1930). For Robert Johnson's legacy, reference is made to Lothrop Withington, "South Carolina Gleanings in England," *South Carolina Historical Magazine,* Vol. V, No. 2 (April, 1904), pp. 100-107; Henry A. M. Smith, "The Baronies of South Carolina: The Seewee Barony," *Ibid.,* Vol. XII, No. 3 (July, 1911), pp. 109-117; and City of Charleston, *Year Book, 1880.*

For the study of Johnson's conduct of the colony's affairs, there is a mass of manuscript material available. The Records in the British Public Record Office Relating to South Carolina (transcripts in the South Carolina Archives Department, Columbia), Vols. VI-XVII, and the Records from the British Public Record Office in the Library of Congress (transcripts and photostats): (1) Additional Manuscripts; (2) Colonial Office 5; (3) Colonial Office 324; and (4) State Papers, Domestic, George II; offer a large amount of official correspondence to and from England and the colonies, in addition to reports, orders, memorials, memoranda, etc. The day-by-day governmental activities of the Province is followed in the Journal of the Commons House of Assembly of South Carolina (South Carolina Archives Department, Columbia), 1717, 1720-1735, and the Journal of the Council of South Carolina (South Carolina Archives Department, Columbia), Vol. V-VI.

Along with official correspondence, insight into the condition and problems of the Province is furnished in Society for the Propagation of the Gospel in Foreign Parts, London: (1) Fulham Palace Manuscripts: N. C., S. C., Ga. series and South Carolina series; (2) Series A: Vols. XIII-XXVI; and (3) Series B: Vol. IV, Parts 1 and 2. For background and a look into the aims, problems, and work of the Society, the following are indispensable: David Humphreys, *An Historical Account of the Incorporated Society for the Propagation of the Gospel in Foreign Parts* (London, 1730); C. F. Pascoe, *Two Hundred Years of the S.P.G.,* 2 vols. (London, 1901); and Frederick Dalcho, *An Historical Account of the Protestant Episcopal Church in South Carolina* (Charleston, 1820).

Another source of much value is the *South Carolina Gazette* whose publication began in 1732. Besides duplicating material found in official records, the *Gazette* contains an amazing amount of original material not to be found elsewhere, plus sometimes offering a surprising variety of ideas and opinions. Also containing many mentions of the colonies, and offering a view of English opinion on colonial affairs, are the *Gentleman's Magazine* (from 1731) and the *London Magazine* (from 1733). Helpful in connection with these is C. Lennart Carlson, *The First Magazine: A History of the Gentleman's Magazine* (Providence, 1938) and Walter Graham, *English Literary Periodicals* (New York, 1930).

Important printed collections of source material include B. R. Carroll (ed.), *Historical Collections of South Carolina,* 2 vols. (New York, 1836); *Collections of the South Carolina Historical Society,* 5 vols. (Charleston, 1857-1897); Thomas Cooper and David J. McCord (eds.), *The Statutes at Large of South Carolina,* 10 vols. (Columbia, 1836-1841); Anne King Gregorie (ed.), *Records of the Court of Chancery of South Carolina, 1671-1779* (Washington, 1950); A. S. Salley (ed.), *Commissions and Instructions from the Lords Proprietors of Carolina to the Public Officials of South Carolina, 1685-1715* (Columbia, 1916), and *Journal of the Commons House of Assembly, for the Session Beginning February 23, 1724/5 and Ending June 1, 1725* [Columbia] 1945. Also, Douglas C. McMurtrie, *A Bibliography of South Carolina Imprints, 1731-1740* (Charleston, 1933), and *Four South Carolina Imprints of MDCCXXXI, Together with Complete Facsimiles of These Imprints from the Presses of George Webb and Thomas Whitmarsh* (Chicago, 1933); and William L. Saunders (ed.), *The Colonial Records of North Carolina,* 10 vols. (Raleigh, 1886-1890).

On matters of defense and settlement, special mention must be given to two outstanding accounts: Verner W. Crane, *The Southern Frontier, 1670-1732* (Durham, 1928), and Robert L. Meriwether, *The Expansion of South Carolina, 1729-1765* (Kingsport, Tennessee, 1940). A rewarding collection of source material is found in *Mississippi Provincial Archives,* ed. by Dunbar Rowland and A. G. Sanders, 3 vols. (Jackson, 1927-1932), that reveals much about the relations and conflicts of the European powers in the southeast. An early account is found in Andrés de Barcia, *Chronological History of the Continent of Florida,* trans. by Anthony Kerrigan (Gainesville, 1951). Various aspects of the tri-power conflict are covered in James G. Johnson, "The Colonial Southeast, 1732-1763: An International Contest for Territorial and Economic Control," University of Colorado *Studies,* Vol. XIX, No. 3 (June, 1932), pp. 163-225, and *The Spanish Period of Georgia and South Carolina History, 1566-1702,* University of Georgia *Bulletin,* Vol. XXIII, No. 9b., Special series: Studies, Vol. I, No. 9 (Athens, 1923); William E. Dunn, *Spanish and French Rivalry in the Gulf Region of the United States, 1678-1702,* University of Texas *Bulletin,* No. 1705, Studies in History, No. 1 (Austin, 1917); Henry Folmer, *Franco-Spanish Rivalry in North America, 1524-1763, Spain in the West* series, Vol. VII (Glendale, Calif., 1953); Herbert E. Bolton, "Spanish Resistance to the Carolina Traders in Western Georgia," *Georgia Historical Quarterly,* Vol. IX, No. 2 (June, 1925), pp. 115-130; and Herbert E. Bolton and Mary Ross, *The Debatable Land* (Berkeley, 1925). Specialized studies pertaining to settlement include Arthur H. Hirsch, *The Huguenots of Colonial South Carolina* (Durham, 1928); Gilbert P. Voigt, "The Germans and German-Swiss in South Carolina, 1732-1765: Their Contribution to the Province," South Carolina Historical Association *Proceedings,* 1935, pp. 17-25; Henry A. M. Smith, "Purrysburgh," *South Carolina Historical Magazine,* Vol. X, No. 4 (October, 1909), pp. 187-219; Harriette D. K. Leiding, "Purrysburg, A Swiss-French Settlement of South Carolina, on the Savannah River," Huguenot Society of South Carolina, *Transactions,* No. 39 (1934), pp. 27-39.

Indian problems and relations are an integral part of defense and settlement, but besides the works already cited, attention should be directed to John R. Swanton, *The Indian Tribes of North America,* Smithsonian Institution, Bureau of American Ethnology, Bulletin

145 (Washington, 1953); James Adair, *The History of the American Indians* (London, 1775); Alexander Gregg, *History of the Old Cheraws* (New York, 1867 and Spartanburg, Reprint Company, 1966); John Pitts Corry, *Indian Affairs in Georgia, 1732-1756* (Philadelphia, 1936); Chapman J. Milling, *Red Carolinians* (Chapel Hill, 1940); and A. S. Salley, *George Hunter's Map of the Cherokee Country and the Path thereto in 1730,* Historical Commission of South Carolina, *Bulletins,* No. 4 (Columbia, 1917), and *Journal of the Commissioners of the Indian Trade of South Carolina, September 20, 1710-April 12, 1715* (Columbia, 1926).

Newest work on Indians is the comprehensive *The Catawba Indians: The People of the River* by Douglas Summers Brown. Mrs. Brown has included information on tribes other than the Catawbas (Columbia: University of South Carolina Press, 1966).

The settlement of Georgia was a major event during the Johnson administration and ultimately was to be of great significance for the defense problem. Important source collections are *The Colonial Records of the State of Georgia,* ed. by Allen D. Candler, 26 vols. (Atlanta, 1904-1916); *Collections of the Georgia Historical Society,* Vol. I (Savannah, 1840); George White, *Historical Collections of Georgia* (New York, 1854); and the intriguing "Azilia: A Discourse by Sir Robert Montgomery, 1717," ed. by J. Max Patrick, Emory *Sources and Reprints,* Series IV, No. 3 (1943).

On the origins and settlement of Georgia, the following are especially noteworthy: R. A. Roberts, "The Birth of an American State: Georgia: An Effort of Philanthropy and Protestant Propaganda," *Transactions of the Royal Historical Society,* 4th series, Vol. VI, pp. 22-49 (1923); U. B. Phillips, "New Light Upon the Founding of Georgia," *Georgia Historical Quarterly,* Vol. VI, No. 4 (December, 1922), pp. 277-284; and Verner Crane, "The Origins of Georgia," *Ibid.,* Vol. XIV, No. 2 (June, 1930), pp. 93-110. No serious student of the period can afford to overlook the information presented by Albert B. Saye, *New Viewpoints in Georgia History* (Athens, 1943). Standard accounts are Charles C. Jones, Jr., *The History of Georgia,* 2 vols. (Boston, 1883); James R. McCain, *Georgia as a Proprietary Province* (Boston, 1917); George G. Smith, *The Story of Georgia and the Georgia People, 1732-1860* (Macon, 1900); and the excellent one-volume work by E. Merton Coulter, *Georgia: A Short History* (Chapel Hill, 1947).

It is of course impossible to separate the founding of Georgia from the name of Oglethorpe, and the following are recommended: Amos A. Ettinger, *James Edward Oglethorpe, Imperial Idealist* (Oxford, 1936); Leslie F. Church, *Oglethorpe: A Study of Philanthropy in England and Georgia* (London, 1932); Austin Dobson, *A Paladin of Philanthropy and Other Papers* (London, 1923): and Henry Bruce, *Life of General Oglethorpe* (New York, 1890). A somewhat different emphasis is found in H. P. Thompson, *Thomas Bray* (London, 1954), and "Letters of Thomas Coram," Massachusetts Historical Society, *Proceedings,* Vol. LVI (1922-23), pp. 15-56. Important source material is found in Historical Manuscripts Commission, *Manuscripts of the Earl of Egmont: Diary of Viscount Percival, Afterwards First Earl of Egmont,* 3 vols. (London, 1920-1923); Benjamin Rand (ed.), *Berkeley and Percival: The Correspondence of George Berkeley, Afterwards Bishop of Cloyne, and Sir John Percival, Afterwards Earl of Egmont* (Cambridge, 1914); *The Parliamentary History of England* (Hansard), Vols. VII and VIII (London, 1811); and E. Merton Coulter (ed.), *The Journal of Peter Gordon, 1732-1735* (Athens, 1963).

While the settlement of Georgia aided South Carolina's defensive position, it also created problems, particularly for the traders, as was soon revealed in *Report of the Committee to Examine into the Proceedings of the People of Georgia, with Respect to the Province of South-Carolina, and the Disputes Subsisting Between the Two Colonies* (Charleston, 1736).

Specialized studies of particular merit are Shirley C. Hughson, *The Carolina Pirates and Colonial Commerce, 1670-1740,* Johns Hopkins University *Studies in Historical and Political Science,* Series 12, No. 5-7 (Baltimore, 1894); Richard M. Jellison, "Paper Currency in Colonial South Carolina: A Reappraisal," *South Carolina Historical Magazine,* Vol. LXII, No. 3 (July, 1961), pp. 134-147.

Other works deserving mention are W.O.B. Allen and Edmund McClure, *Two Hundred Years: The History of the Society for Promoting Christian Knowledge, 1698-1898* (London, 1898); W. Chappell, *The Ballad Literature and Popular Music of the Olden Time* (London, n.d.); St. Julien Ravenel Childs, "Notes on the History of Public Health in South Carolina, 1670-1800," South Carolina Historical Association, *Proceedings,* 1932, pp. 13-22;

J. B. O. Landrum, *Colonial and Revolutionary History of Upper South Carolina* (Greenville, 1897); Edward McCrady, "Slavery in the Province of South Carolina, 1670-1770," American Historical Association, *Annual Report, 1895,* pp. 631-673; Newton D. Mereness (ed.), *Travels in the American Colonies* (New York, 1916); Robert Mills, *Statistics of South Carolina* (Charleston, 1826); Vere L. Oliver, "Carolina Wills," *South Carolina Historical Magazine,* Vol. XII, No. 4 (October, 1911), pp. 215-9; A. S. Salley (ed.), *Marriage Notices in the South Carolina Gazette* (Albany, 1902); Leila Sellers, *Charleston Business on the Eve of the American Revolution* (Chapel Hill, 1934); Society of Antiquaries of Newcastle-upon-Tyne, *Proceedings,* 3rd and 4th series (1920-1925); South Carolina State Board of Agriculture, *South Carolina, Resources and Population, Institutions and Industries* (Charleston, 1883); "A Treaty Between Virginia and the Catawbas and Cherokees, 1756," *Virginia Magazine of History and Biography,* Vol. *XIII,* No. 3 (January, 1906), pp. 225-264; David Duncan Wallace, *Constitutional History of South Carolina, from 1725 to 1775* (Abbeville, S. C., 1899); and Mabel L. Webber, "Ralph Izard," *Dictionary of American Biography,* Vol. IX, pp. 524-5.

INDEX